This volume surveys the history of United States foreign relations from 1913 to 1945, covering the presidencies of Woodrow Wilson, Warren Harding, Calvin Coolidge, Herbert Hoover, and Franklin D. Roosevelt. Professor Iriye first provides an overview of the international system as it evolved through the seventeenth, eighteenth, and nineteenth centuries and came to be dominated by the European nation-states. This introduces his thematic framework of America's "globalization," for the first half of the twentieth century saw the United States supplant Europe as the world's leader, not just in terms of military force but also in economic and cultural influence.

Iriye discusses America's shift from neutrality to eventual involvement in World War I. Americans believed that domestic stability and global economic development and interdependence were interchangeable propositions, all contributing to peace at home and abroad. Ironically, it was this certainty that first involved the United States in the European war. Iriye explains how America's continuing commercial involvement with Europe complicated U.S. neutrality but also sped the emergence of the United States as the world's leading economic power. America became a creditor nation virtually overnight, and this economic heft, as much as the moral suasion of Wilsonianism, gave the United States a new opportunity to shape the European political order.

Iriye describes the American response to the Bolshevik Revolution, which presented an ideological challenge to the new American hegemony. He shows how the Versailles Treaty fulfilled some of the Wilsonian aims, such as the creation of new states on the basis of ethnic nationalism, while betraying the spirit of the peace by imposing punitive reparations and a pronouncement of war guilt on defeated Germany.

The penetration of world markets by American goods as well as capital and technology provided the economic foundation for the postwar international order. Iriye tells the story of the economic boom of the new peace and describes the cultural and intellectual internationalism that the worldwide peace movement inspired. Interelite exchanges, accompanied by the extensive spread abroad of American goods and popular culture, helped develop a global cultural order with a distinctly American character.

Cultural internationalism could not prevent the terrifying collapse of international order in the 1930s under the onslaught of a worldwide economic depression. This period saw the rise of fascism and national socialism, and the atrocities of the concentration camps. World War II was far more global in scope than World War I, but only the United States was involved in all theaters of the war: in the Atlantic as well as the Pacific, in North Africa as well as Southeast Asia, and in the Middle East as well as South America. In this sense, World War II is the culminating point in the story of the steady globalization of the United States. It was to be the nation's task to help shape a more stable world order that would be at once true to the American traditional values and responsive to the new challenges of the twentieth century. Throughout Iriye's survey of global developments, he discusses America's position and role as an emerging world power.

The Cambridge History of American Foreign Relations

Volume III
The Globalizing of America, 1913–1945

THE CAMBRIDGE HISTORY OF AMERICAN FOREIGN RELATIONS

Warren I. Cohen, Editor

Volume I: The Creation of a Republican Empire, 1776–1865 – Bradford Perkins
Volume II: The American Search for Opportunity, 1865–1913 – Walter LaFeber
Volume III: The Globalizing of America, 1913–1945 – Akira Iriye
Volume IV: America in the Age of Soviet Power, 1945–1991 – Warren I. Cohen

THE CAMBRIDGE HISTORY OF AMERICAN FOREIGN RELATIONS

Volume III
The Globalizing of America, 1913–1945

AKIRA IRIYE

Published by the Press Syndicate of the University of Cambridge
The Pitt Building, Trumpington Street, Cambridge CB2 1RP
40 West 20th Street, New York, NY 10011-4211, USA
10 Stamford Road, Oakleigh, Melbourne 3166, Australia

First published 1993

Printed in the United States of America

Library of Congress Cataloging-in-Publication Data

Iriye, Akira
The Cambridge history of American foreign relations / Akira Iriye.
p. cm.
Includes bibliographical references and index.
Contents: v. 1. The Creation of a Republican empire, 1766–1865 – v. 2.
The American search for opportunity, 1865–1913 – v. 3. The globalizing of
America, 1913–1945 – v. 4. America in the age of Soviet power, 1945–1991.
ISBN 0-521-38209-2 (vol 1). – ISBN 0-521-38185-1 (vol 2)
1. United States – Foreign relations. I. Title.
E183.7.P45 1993
327.73 – dc20 92-36165
CIP

A catalog record for this book is available from the British Library

ISBN 0-521-38206-8 hardback

Contents

Maps

General Editor's Introduction

My goal for the Cambridge History of American Foreign Relations was to make the finest scholarship and the best writing in the historical profession available to the general reader. I had no ideological or methodological agenda. I wanted some of America's leading students of diplomatic history, regardless of approach, to join me and was delighted to have my invitations accepted by the first three to whom I turned. When I conceived of the project nearly ten years ago, I had no idea that the Cold War would suddenly end, that these volumes would conclude with a final epoch as well defined as the first three. The collapse of the Soviet empire, just as I finished writing Volume IV, astonished me but allowed for a sense of completion these volumes would have lacked under any other circumstances.

The first volume has been written by Bradford Perkins, the preeminent historian of late eighteenth- and early nineteenth-century American diplomacy and doyen of currently active diplomatic historians. Perkins sees foreign policy in the young Republic as a product of material interests, culture, and the prism of national values. He describes an American pattern of behavior that existed before there was an America and demonstrates how it was shaped by the experience of the Revolution and the early days of the Republic. In his discussion of the Constitution and foreign affairs, he spins a thread that can be pulled through the remaining volumes: the persistent effort of presidents, beginning with Washington, to dominate policy, contrary to the intent of the participants in the Constitutional Convention.

The inescapable theme of Perkins's volume is presaged in its title, the ideological commitment to republican values and the determination to carry those values across the North American continent and to obliterate all obstacles, human as well as geological. He sees the

American empire arising out of lust for land and resources rather than for dominion over other peoples. But it was dominion over others – native Americans, Mexicans, and especially African Americans – that led to the last episode he discusses, the Civil War and its diplomacy. This is a magnificent survey of the years in which the United States emerged as a nation and created the foundations for world power that would come in the closing years of the nineteenth century.

Walter LaFeber, author of the second volume, is one of the most highly respected of the so-called Wisconsin School of diplomatic historians, men and women who studied with Fred Harvey Harrington and William Appleman Williams and their students, and were identified as "New Left" when they burst on the scene in the 1960s. LaFeber's volume covers the last third of the nineteenth century and extends into the twentieth, to 1913, through the administration of William Howard Taft. He discusses the link between the growth of American economic power and expansionism, adding the theme of racism, especially as applied to native Americans and Filipinos. Most striking is his rejection of the idea of an American quest for order. He argues that Americans sought opportunities for economic and missionary activities abroad and that they were undaunted by the disruptions they caused in other nations. A revolution in China or Mexico was a small price to pay for advantages accruing to Americans, especially when the local people paid it. His other inescapable theme is the use of foreign affairs to enhance presidential power.

The third volume, which begins on the eve of World War I and carries the story through World War II, is by Akira Iriye, past president of the American Historical Association and our generation's most innovative historian of international relations. Japanese-born, educated in American universities, Iriye has been fascinated by the cultural conflicts and accommodations that permeate power politics, particularly as the United States has confronted the nations of East Asia. Iriye opens his book with a quick sketch of the international system as it evolved and was dominated by Europe through the seventeenth, eighteenth, and nineteenth centuries. He analyzes

Wilsonianism in war and peace and how it was applied in Asia and Latin America. Most striking is his discussion of what he calls the "cultural aspect" of the 1920s. Iriye sees the era about which he writes as constituting the "globalizing of America" – an age in which the United States supplanted Europe as the world's leader and provided the economic and cultural resources to define and sustain the international order. He notes the awakening of non-Western peoples and their expectations of American support and inspiration. In his conclusion he presages the troubles that would follow from the Americanization of the world.

Much of my work, like Iriye's, has focused on American–East Asian relations. My friend Michael Hunt has placed me in the "realist" school of diplomatic historians. Influenced by association with Perkins, LaFeber, Iriye, Ernest May, and younger friends such as John Lewis Gaddis, Michael Hogan, and Melvyn Leffler, I have studied the domestic roots of American policy, the role of ideas and attitudes as well as economic concerns, the role of nongovernmental organizations including missionaries, and the place of art in international relations. In the final volume of the series, *America in the Age of Soviet Power, 1945–1991,* I also rely heavily on what I have learned from political economists and political scientists.

I begin the book in the closing months of World War II and end it with the disappearance of the Soviet Union in 1991. I write of the vision American leaders had of a postwar world order and the growing sense that the Soviet Union posed a threat to that vision. The concept of the "security dilemma," the threat each side's defensive actions seemed to pose for the other, looms large in my analysis of the origins of the Cold War. I also emphasize the importance of the two political systems, the paradox of the powerful state and weak government in the United States and the secrecy and brutality of the Stalinist regime. Throughout the volume, I note the importance of the disintegration of prewar colonial empires, the appearance of scores of newly independent states in Africa, Asia, and Latin America, and the turmoil caused by American and Soviet efforts to force them into an international system designed in Washington and Moscow. Finally, I trace the reemergence of Germany and Japan as major powers, the collapse of the Soviet Union, and the drift of the United States, its course in world affairs uncertain in the absence of an adversary.

There are a number of themes that can be followed through these four volumes, however differently the authors approach their subjects. First, there was the relentless national pursuit of wealth and power, described so vividly by Perkins and LaFeber. Iriye demonstrates how Americans used their wealth and power when the United States emerged as the world's leader after World War I. I discuss America's performance as hegemon in the years immediately following World War II, and its response to perceived threats to its dominance.

A second theme of critical importance is the struggle for control of foreign policy. Each author notes tension between the president and Congress, as institutionalized by the Constitution, and the efforts of various presidents, from 1789 to the present, to circumvent constitutional restraints on their powers. The threat to democratic government is illustrated readily by the Nixon-Kissinger obsessions that led to Watergate and Reagan's Iran-Contra fiasco.

Finally, we are all concerned with what constitutes American identity on the world scene. Is there a peculiarly American foreign policy that sets the United States off from the rest of the world? We examine the evolution of American values and measure them against the nation's behavior in international affairs. And we worry about the impact of the country's global activity on its domestic order, fearful that Thomas Jefferson's vision of a virtuous republic has been forgotten, boding ill for Americans and for the world they are allegedly "bound to lead."

WARREN I. COHEN

Preface

The story of American foreign relations during the turbulent years 1913–45, encompassing the two world wars, is sufficiently well known to the general reader that it would make little sense to write yet another survey, chronicling detailed data and accumulating episodes. In this volume, I have tried to be more analytical in order to highlight the ways in which the United States steadily became globalized, that is, involved in security, economic, and cultural affairs in all parts of the world. The phenomenon was by no means unidirectional, nor did it always bring about the same results in international affairs. Nevertheless, to describe the evolution of American foreign relations during these years without trying to understand how the world was transformed through American power, influence, and will would be to treat the subject in a vacuum. For this reason, I have decided to include references to other countries to a greater extent than is usual in a book of this kind.

The scholarly literature on international affairs and American foreign relations during this period is enormous, not only in the United States but also elsewhere. The notes and the bibliography indicate only a fraction of it. I am pleased that scholars in many parts of the world are producing important monographs and essays free of dogmatism and chauvinism. I am indebted to their labor and encouraged by the growing internationalization of the historical scholarship. That, too, is an important aspect of the globalization of America.

Warren Cohen, who, together with Frank Smith of the Cambridge University Press, took the initiative to launch a four-volume history of U.S. foreign relations and invited me to contribute this volume, went over the manuscript with meticulous care. To him and to the authors of the first two volumes of this work (Bradford Perkins and Walter LaFeber), who also read the draft and gave me valuable suggestions, I should like to express my appreciation. In the final stages of the book's preparation, I was a beneficiary of the careful reading of the text by Robert David Johnson and Brian MacDonald, and of the warm and lively family environment created by my wife and two daughters.

1. *The Age of European Domination*

The Rise of the West

The world on the eve of the Great War was European-dominated. As we trace the history of American foreign relations from 1913 to 1945, it is important to recall that the United States had come into existence and conducted its external affairs in a world system in which European military power, economic pursuits, and cultural activities predominated. This had not always been the case. Before the eighteenth century, the Ottoman Empire in the Middle East and the Chinese Empire in East Asia had been equal contenders for power and influence. In fact, as the European nation-states had fought one another almost without interruption throughout the seventeenth and eighteenth centuries, a dispassionate observer might have predicted that those states would soon exhaust themselves and that the more unified empires of the Middle East and East Asia – collectively known as "Asia," the "Orient," or the "East" – might in the long run prove much more important determinants of world affairs.

As Paul Kennedy and others have argued, however, it was the very divided nature of European affairs that proved decisive in the ascendance of the region in the international community.[1] Because the nation-state was in a virtually constant state of war or of war preparedness, it had to develop a centralized administrative structure for mobilizing armed forces and collecting taxes to pay for them. These, which John Brewer has termed the "sinews of power," were systematically developed by the European monarchies throughout the seventeenth century, and during the following century the struggle for power among the nation-states came to define the basic

1 Paul Kennedy, *The Rise and Fall of the Great Powers* (New York, 1987).

nature of European international relations.[2] Concepts of "great power," "balance of power," and "reason of state" were developed as guides to national policy, justifying domestic and external measures for the enhancement of each state's relative power.

Such competitiveness, while fragmenting Europe into contending units, also had the effect of increasing the region's overall power in relation to the more unified and thus less militarily oriented empires elsewhere. Because successful wars entailed effective strategies and advanced military weaponry, it is not surprising that the European wars coincided with vast developments in science, technology, and strategy. By the end of the eighteenth century, European armies and navies were equipped with arms far more sophisticated than those in use in the Middle East or East Asia.

Such a situation alone, however, would not have ensured European predominance in world affairs. The pursuit of power, as William McNeill has noted, is ultimately wasteful of national resources.[3] If the rise to power of Spain, the Dutch republic, and France in the seventeenth and eighteenth centuries had been a product of their respective military strengths and successfully waged wars, these same phenomena exhausted their resources and divided national opinion, thus undermining domestic unity that was essential for the augmentation of power. The same fate appeared to visit Great Britain, a latecomer to the European power scene, as it fought the American colonies during the 1770s and the 1780s.

What saved, and indeed perpetuated, European predominance were two additional factors, also making their appearance during the eighteenth century: the Industrial Revolution and the Enlightenment. The two were connected in the sense that modern rational thought, unfettered by traditional constraints, made possible the phenomenal growth of productivity, turning first Britain and then other countries into the workshops of the world.

Economically, it is well to recall that as late as 1800 China was producing more manufactured goods than any other country.[4] Al-

2 John Brewer, *The Sinews of Power* (New York, 1989).
3 William H. McNeill, *The Pursuit of Power* (Chicago, 1984).
4 Kennedy, *Rise and Fall,* 149.

ready by then, however, the Industrial Revolution had come to Britain and was beginning to turn that island country into the world's center of textile manufacturing. More efficiently produced and consequently cheaper cotton yarn and fabrics were spreading out to all parts of the globe, bringing with it immense trade and shipping revenues. With an increasing working population employed at factories, and with the building of railroads that connected city with countryside, the demographic landscape of the country was changing, increasing the overall population but also creating new classes of people, now more subject to laws of supply and demand on a worldwide scale than earlier. Overseas sources of cotton and other raw materials as well as food were sought, and new markets had to be found to sell goods produced at home. The increasing wealth of Britain would spill over other European countries as they would sell more to an increasingly prosperous British population, and as British capital would be brought over to modernize their own economic systems. The result was that Europe's relative economic position was fast improving, soon to overtake that of China and all other parts of the globe.

Culturally, the Enlightenment ideology, with its emphasis on rationalism, combined with earlier traditions of British liberalism and produced the typically eighteenth-century idea of history as progress, in which humanity was pictured as being capable of unlimited development. Underlying were the concepts of human rights and liberty. Collectively, groups of people were said to possess inalienable rights as citizens, equal before the law, and individually each person was seen as endowed with a right to pursue material well-being as well as spiritual contentment. Such concepts pitted men and women against larger entities such as the church and the state, and for this reason the clash of perspectives between individual conscience and religion – and, more seriously, between citizen and state – would become a key theme of eighteenth-century European thought.

To return to the observation made at the outset, it is important to note that the United States emerged on the world stage as it was being molded by the military, economic, and cultural developments in Europe. They provided the point of departure for the young nation's foreign and domestic affairs. Its very existence as an independent republic was aided by the European military rivalries, in particular the French-British struggle for power. The Founding Fathers took it for granted that if the nation were to protect its independence, it would have to be prepared for war, which would necessitate military force and a bureaucracy to pay for and administer it. Furthermore, national power would be enhanced through territorial expansion and the removal of potential threats nearer home. All these objectives were pursued by the U.S. government, formally established under the Constitution in 1787.

Economically, too, the nation was no less part of the European developments. It was cut off from the protective arms of the British Empire and shut out of the West Indies markets, but otherwise the Americans continued their economic activities as they had done as British colonials, producing food, selling its surpluses overseas, and sending ships abroad to engage in carrying trade. The independence gave such activities further impetus as it coincided with the Industrial Revolution in England. Demands for American wheat, fish, lumber, and other primary products increased. Their carrying trade took them to North Africa, the Indian Ocean, and East Asia. Apart from their political identity as citizens of the newly independent United States, their economic activities distinguished them little from those of the Europeans. They were part of the global economic penetration by the West.

Culturally, America was as much a product of British liberalism and the Enlightenment as of the indigenous conditions. From the beginning, to be sure, Americans were self-conscious people, considering themselves exceptional – citizens of the New World, not tainted by the ills of the Old. But the revolt against Old World traditions was also a European phenomenon, going back to the Reformation and to early modern currents of thought, and therefore American exceptionalism was in part an extension, a further development, of the European phenomena. Republicanism was a good example. It was an ideology that stressed a community of virtuous citizens who were imbued with a concern for public welfare even as they pursued their individual interests. The ideals had been in England for a long time, but they were taken seriously by the American leaders who believed in the possibility of their implementation in the New World. Here the physical environment of the American continent, with its rich soil and expanding horizons, seemed well suited for the experiment. As best exemplified in James Madison's thought, republicanism had a rare opportunity to flower in the new land, as the population would multiply without producing a concentration of wealth and power. Instead, the people would live in frugal prosperity, conscious of their precious liberties.[5] It is clear that these ideas grew out of the European background and that viewed from outside the West, they could be seen as a refinement of, not a departure from, European thought.

In one sense, however, America was unique, or at least significantly different from Europe in the late eighteenth century. American society was more cohesive in the absence of feudalism, the established church, monarchical institutions, and other privileged classes. To be sure, the existence of slavery and of the indigenous Indian populations, who never acknowledged the independence of the thirteen colonies, meant a society that was deeply divided, and the division would steadily undermine national unity.[6] But in the early stages of the Republic's history, the nation was spared serious cleavages of the kind that rent France and other countries apart in Europe. Among the white majority in America, there were occasional crises and even uprisings, but on the whole they did not threaten to tear apart the political entity or the social fabric. There was a cohesiveness in America that could create a sense of nationhood – a nationalism that transcended the factional alignments or ethnic traditions of the citizens and was founded upon a shared consciousness of how the independence had been won. The absence of a serious division was a source of strength for the new nation, perhaps the key to its acceptance as a member of the European-defined community of nations.

If such was the world of the late eighteenth century in which the United States made its appearance, the following century at once

5 Drew McCoy, *The Elusive Republic* (Chapel Hill, 1988).

6 On native-American responses to the independence of the thirteen colonies, see J. L. Wright, *Britain and the American Frontier* (Athens, Ga., 1975).

confirmed and added variations to the picture. The nineteenth century opened with French revolutionary wars in which France, led by Napoleon Bonaparte, sought to establish its military, political, and ideological domination over Europe and the world beyond, and in the end failed in the face of a determined opposition on the part of most other countries. The Napoleonic wars brought much destruction to European nations but, significantly, did not diminish the relative power of Europe in the world. On the contrary, as they continued with their Industrial Revolution, mobilized masses for warfare, improved military technology, and absorbed Enlightenment thought, the Europeans emerged out of the wars in an even superior position to people in other areas of the globe than before. The United States, even as it collided with France and Britain over its rights as a neutral in the European wars, did not remove itself from the overall trend. It continued to constitute part of the Western-dominated world.

At the same time, however, America's one strength, national unity or domestic cohesiveness, began to erode to such an extent that by the middle of the nineteenth century the nation had come to exist in separate compartments, defined in economic and geographic terms. The North on the whole stood for a conception of the nation in which free white labor would develop the economy, protected by a system of import duties on manufactured foreign goods, whereas the South, pursuing a slavery-based economy and in need of free trade to market its cotton and to obtain cheap consumer goods, held to a view of the nation as a compact, dissolvable when some segments felt they no longer benefited from the association. Such cleavages made it difficult for the United States to conduct itself as a unified nation. At a time when in Europe nationalistic movements were creating a potent force for the establishment of unified states, America, even as it extended its territorial domain beyond the Mississippi and eventually to the Pacific, threatened to become fractured. It was fortunate that in the mid-nineteenth century the European powers on the whole maintained a stable relationship with each other and more or less left the United States alone.

It is all the more remarkable, therefore, that outside of Europe Americans continued to expand their activities and interests – as part of the expansion of the West in the wake of the Industrial Revolution. America's own industrialization began during the War of 1812 against England, although it would pick up momentum only after the Civil War. In the meantime, it was in trade and shipping that the Americans excelled; their ships were almost as numerous as British, prying open new markets in the Middle East and East Asia and establishing connections with the newly independent states of Latin America. Clearly, such activities added to the wealth of individual Americans, but whether they also augmented national power on the whole was in question in the absence of domestic unity. In the middle of the century, the United States was already being recognized as a would-be economic giant, but that did not translate into a formidable power in world affairs. In the Middle East, Asia, and Latin America, where "informal empire" held sway – ad hoc systems of control exercised by the West over indigenous peoples for facilitating trade – the American presence was conspicuous.[7] That such informal empire might have brought about an enhancement of American power in the global picture could be seen in Commodore Matthew Perry's expeditions to Japan, undertaken in 1853 and 1854. It was a dramatic moment, revealing America's emergence as a Pacific nation. Perry himself had visions of American power holding sway over the western Pacific. Such visions, however, had no way of becoming realized while the nation grew steadily divided. It should be noted, however, that at this time few European nations were intent upon systematically extending formal control over other parts of the globe. In this sense, too, America was still part of the West.

The same can be said of the cultural dimension. The nineteenth-century world continued to be dominated by European culture, but European culture underwent significant transformation. To the eighteenth-century legacies were now added romanticism, socialism, and a host of other ideologies that brought about new perspectives on national and international affairs. Romanticism, by exalting emotion over intellect, and the primeval over the modern, generated

7 On "informal empire," the pioneering study is Ronald Robinson and John Gallagher, *Africa and the Victorians* (New York, 1961).

nationalistic movements all over Europe – not the nationalism of the French Revolution espousing universalistic values but rather ethnic nationalism, each ethnic group stressing its own tradition and developing a political self-consciousness opposed to domination by others. Socialism, on the other hand, created self-consciousness among certain classes of people in an industrializing society, giving workers a sense of group solidarity. Thus both romanticism and socialism abetted particularistic tendencies, exalting the role of community or class as an intermediate existence between state and individual.

Because earlier traditions had focused on the rights and interests of the state or the individual, these nineteenth-century additions complicated perceptions, nowhere more so than in discussions of international affairs. Earlier, statecraft (reasons of state, balance of power, national interests) and human rights (equality, liberty, pursuit of happiness) had been the two guiding principles, often at variance with each other. Romanticism and socialism both questioned the bases of the existing state boundaries and organizations, and at the same time placed individual rights in the larger framework of a community. International relations, in such a context, would mean much more than interstate relations, on one hand, or individual pursuits of commerce and other activities, on the other. War, for instance, would signify much more than clashes over territorial boundaries or trading rights, and peace more than a product of rational human behavior. Instead war could come from romantic forces – the shedding of blood for noble causes, defined ethnically – or from a class collision between capitalists and workers. Peace might be defined as an ultimate goal after romantic aspirations had been satisfied, or after a classless world had been established and states had withered away.

The divisiveness of nineteenth-century thought was accentuated by developments in the biological sciences, some of which stressed distinctions among different races. Away from the conception of unity of man, various theories of racial distinctions postulated autonomous and unchanging characteristics of racial groups, with almost always the white race viewed as the norm, the most advanced. Then there were developments in anthropology, linguistics, historical study, and other subjects in which racial, ethnic, and national differences were likewise emphasized. The revival of Protestant Christianity fitted into the picture insofar as Protestant missionaries redoubled their efforts to proselytize among the less enlightened. Of course, they believed it possible to save the unenlightened from their "moral darkness" and, in so doing, assumed it was possible to change even the heathen. There was a tension between such a belief in the malleability of man and the cultural determinism inherent in various theories of racial distinctions. But the two were joined by a firm belief in Western superiority.

American culture in the nineteenth century was part of the broader Western civilization in that these European ideas had their counterparts in the United States. Not all of these ideas were taken with the same degree of seriousness; romanticism was most conspicuous among Southern sectionalists, and socialist experiments in the Midwest. But theories of race differences were virtually universally accepted. By the 1840s, apart from a tiny minority who believed in complete racial equality, Americans in all parts of the world had come to take the superiority of the white race for granted.[8] In this respect, too, they belonged to the same universe as Europeans. Americans were Westerners, culturally as well as economically, and the temporary passivity of U.S. foreign affairs, induced by growing domestic tensions, did not alter the equation.

The Emergence of Modern States

The Civil War forever put to rest the question of national unity of the United States. There might still continue sectional differences, and most certainly ethnic cleavages would not disappear, but the political unity of the nation would never again be challenged. The significance of this for American foreign relations is obvious. The government would be able to conduct foreign affairs without fearing their immediate impact on domestic cohesiveness. To be sure, elected leaders would have to be sensitive to various interest groups and proclivities of the population, but at least they would be able to

8 Reginald Horseman, *Race and Manifest Destiny* (Cambridge, Mass., 1981); Michael H. Hunt, *Ideology and U.S. Foreign Policy* (New Haven, 1987).

take for granted the continued existence of the nation as a unified entity.

The timing of this phenomenon could not have been more opportune, for the end of the Civil War coincided with significant developments in Europe – Italian unification, German unification, the Franco-Prussian War, and the birth of the Third Republic in France, the reform bill of 1867 in Britain, the emancipation of serfs in Russia in 1861 – all of which added up to bringing Europe to the age of the modern states.

The modern state, characterized by centralized administration and armed forces, secular public authorities and institutions defining the limits of acceptable behavior for people within the boundaries, mass participation in the political process, unified domestic markets and systems of production and distribution, extensive networks of transportation and communication, and legal codes distinguishing citizen from foreigner – such a state was an outgrowth of the earlier nation-state that had come into existence in the seventeenth century, but it was built upon a society that was more cohesive and integrated a far greater segment of the population into the entity. A modern state was a greater power than its earlier manifestation in that it possessed nationalized mass armed forces equipped with ever newer weapons, products of rapidly advancing technology, and because the state itself, rather than a monarchy or an aristocratic order, was the focus of loyalty.

Of course, some modern states were more authoritarian than others, and some were more fragile than the rest. Citizens and social classes in some states were more aware of their rights than those elsewhere. Differences among the modern states, as much as their common characteristics, affected their interrelationships, as the subsequent history of international affairs was to show. But one point should be emphasized: During the last decades of the nineteenth century, several nations emerged as modern states, and they were by definition military and economic powers. Their power might not always be fully mobilized, but they could count on the loyalty of their citizens, particularly in times of foreign crises. International relations, therefore, in this sense became interpower relations.

Toward those countries and peoples lacking in similar power, there was an inevitable tendency on the part of the modern states to extend their sway, both in order to enhance their respective power positions in the world and also to minimize areas of instability that might adversely affect international order. This was the phenomenon known as imperialism, or the new imperialism to distinguish it from earlier varieties of colonialism.

Lest it should be thought that the modern states were always trying to augment their respective power positions and engaging in a constant struggle for power, it should be noted that they also interacted with one another peacefully, through trade, investment, and other forms of economic transaction as well as through cultural pursuits such as tourism and scholarly interchanges. Although they too were increasingly brought under the control of state authority, these transactions created networks of personal ties that did not always duplicate state-level interactions. More important, such transactions affected the social developments of all countries so that the latter did not follow preordained paths of history. This dynamism – how interstate relations transformed modern states, even as the emergence of modern states transformed international relations – provides a key to the understanding of world affairs since the 1860s.

As a newly reunified modern state, the United States shared many features with the modern states of Europe. Although, after 1865, the nation was led by politicians whose stature did not match Germany's Otto von Bismarck or Britain's William Gladstone, the authority of the federal government in upholding domestic order was unquestioned. It had at its disposal U.S. armed forces and "national guards," state-level forces. Although much smaller in scale than continental European forces, they were steadily modernized to cope with possible crises overseas. It is true that prior to the 1890s American military power was less conspicuous than most European countries'; during the Cuban crisis of 1868–78, when the island's rebels turned to the United States for support, Washington refused to act for fear that the nation might become involved in a war with Spain, which then was considered superior militarily to the United

States. But it was only a matter of time before the latter would catch up, and indeed in 1898 it fought a highly successful war against Spain.

In another area American power also lagged behind European: overseas colonization. In Europe it came to be taken for granted, from the 1870s onward, that a great power acquired overseas possessions both in order to demonstrate that it *was* a great power and also because colonies, bases, and spheres of influence were considered to be major assets that augmented the nation's resources and made more effective its strategic position in world affairs. The United States was slow to join the trend. To the country's leaders, distant lands in Africa, the Middle East, or Asia held little attraction beyond offering markets. But even here, over four-fifths of American trade was carried on with European countries, and there was no pressing need to establish enclaves of special interests abroad. It was not that the United States was unconcerned with developments outside of Europe, especially after the 1880s when the great powers began in earnest the process of dividing up Africa, the Middle East, and parts of Asia and the Pacific Ocean into their respective spheres of influence. For the time being, however, the United States emulated the European powers only in Hawaii, which was turned into a virtual protectorate in 1876 when the two countries signed a treaty binding the Hawaiian monarchy to refrain from leasing its ports to any other power and establishing a reciprocity arrangement regarding trade.

After a brief moment of passivity, however, the United States redefined its approach to world affairs and, during the 1890s, undertook military strengthening and colonial expansion. The two were in part interconnected; naval strengthening would not be complete without the building of an isthmian canal, which in turn would call for establishing an American presence in Central America. Also, an expanding navy would require coaling stations and bases in distant lands.

Most crucial was the consideration that the United States should not "fall behind the march" of other powers, as many argued. To do nothing when the European nations were carving up the world appeared to be tantamount to falling behind; and to fall behind seemed to spell inaction, doldrums, decay, even death for the nation. When the traditionalists argued that an aggressive foreign policy would be divisive domestically, the expansionists answered that, quite the contrary, inaction would have that consequence; if the United States remained stationary when every other power was moving rapidly, it would sap national energies and lead to the country's atrophy. The only course open, to demonstrate vigor and to prevent internal disunity, was to act like a great power, including overseas territorial expansion. Although it would be difficult to test such a proposition, the fact remains that America's colonial expansion did not bring domestic disunity; rather, domestic unity achieved through the Civil War ensured that foreign policy initiatives could be undertaken without much fear of losing internal cohesiveness.

Thus, as several European states were now becoming global powers, the United States entered the twentieth century as a global power. Having launched programs of military strengthening and colonial control, the nation was ready to assert its presence in the world arena. Instead of merely being part of the West and following in the footsteps of the European countries, the United States would now act on its own initiative, clarify its own conception of its position in the international system, and use its own power to contribute to defining world order. The globalization of America had begun.

One can see this not only in military and territorial affairs but also, and particularly, in American economic resources and performance. Already at the turn of the century, its manufacturing output was second only to Britain's, and America's rapid industrialization was reflected in the relative rise in importance of the areas outside of Europe for its export trade. The policy of the Open Door, first promulgated in 1899, signaled the U.S. government's concern with participating in the trade of less industrialized parts of the world. Foreign investment was another example. Although the nation continued to obtain funds for its industrialization from Europe, especially Britain, American financiers increasingly turned their attention to investment opportunities in less developed areas of the globe, such as Mexico and China. It is no accident that at first they concentrated on railway development in these countries. More miles of railways (182,000) had been built in the United States than anywhere else, and the Americans were convinced that by building more railways in Latin America, Asia, and possibly even the Middle East, they could develop these lands and turn them into huge markets for American goods. Establishing global linkages to the American economy impressed the political and business leaders as essential to the health of the domestic political and social system.

Growing American assertiveness in foreign affairs was buttressed by certain ideologies that stressed power, order, and civilization. Much of this was part of the trends in European thinking. It may be noted that while Western cultural dominance in the world continued, there was now also a greater degree of self-consciousness, even of defensiveness, in the age of imperialism. Of course, the West continued to excel in science, medicine, and technology, and enjoyed better health care and sanitation than elsewhere, with the result that life expectancies were longer and infant mortality lower in Europe and the United States than ever before. It was to Western countries that aspiring young students from other parts of the world went. In housing, in infrastructure such as roads, plumbing, and sewage, or in recreational activities, Westerners could be said to have better qualities of life than people elsewhere. Their literacy rates were on the whole higher, although that would not be true of Russia or the complex nationality groups comprising the Austro-Hungarian Empire. Above all, Europeans and Americans had developed modern systems of government, including legal frameworks, conceptions of citizenship with specified rights and duties, and community services. It was these things that attracted the attention of visitors from Asia, the Middle East, or Africa.

At the same time, Western thought came to lay unusual stress on power. This, to be sure, was not a new phenomenon; since the seventeenth century, writers had developed theories on how to measure and enhance national power. This continued, but at the end of the nineteenth century and the beginning of the twentieth, power also came to be put in the context of the West's relationship with the non-West. Power often meant control over distant lands. Civilization, another term that was widely used, was synonymous with power; those nations that were more powerful were by definition more civilized, and vice versa. Those less civilized remained less powerful, incapable of maintaining their existence without some supervision and protection by the West. Indeed, the more civilized had an obligation to exercise such supervision in order to help the less powerful. Best expressed in Rudyard Kipling's phrase, "the white man's burden," the equation of power and civilization provided the ideological framework in which international affairs were discussed.

The burden was the white man's, for at that time only the white race appeared to be among the most powerful and the most civilized. Other races seemed to be in a state of passivity, weakness, and disorder and threatened with extinction unless the white race came to their rescue – by controlling them; by providing for law and order, health care, and education; in short, by civilizing them. All such activities confirmed the conception of race hierarchy that had always existed but which now became more relevant in view of the coming closer together of various races of mankind.

Americans partook of this ideology. They, of course, prided themselves as being among the most civilized; they enjoyed the highest standard of living in the world, roads and sewage systems were fast covering the whole continent, their schools were socializing millions of newcomers, and innovations in refrigeration, meat packing, and wholesale merchandising were creating a huge national middle class. As in the European countries, the distance between government and society (or the state and civil society, as some have termed the dichotomy) was narrowing, with the state becoming increasingly concerned over social order and welfare. In such a situation, both domestic and external affairs came to be products of closer coordination between governmental authorities and private citizens than had been the case earlier. That was probably why the concepts of power and civilization were interchangeable. The state, exercising power, was in charge of protecting the civilization, the sum of private endeavors. That even in the United States, where traditionally the private sector (society) had been far more important than the government (the state) as a regulator of national life, power and civilization became synonymous indicates the approximation of ideological developments on both sides of the Atlantic.

At the same time, such self-assertiveness both in Europe and the United States concealed a growing defensiveness, a fear of the consequences of the new imperialism in transforming the entire world. For the new imperialism contained an internal paradox; it confirmed the West in the position of dominance over the non-West, but in such a way as to transform the latter. Once the transformation had occurred, there was no assurance that the non-West might not come to challenge the West's supremacy. This possibility already attracted lively interest at the turn of the century as Japan emerged as one non-Western country that was administratively centralized, economically unified, and militarily powerful – in other words, a modern state. Its victories over China and Russia (in the wars of 1894–5 and 1904–5, respectively) and its acquisition of colonies and spheres of influence in nearby areas marked Japan's emergence as a Western-style power and imperialist. Its transformation was a result of the nation's leaders having avidly emulated the West and eagerly sought to catch up with the latter in political, economic, and military affairs. If Japan, little endowed with natural resources and already overcrowded, could so transform itself, why not China, or India, or Turkey, or any other country willing to exert itself in similar fashion? And what if all these countries successfully modernized themselves? Surely, their modernization would make them less willing to tolerate Western dominance, and they might even come to threaten Western supremacy. The West might still retain its superiority in science or medicine; it might continue to uphold human rights and individual liberties better than other parts of the globe, but how good would they be if the non-Western peoples – numerically far surpassing Westerners – should decide to arm themselves and turn on the latter?

Of course, such nightmares were too extreme, derived from visions of essential incompatibility between West and non-West, between white and nonwhite peoples. (The "yellow peril" concept best described the racism underlying these fears.) What is interesting is that Americans, when they talked of such matters, invariably identified with Europeans. They viewed themselves as part of the Western minority that enjoyed momentary ascendancy but who feared its consequences. Henry Adams, his brother Brooks, and Alfred Thayer Mahan were among the most sophisticated writers of the time who earnestly wrote of the coming end of the age of Western dominance, and they were joined by thousands of others who used the same language in advocating immigration restriction, in particular the exclusion of Asian immigrants. They inhabited the same mental universe as Europeans insofar as the question of the West's relations with the non-West were concerned. Both in their self-assertiveness and self-defensiveness, Americans were very much part of the larger Western community.[9]

This does not mean, however, that Americans simply followed their European cousins in conceptualizing international affairs. One important development in the several years before the outbreak of the Great War in 1914 was the growing self-confidence with which American leaders in and out of government came to argue for their nation's special role in, or unique contribution to, the world. One may point to two particularly significant formulations: President William Howard Taft's "dollar diplomacy" and his and others' espousal of world peace through international law.

Taft's idea was to make use of the nation's financial resources in promoting an economically more interdependent – and therefore, he believed, politically stabler – international order. By substituting "dollars for bullets," the United States would seek to put an end to the seeming chaos in the world, which saw increasing arms, colonial rivalries, and military alliances. Instead of these, the nations would do well to devote their resources to economic endeavors. As the fast rising economic power, the United States could show the way. The nation was spending proportionately less of its income on government outlays and on armament than any other power, and so should persuade others to do likewise.

This stress on economic development and interdependence as a key to world order was reinforced by an increasingly active peace

9 For a discussion of Western perceptions of the non-West's modernization, see Akira Iriye, *Across the Pacific* (New York, 1967; repr., Chicago, 1992), chap. 3.

movement in the United States. Pacifism, of course, had existed for ages, in Europe as well as in the United States, but much of it had been inspired by Christian piety. Of late socialism had added a new variety, visualizing peace as a product of workers' control of decision making. (Presumably, they were more cosmopolitan than capitalists, especially arms manufacturers and bankers who financed them.) America's peace activists in the early twentieth century were different in their emphasis on international law. They reasoned that peace was a legally definable phenomenon, with nations agreeing to abide by certain principles of international law. It is no accident that they were particularly interested in arbitration as a way of resolving disputes among nations. If they accepted international law as a basic guide to their conduct, then they should be able to reconcile their differences through arbitration, not through military force.[10]

Both the ideas of economic interdependence and of peaceful settlement of disputes were to be incorporated into a new American agenda for world affairs that would be formulated by President Woodrow Wilson. But even before 1914 they were sufficiently advanced in the United States to constitute a vision of American leadership in international relations. Not just in the military sphere or in colonial questions, but also in organizing the world for a more peaceful order, the nation was preparing itself for a global role.

10 Sondra Herman, *Eleven Against War* (Stanford, 1969); Warren Kuehl, *Seeking World Order* (Nashville, 1969); C. Roland Marchand, *The American Peace Movement and Social Reform* (Princeton, 1972). The stress on international law as an instrument for preserving world order was also part of European thought since the seventeenth century. See Terry Nardin and David R. Mapel, *Traditions of International Ethics* (Cambridge, 1992).

2. *The Great War and American Neutrality*

The American Question in the War

The coming of the Great War had little or nothing directly to do with the United States. It was a culmination of complex intra-European conflicts which had at least four dimensions: the French-German contention over Alsace-Lorraine, the Balkan crisis brought about by efforts of various nationality groups to assert their independence of the Austro-Hungarian Empire or of the Ottoman Empire, the German-British rivalry over naval expansion, and the general colonial disputes.[1] In none of these conflicts had the United States been directly involved. Its military power had grown considerably, and it had come to possess an overseas empire. But its presence in global geopolitical affairs had been primarily confined to the Caribbean and the Pacific, even though it had developed extensive economic and ideological influences throughout the world. The very fact that war broke out in Europe without any sense of American involvement revealed that, much as the United States had begun to make itself conspicuous on the global stage, its mere existence and power alone were insufficient to prevent a major catastrophe in international affairs. As the great powers of Europe one after another mobilized for war in July 1914, and as they formally began fighting against one another in August, the United States recoiled in disbelief, incredulous that the civilized nations should thus stumble into fratricide but, all the same, relieved that at least the American people were spared the tragedy.

So it was natural that the United States should proclaim its neutrality as soon as war came. Although some, notably former President Theodore Roosevelt, warned that the war would alter the

1 On the origins of World War I, the best summary may be found in James Joll, *The Origins of the First World War* (London, 1984).

Europe
in 1914
European allied states
of World War I
Central states
of World War I
Neutral states
Arctic Ocean
Iceland
Atlantic
Ocean
Ireland
Scotland
Great
Britain
England
London
Denmark
The
Netherlands
Amsterdam
Norway
Sweden
Finland
Baltic Sea
Copenhagen
Archangel
Siberia
St. Petersburg
(Petergrad)
Moscow
Samara
Russia
Kharkov
Aral Sea
Vilna
Warsaw
Poland
Kiev
Ukraine
Rostov
Caspian Sea
Turkestan
Berlin
German
Frankfurt
Empire
Brest
Paris
France
Bordeaux
Galeat
Switz
Marseilles
Vienna
Austria-
Hungary
Bosnia
Romania
Black Sea
Portugal
Madrid
Lisbon
Spain
Barcelona
Gibraltor
Corsica
Sardinia
Italy
Rome
Naples
Adriatic Sea
Belorade
Serbia
Albania
Bulgaria
Sofia
Constantinople
Persia
Tangier
Sicily
Mediterranean
Sea
Greece
Athens
Ottoman Empire
Morocco
Algiers
Tunis
Crete
Cyprus
Aleppo
Damascus
Syria
Jerusalem
Tripoli
Algeria
Tripolitania
Benghazi
Cairo
Egypt
Arabia
Persian Gulf
Rio De Oro
(Spanish)

global balance of power and thus could not but affect the security of the nation, initially, at least, this did not seem to be the case. As the German forces sped across the western front to conquer Belgium and march on to the heart of France, and as German and British ships exchanged fire in the North Sea, there was little concern that whatever happened in Europe would immediately involve the United States. The only possible threat in the summer of 1914 lay in Asia, where Japan, which had emerged as a rival of the United States, seized upon its alliance with Britain, declared war on Germany, and proceeded to drive Germans out of China (Shantung Peninsula) and the western Pacific (the Carolines, the Marianas, and the Marshalls). Some naval strategists in Hawaii and Washington were alarmed, but President Woodrow Wilson was not. He, in fact, had forbidden the navy to undertake hypothetical war planning against Japan. He was not unaware of sources of conflict with Japan, especially the immigration dispute on the West Coast, but he did not believe the two countries were potential enemies at this time. The Japanese occupation of Shantung province and the German islands in the Pacific was viewed with essential equanimity. Events in Asia would not affect American neutrality in Europe.

Neutrality, however, did not mean severing of connections with Europe. On the contrary, Americans were eager to continue their commercial activities across the Atlantic, just as their forebears had done during the Napoleonic wars. As they did so, they soon learned that official neutrality did not prevent the nation from having an impact on the course of the war, that their very neutrality could end up favoring one side in the conflict over the other.

Activities by Americans as citizens of a neutral nation included carrying goods from the United States to Europe, and from one European country to another, traveling on American and European vessels, and engaging in financial and other transactions with the belligerent governments and their citizens. Washington claimed that all these were legitimate activities of a neutral nation. At the same time, it also recognized that under existing international law, the belligerents had certain rights with regard to neutral trade. They could intercept neutral ships to inspect their cargo, confiscate goods that were deemed contraband, take away enemy personnel who might be traveling on board, or even take such ships to port for detention to deny their seizure by the enemy.

Such broad agreement was no guarantee that the rights of a neutral nation would be respected, however, for all belligerents would try to restrict such rights lest they should benefit the enemy side. Britain made this quite clear when it defined contraband very broadly in order to stop shipments from the United States to Germany of all but obviously nonmilitary goods such as food and medicine. After March 1915, moreover, the British Navy was authorized to stop all goods destined for Germany through the institution of a blockade. Blockading the enemy coast was acceptable in international law so long as it was effective; the belligerent power establishing it must not simply declare a blockade but must use its force to divert ships entering the blockaded area to other destinations. The cargoes of such ships would be detained or paid for as compensation. However, as neutral (e.g., U.S.) goods could reach Germany through another neutral port (for instance, in Sweden), Britain forbade such practice ("continuous voyages") and stopped American contraband from reaching neutral destinations.

Predictably, these strong measures provoked countermeasures by Germany. To deny Britain and its allies their advantages at sea, the German Navy began, in 1915, employing U-boats or submarines against enemy warships and other categories of vessels. Existing international law did not explicitly forbid submarine warfare (unlike poison gas, whose use had been declared illegal in 1899 at the International Peace Conference at The Hague), although there was considerable murkiness as to whether it was lawful for a submarine to fire at an enemy merchantman without warning. In any event, the U-boat campaign had immediate implications for the United States as the rights of Americans to travel on nonmilitary belligerent ships would be compromised.[2]

In such a situation, it was no simple matter for the United States to maintain its neutrality. Because Washington was determined to protect U.S. citizens' neutral rights, there ensued, from the very

2 For an extensive discussion of the wartime disputes concerning neutral rights, see Arthur S. Link, *Wilson: The Struggle for Neutrality* (Princeton, 1960).

beginning of the war, an acrimonious series of exchanges with the belligerent governments on the legality of what they were doing. It will be recalled that there had developed a strong movement in America to promote a world order on the basis of international law. In a sense, then, to protest against violations of American neutral rights reflected a determination to continue to play a role in world affairs even in a period of conflict, to remind the great powers that they had an obligation to observe international law in war as in peace.

Thus, by its very decision to remain neutral, the United States found itself becoming part of the European conflict. For the belligerents were forced to balance their strategic needs with diplomatic considerations toward the United States. Both Britain and Germany were determined to avoid a serious crisis with America even as they carried on their fierce war at sea. But it was very difficult to do so. Britain, for instance, tried to mollify American opinion by exempting cotton from the list of embargoed goods. But this did not prevent serious disputes between the two countries. Washington and London exchanged many notes during 1914 and 1915, the former protesting against Britain's infringement on neutral rights and the latter justifying its action on legal grounds. The disagreement between the two positions was virtually irreconcilable and might have led to a grave crisis but for other circumstances.

One was the nature of American opinion, official and at large. President Wilson, to be sure, declared on a number of occasions that the nation must maintain its neutrality in thought and behavior. The war, he repeatedly told his countrymen, was a European affair involving disputes over matters about which the United States was not concerned. At the same time, however, in private conversations and correspondence he did not conceal his sympathies with Britain. As a political science scholar and as a practicing politician, he had looked on the British system of government as an exemplary form of democracy, which he considered was being challenged by German autocracy.[3] Many advisers around him – Colonel Edward House, Robert Lansing (secretary of state after May 1915), and others –

3 Ibid., 50–2.

were outspoken supporters of the British side in the war, as were highly vocal public figures such as Theodore Roosevelt and presidents of prestigious East Coast universities. Their proallied sentiment was reinforced by a highly effective propaganda campaign organized in London. Through its diplomats and other agents (the most successful of them was Sir William Wiseman, who established his headquarters in New York and kept in close touch with prominent Americans), the British government disseminated anti-German propaganda, fed high officials in Washington confidential information that was favorable to the allies, and sought to influence local opinion by contacting newspaper editors. The Germans, of course, were by no means inactive. They too organized public relations networks to incite anti-British sentiment, especially in rural areas and small towns with sizable populations of German background. A large number of them, as well as those of Irish origin, insisted that the nation should maintain strict neutrality in the war. Few of them advocated outright support of Germany, but many were opposed to any action on the part of the United States that benefited Britain and its allies. The influence of pro-German opinion would have remained strong and might even have grown if America's dispute had been confined to Britain.[4]

Starting in 1915, however, the assertion of American neutral rights came to involve Germany as much as Britain as Berlin commenced its U-boat campaign, not just against warships but also nonmilitary freighters and passenger liners. One dramatic incident occurred in May 1915 when the *Lusitania,* a British ocean liner with American travelers aboard, was sunk, with the loss of 128 American lives. The public was incensed, as this was a clear violation of what the American people believed to be one of their fundamental rights. Washington immediately fired off a stiff protest, holding Germany strictly accountable for further loss of American lives and infringement on neutral rights. Alarmed at the possibility of driving the United States to the other side, Berlin quickly expressed its regrets

4 One of the best studies of wartime American society is David Kennedy, *Over Here* (New York, 1980).

over the affair and pledged to exercise more caution in dealing with American lives.

Secretary of State William Jennings Bryan resigned over what he considered Wilson's needlessly harsh reaction to the *Lusitania* affair, an indication that an event as serious as this still was not sufficient to unite American opinion against Germany. Many Americans undoubtedly agreed with Bryan that while the loss of American passengers was regrettable, it was equally deplorable that Britain, through its blockade, was starving an entire nation.[5] It was difficult to decide on the moral merits of such an issue, but at least the U-boat campaign checked the tendency of wartime U.S.-British relations to deteriorate to a point of severe crisis.

Finally, despite the acrimonious debate over neutral rights, economically the United States became tied almost exclusively to the British side in the war. In theory, of course, neutral trade would have involved the nation in trade with all belligerents, but given the blockade of the Continent, little could reach Germany. Britain, on the other hand, freely obtained from America what it and its allies needed, especially arms and munitions. Altogether some $2.2 billion of arms were sold by the United States to Britain and its allies between August 1914 and March 1917, the period of American neutrality, a considerable sum when one recalls that the export of U.S. merchandise in 1913 had amounted to a little over $2.4 billion. Such large shipments – and, of course, other items such as iron, steel, and foodstuffs were also sent to Britain in increasing quantities – could not be paid for by the latter through its own exports to the United States or through the transfer of gold. (All belligerents embargoed the export of gold, thus effectively putting an end to the gold standard, which had sustained world commercial transactions since the 1890s.) Nor were British assets in the United States sufficient to cover the costs. At first, short-term credits of six months' duration and then, when the war did not end, longer-term credits had to be extended to British purchasers of American goods. These credits amounted to loans extended by American bankers, and

5 Charles Tansill, *America Goes to War* (Boston, 1938), 258–9.

Wilson and Bryan were initially uneasy about the possible implications of this for the nation's neutrality. But they ultimately supported the financial transactions, because without them wartime trade could not be carried out.

If these increasingly close commercial and financial ties with Britain did not alter the nation's policy of neutrality, at least they mitigated the atmosphere of crisis in U.S.-British relations arising out of the disputes at sea. For it could not be denied that the increasing amounts of American trade, shipping, and loans were making the nation a virtual participant in the war, and that most certainly these activities were benefiting the British side to the detriment of the Central Powers. Thus, ironically, the more extensively the United States engaged in neutral trade, the less could it remain a neutral in the struggle. The belligerents, on their part, understood the situation, recognizing only too well that the American question, which had played no part in the European war's origins, was now becoming a crucial issue, possibly even the decisive factor in determining the course of the conflict.

American Visions

One consequence of this growing importance of the American question in the European war was the need to persuade the Americans themselves of this fact – that is, to make them realize that, despite their official neutrality and widespread aversion to becoming involved in the conflict, they were in fact playing an increasingly vital role in it and that their actions even as nonbelligerents would have serious implications for the outcome of the struggle.

First of all, Americans quickly recognized that the European war was turning the nation into the strongest economic power in the world, with implications not only for U.S. foreign affairs but also for the future development of other countries as well. For it was not just in Europe that American trade and shipping expanded. As the European merchant marine virtually disappeared from Asia, the Middle East, and Latin America, American ships took its place, carrying not only domestic merchandise but other countries' products as well to various ports throughout the world. These activities were accompanied by rapid increases in American investments and loans abroad. Hitherto the United States had been a net importer of capital, but virtually overnight it became a creditor nation as the European powers liquidated their holdings in the United States to pay for their purchases and then turned to the latter to obtain loans and credits. Outside of Europe, increasing amounts of American capital were imported and invested in banks, railways, and factories. (Nascent industrialization began in Asia and Latin America to make up for the lost European imports.)

The United States would have emerged as the leading economic power in the world even without the European war, but now this was fast becoming a reality. The American government and people welcomed this, and their adamant insistence on protesting any infringement of neutral rights indicated the widely shared view that if Europe's distress was America's gain, there was nothing to apologize for. In fact, by carrying on its commercial activities, the United States could be said to be ensuring that global economic transactions were disrupted as little as possible during the conflict. Those who had envisioned stable international order in economic terms could only congratulate themselves that with their nation's impressive economic performance, the cause of world peace had a better chance of being served than ever before.

It was a step from such thought to the idea that the nation should not simply engage in neutral commercial activities but try to use its newly gained power and influence to help bring the European war to an end. Not through entering the war as a belligerent but through some constructive mediatory role could the United States make a worthy contribution to world affairs. That would be the most satisfying way the nation could utilize its resources and influence. Precisely because the European war's origins had had nothing to do with the United States, the latter would be in a position to offer its good offices to the belligerents. Thus already in early 1915 Wilson dispatched Edward House to England, France, and Germany on a peace mission, in order to ascertain these powers' interest in a mediated end to the hostilities. Wilson's and House's thinking at this time did not go much beyond restoring the prewar status quo, coupled with some reduction of armaments and the reestablishment of a regime of global economic interdependence.[6]

Unfortunately, nothing came of the House mission; he was told in London that Britain would accept a peace only if it meant the destruction of German militarism. Not discouraged, Wilson tried again in 1916, sending House back to the European capitals. This time, however, House would not just offer America's good offices or sound out the thinking of the belligerent governments but would actually summon them to a peace conference. The United States would invite both sides to attend the conference where it would specify certain conditions for peace. It is indicative of much thinking that had gone on in Washington that the 1916 House mission went far beyond postulating the restoration of the status quo ante bellum, as had been the case in 1915. Now House (and, of course, Wilson) spoke of the cession of Alsace and Lorraine to France, and of Constantinople to Russia – terms that clearly favored the allied side. More important was the proposal for the establishment of an international organization to ensure the postwar world order. The idea had emerged among certain leaders, such as former President William Howard Taft, who had begun calling for the creation of "a league to enforce peace." (The British foreign secretary, Edward Grey, also advocated a similar idea.) Wilson wanted to make the idea his own and likewise began urging the establishment of some such organization after the war. Taft, Wilson, and other advocates of the idea believed that merely to restore the prewar status quo would bring the world back where it had been in 1914 and would have solved nothing. Another war would most surely break out. What was needed was a new world organization to replace the traditional mechanism of balance of power. With prominent Republicans and Democrats supporting such a proposal, the new Wilsonian initiative might well have served to signal America's emergence as the arbiter of the European conflict without itself becoming involved in the fighting.

The European governments, however, were not yet ready for the

6 N. Gordon Levin, *Woodrow Wilson and World Politics* (New York, 1968), 38–9.

American initiative. To be sure, Britain, France, and Germany – the three countries visited by House in 1916 – did not flatly turn down Wilson's offer of mediation. To do so would have antagonized the United States, so their leaders listened to House and expressed a willingness to explore the possibility of a negotiated peace. Berlin, in particular, sought to embarrass the British and the French by agreeing to let the United States proceed with the peace efforts. Underneath, however, the German Navy was planning for an all-out submarine campaign as the ultimate weapon to bring down the allies, after the war on land had bogged down in trench warfare. Supremely confident of success, the naval strategists, with the support of the kaiser, held firm against any premature truce. Britain and France, on their part, had entered into secret negotiations with each other and with the other allies (Russia, Japan, and Italy) to divide up the spoils of victory. Assuming that the war would ultimately be won, they wanted postwar territorial dispositions to reflect the victory, at the expense of Germany and its overseas empire. These negotiations were kept secret from the Americans and could not, for obvious reasons, be the rationale for rejecting American mediation. Rather, officials in London and Paris encouraged House's efforts so as to curry favor with the United States. They agreed to Wilson's terms as the basis for negotiation and even succeeded in having the latter pledge that if Germany and its allies should not agree to attend a peace conference the United States was to call, the latter "would probably enter the war" on their side. This was an unusual commitment on Wilson's part and may have reflected his confidence that the pledge would not have to be honored, because Germany would see the wisdom of a mediated peace.

In any event, by then America's strong interest in playing the role of peacemaker was abundantly clear. This went much beyond anything Washington had ever attempted in European affairs. Clearly it reflected the sense that the Europeans were incapable of managing their own, and by extension the world's, affairs, and that without some leadership role played by the United States, there could be no stable international order. Although the precise nature of that role or of the international order the United States would seek to promote remained vague, the Americans did not have to start from scratch but could build on many years of preparation. They had come to assume that world peace, global economic development and interdependence, and domestic stability were interchangeable propositions, all contributing to peace at home and abroad. From such a perspective, a war among the economically developed and politically advanced nations of Europe was nothing but a disaster. Because they nevertheless were destroying one another, something was lacking there. The United States would provide that something and bestir itself so as to minimize the damage to civilization and establish a stable international system in which such wars would become less likely.

The ultimate failure of America's mediation efforts – which became evident when Germany announced the resumption of unrestricted submarine warfare in January 1917 – should not detract from the historic significance of these developments. The United States had prepared itself economically and intellectually for a crucial role in the European conflict. And now, in 1917, it was about to define its role in military, strategic terms and to assume a leadership position not only in European but also in global affairs from which it would not retreat for decades to come, except for a brief interlude in the mid-1930s. In that sense, the twentieth century, as the century in which the United States emerged as the principal world power, may be said to have begun in 1917.

America in Asia and Latin America

In the meantime, as the United States was preparing itself for an ultimate involvement in the European war, it was pursuing active, interventionist policies in East Asia and the Caribbean, something of a rehearsal for what was to come in Europe.

First of all, the United States found itself becoming more and more deeply involved in Asian affairs because it was the only power capable of influencing the course of acrimonious, often violent relations between China and Japan. It should be noted that the coming of the European war coincided with important changes within both these countries. The Meiji emperor, under whom Japan had undertaken successful programs of military strengthening and colonial acquisitions, died in 1912, and the coming of the Taisho era triggered movements against the continuation of those programs. Some called for a cutback in military spending, and others for more democratic government. But then war came in Europe, and Japan's expeditions to Shantung and the German islands further expanded the power of the military, which sought to take advantage of the temporary absence of European nations from China by entrenching Japanese influence there. One climax came in May 1915 when Japan presented a list of twenty-one demands to China, including the renewal of the lease of south Manchurian bases, the transfer of the German rights in Shantung to Japan, and Japanese supervision of Chinese police.

China was vulnerable to such strong tactics on the part of Japan because it, too, was undergoing transformation. In 1911 a revolt had erupted against the reigning Ch'ing dynasty, and in the following year the three-century-old dynasty came to an end, unable to withstand either the revolutionary movements or its own internal decay as manifested by the unwillingness of the scholar-gentry class to come to its rescue. Instead, these erstwhile elites combined with the revolutionaries to proclaim the Republic of China. Much confusion and disunity ensued, but by 1913 Yüan Shih-k'ai, a former high Ch'ing official, emerged as the new leader, assuming the title of provisional president. He was opposed, however, by more radical groups led by Sun Yat-sen and by other former leaders, some of whom held sway over various regions of the country. They soon developed their own military bases and became warlords, effectively dividing the young republic into so many subunits. Underneath all this turmoil, at the same time, new political and intellectual winds were blowing. Deeply influenced by what they took to be China's embarrassing weakness in international affairs, the "young China" leaders were determined to put an end to the country's humiliation. The emerging opinion leaders – university professors and students, merchants, journalists, and even some army officers trained abroad (including Japan) – were a force to be reckoned with. Thus, an episode like the twenty-one demands both revealed China's weakness and produced a nationalistic reaction, making it extremely difficult for the government to accede to Japanese pressure.

It was in such a situation that the United States found itself becoming more deeply involved in Asian affairs than it might have anticipated. In part this was due to Europe's temporary absence from the scene and, even more pertinent, its diminished prestige in the non-Western parts of the world. There is little doubt that the prestige that the European nations had enjoyed as the center of civilization and of power was shattered by the war. Liang Ch'i-ch'ao, the leading Chinese intellectual, spoke for millions outside the West when he wrote that Europe was no longer the model for others to emulate and that its very greatness had concealed flaws and sicknesses that had come out in the open in the bloody war.[7]

The fact that even the finest of European cultural figures as well as leaders of the Socialist International had almost overnight become ardent patriots, urging their respective countrymen to put country above all other considerations, was deeply disturbing to those Asians who had looked up to them for guidance and inspiration. No longer able or willing to do so, they naturally looked in the direction of the United States, one country that had refrained from entering the conflict. Of course, Asians had viewed America with admiration tinged with awe because of its natural resources and technological skills. Now, however, the United States also seemed to possess wisdom when Europe was discarding it, to exemplify progress when Europe had apparently deviated from its paths, and to stand ready to replace the latter as the world's new leader.

The situation augured well for China, which many Americans now called their "sister republic." The new Chinese leaders could surely expect to benefit from the emerging presence of the United States in the international arena as they undertook to reorganize their own national affairs. And President Wilson obliged without hesitation. Even before the republican revolt began in 1911, he had shown a strong interest in missionary activities, and as president he was eager to promote American influence in China, Christian and secular. He appointed a scholar, Paul Reinsch of the University of Wisconsin, as minister to Peking, and sent another, Frank Goodnow

7 Joseph Levenson, *Liang Ch'i-ch'ao and the Mind of Modern China* (Cambridge, Mass., 1953), 203.

of Johns Hopkins, as special adviser to Yüan Shih-k'ai. He also sought to interest American bankers in investing in China's future by providing funds for the development of railways and industry. It was quite natural, then, that Yüan and his aides should have turned to the United States for help when they were confronted with wartime Japanese imperialism, in particular the twenty-one demands of 1915.

The Japanese, on their part, realized that henceforth they would have to reckon with American reaction whenever they dealt with China. Many Japanese leaders, it should be noted, shared their Chinese counterparts' perception about the rising prestige and importance of the United States in the world scene, but for this very reason they were nervous about the developing Chinese-American ties. They sought to assure Washington that Japan was not contemplating anything unusual in China, but simply acting in self-defense by adjusting itself to the changed circumstances brought about by the European war. In a sense the Japanese were putting the United States in the traditional framework of big-power diplomacy, whereas the Chinese were more eager to see an America that stood for new principles, for a new way of conducting international affairs.

Both Japanese and Chinese were right, for American policymakers were in fact divided over the question of how far they should become involved in the Chinese-Japanese dispute. Some, echoing Theodore Roosevelt's pragmatic argument, believed little would be gained by backing China against the stronger Japan, which was in a position to threaten American security and interests in Asia and the Pacific. Others asserted that such old-fashioned thinking should be discarded in favor of a more forthright and righteous policy, especially because the new Chinese republic desperately needed American support.[8] The result was a compromise; Washington quietly expressed its opposition to the more obnoxious aspects of the twenty-one demands while at the same time openly declaring that the United States would not recognize any agreement between the two Asian

8 For a discussion of the origins of "missionary diplomacy" in China, see James Reed, *The Missionary Mind and American East Asian Policy* (Cambridge, Mass., 1983).

countries that infringed on the Open Door principle or the territorial integrity of China. These expressions of helpfulness toward China, however, were combined with a statement made to the Japanese government that the United States well recognized Japan's special interests in areas of China that were closest to it, such as Manchuria.

Such a policy of support for China combined with the placating of Japan did not satisfy President Wilson, whose sympathies lay mostly with the former. In order to help China more effectively, he decided to encourage its entry into the European war. It would be primarily of symbolic significance alone, but by declaring war against Germany and Austria, China would be able to confiscate enemy property, put an end to the old treaties that had given these countries their "unequal" rights, and treat Germans and Austrians as enemy aliens subject to incarceration. If nothing else, such steps would demonstrate that the Chinese were not powerless and that they could take on some of the world's mightiest powers. The Japanese well understood such logic and symbolism, and for that reason opposed China's entering the war. By the beginning of 1917, however, they had come to reconcile themselves to the situation and even to see the wisdom of supporting China's war against Germany. By then Yüan was dead (he had died in June 1916), and Peking was under the control of warlords, at least some of whom were considered to be pro-Japanese. So, by not standing in the way of China's entering the war, Tokyo hoped to smooth the path for improved relations between the two countries.

Thus it was that the war among the European powers, whose origins had little to do with either America or Asia, ended up bringing the United States, Japan, and China into the conflict as cobelligerents of one side against the other. These extra-European nations would surely have a greater say in postwar international affairs – another sign of the relative decline of Europe in the world.

In the meantime, the United States was establishing its firmer presence in Central America and the Caribbean than had been the case before the war. There was, to be sure, little new about U.S. assertiveness or interventionism in the region; in the wake of the Spanish-American War, the nation had steadily extended its influence through various means: annexation (Puerto Rico), a protectorate (Cuba), military occupation (the Canal Zone), customs receivership (Santo Domingo), and political intervention (Nicaragua). While the attention of the European powers had been focused elsewhere, the United States had virtually established its sphere of influence in the area.

The Great War provided an opportunity to consolidate such control, which appeared justified in order to prevent the region from becoming involved in the European antagonisms. President Wilson, however, wanted to go a step beyond traditional gunboat diplomacy, to indicate that U.S. policy in Central America and the Caribbean was different from other imperialists' policies. He could not have done otherwise, given his growing conviction that the nation must bestir itself to play a leadership role in international affairs. If the United States was to be more than a regional power and globalize its commitments, it would be important to demonstrate that, in dealing with nearby countries, the nation pursued more than self-interest. That was why wartime U.S. interventions in Mexico, Haiti, and Santo Domingo were couched in language that suggested connections with the larger goals of American foreign policy. Earlier, interventionism in the region had been justified in the name of the Monroe Doctrine (Theodore Roosevelt) or of the dollar diplomacy (Taft). Now, under Wilson, it was couched in the vocabulary of political reform, precisely the language in which the Wilsonian administration was trying to cope with developments in Asia and Europe.

To be sure, each country represented its unique problems. In Mexico's case two American interventions (in 1914 and 1916) were bound up with the country's internal turmoil following the overthrow of the 35-year dictatorship of Porfirio Díaz in 1911. Out of the chaos, one power contender, Victoriano Huerta, emerged as the strongman and proclaimed himself the new president, just before Woodrow Wilson entered the White House. Unlike China's Yüan Shih-k'ai, however, Huerta did not impress President Wilson as worthy of America's support. On the contrary, Wilson believed the Mexican had come to power through intimidation and even assassination of his opponents. The Mexican people, he was convinced, deserved better, and until a more democratically elected leader emerged, the United States would withhold formal recognition. De facto relations continued to exist between the two countries, but even these were jeopardized when, in the spring of 1914, U.S. troops landed in and occupied Vera Cruz in retaliation against the arrest of several American sailors in Tampico, to which they had been sent from a warship to obtain gasoline. The strong action was intended to force Huerta's resignation, which was eventually accomplished, but not until after even his opponents denounced the U.S. intervention.

The affair was a good example of complications that accompanied America's emerging global role: the conflict between the American policy of promoting reformist government in another country, on one hand, and the latter's nationalism that often transcended its internecine strife, on the other. A particularly unfortunate variant of the theme was the U.S.-Mexican altercation of 1916, which resulted from an American expedition into northern Mexico in pursuit of troops loyal to Francisco Villa, who, challenging the authority of the new provisional president, Venustiano Carranza, had invaded U.S. territory (New Mexico) in order to embarrass the latter. He almost succeeded, as Carranza protested against the expedition, which was led by General John J. Pershing. There was talk of war between the two countries, but they desisted from that step, in part because President Wilson could not justify such a development in view of the deepening U.S. involvement in the European hostilities, but also because Carranza preferred to end the crisis and win American diplomatic recognition as a reward. He got what he wanted.

That was not the end of the U.S.-Mexican crisis, however. Just before Carranza's formal recognition by Washington, Mexico had promulgated a new constitution providing, among other things, for universal suffrage, agrarian reform, and, most important for the United States, restrictions on foreign ownership of land and subsoil resources, notably oil. This last provision, included in Article 27 of the constitution, was ominous for American and other (mostly British) investors who had obtained oil-mining concessions.[9] The clash

9 Robert Freeman Smith, *The United States and Revolutionary Nationalism in Mexico* (Chicago, 1972), chap. 4.

between Mexican nationalism and the American insistence on the sanctity of contracts would complicate their relations for years to come. Whereas aspects of the new Mexican nation – democratization, constitutionalism – were no doubt welcome to America, the latter could not accept unconditionally the implied radicalism of Article 27. This was a harbinger, for the United States would encounter similar challenges in many other parts of the world.

United States expeditions to Haiti (1915) and Santo Domingo (1916) were less complicated because in neither country was there a unified movement to mobilize nationalistic opinion against foreign intervention. But the situation in Hispaniola was analogous to that in China or Mexico in that in both Haiti and Santo Domingo there was apparently endless political disorder, with politicians assassinating one another and ordinary people helpless to stop corruption and turmoil. The situation persuaded President Wilson that the United States would have to step in to "teach" these people "how to elect good men." This was the Caribbean version of what would soon emerge as the "safe for democracy" principle. American Marines and naval forces were the instrument for this educational process; they supervised elections, maintained law and order, and, in the case of the Dominican Republic, even took over cabinet posts. The protectorate over these countries went beyond the scope of the Roosevelt Corollary (which had led to the establishment of customs receiverships) and included the appointment of American financial advisers, sanitation engineers, and police instructors.

Even as Washington supported China's vehement opposition to Japan's twenty-one demands, which would have turned the former into the latter's protectorate and which the Japanese justified as a means for putting an end to Chinese chaos, the Wilson administration was establishing military rule over two Caribbean countries. It would be continued for many years; U.S. forces would be withdrawn from Santo Domingo only in 1924, and from Haiti not until 1934. Combined with America's military presence in Nicaragua, where Wilson maintained his predecessor's policy of stationing U.S. Marines (they would stay till 1925) and establishing a customs receivership, the United States was clearly turning itself into the overlord of the region. How different was such behavior from Japan's in Asia or Germany's in Europe? At least as far as Wilson was concerned, there was no contradiction at all between his espousal of a peaceful world order and the use of military force in the Caribbean. A future peace that he was then envisioning would be a cooperative one in which international action might sometimes have to override parochial concerns. Force would have a role to play so long as it was employed for nobler, not traditional, objectives.[10] Indeed, the United States was about to become engaged in a massive war – for a noble end. In that sense, the Mexican and Caribbean expeditions may be considered a rehearsal for preparing the nation for the grand task of global reconstruction.

10 The best discussion of Wilson's use of force in the Caribbean is Frederick Calhoun, *Power and Principle* (Kent, Ohio, 1986). See also the same author's *Uses of Force and Wilsonian Foreign Policy* (Kent, Ohio, 1993).

3. The United States at War

America Goes to War

Few countries had been as well prepared to go to war as the United States in 1917. Not that the nation had made specific preparations to enter the European conflict on the side of Britain and its allies against Germany and other "central" powers. Officials in Washington as well as the American people would have welcomed a peace if it had been arranged by the combatants without their military intervention. Yet if intervention were to come, the United States was in an excellent position to make a decisive difference. It had strengthened itself economically and militarily during the years of neutrality, the people had had ample time to educate themselves about world affairs and their country's potential role in them, and American foreign policy had been so conducted as to ensure the nation's leadership position once it entered the war.

In the military sphere, President Woodrow Wilson had, in 1916, begun calling for preparedness – at first in order to keep the nation so prepared militarily that no power would dare challenge its security and interests. After 1917, of course, the purpose changed to creating a strong armed force to fight a war. The Selective Service Act of May 1917 established a system for registering Americans for military service, and within a year the army was able to send over two million "doughboys" to Europe. The navy would in the meantime be augmented, and the naval building program of 1918 envisaged making the U.S. Navy the most powerful in the world. The armed forces would be equipped with arms and munitions all produced domestically, and a governmental bureaucracy was created to establish priorities in allocating resources. All this might have cost other countries much time, not to mention money, and strained the social order, but in the United States the transition from peace to war was relatively smooth and painless. The nation could "afford" the war economically and politically. The government had sufficient revenue, there was no diminution of consumer goods even while factories produced military hardware, and the Progressive ideology of state-society cooperation (that the government and the people should cooperate closely to effect necessary reforms) could be applied to war as well as to peace.

Even so, America's entry into the European war, making the conflict a "world" war, was not something the nation chose deliberately. Had there been an easing of U.S.-German tensions following Berlin's announcement of an unrestricted U-boat campaign in January 1917, Washington might have decided to go back to its mediatory endeavor. During the next three months, however, developments in Europe and elsewhere conspired to lead to the American decision for war. First, despite Wilson's denunciation of the renewed U-boat campaign, the German Navy went ahead with the deployment of submarines, which promptly sank American mercantile vessels in addition to British warships. The hostile behavior of the German admiralty, and the Berlin government's apparent capitulation to the latter, persuaded Wilson that Germany was not interested in a negotiated end to the war and that German militarism was the main obstacle to peace. This, of course, had been the British position all along, so the United States was belatedly embracing it. All the acrimonious disputes with London regarding neutral rights seemed to pale in significance in comparison with this fundamental issue of the war.

Relations between the United States and Germany deteriorated further in late February, when the United States intercepted a message from Alfred Zimmermann, the German foreign secretary, to the Mexican government offering an alliance between the two countries (with the possible addition of Japan) against the United States. Zimmermann even hinted that Germany might help Mexico recover the lands it had lost to its northern neighbor in 1848. American officials had already been alarmed over the growth of German influence in Mexico, and the Zimmermann telegram, which was widely published in the United States, inflamed public opinion.[1] Then in March Russian revolutionaries rose against the tsarist regime and established a reformist government, which, on its surface, appeared more democratic and attuned to the wishes of the people. The event had immediate implications for American policy as President Wilson interpreted it as evidence of the rising democratic tide throughout the world. That was a most heartening development and needed strong support by the United States lest it be crushed by autocratic forces – and Germany now exemplified the latter. The time had come for the United States to enter the fray.

American entry into the war became official on April 2, 1917, when President Wilson presented his war message to Congress. The message was a clear statement of American grievances against Germany, in particular the latter's unrestricted U-boat campaign. But Wilson went much beyond listing specific grievances and couched the war decision in broader, ideological terms. The United States was going to fight Germany, he said, because the latter had proved to be a menace to world peace and civilization. So long as German militarism remained, there could be no secure peace. This much was a reiteration of Wilson's as well as Grey's ideas, which they had already expressed on a number of occasions. The president now put the struggle against German militarism in a universalistic, historical framework by asserting that the militarism itself was a product of an autocracy that had long suppressed democratic aspirations of the people. Echoing Immanuel Kant more than a century earlier, Wilson argued that only a democratic government could be counted upon to pursue a peaceful foreign policy. The growing sentiment for democracy and peace was a historical inevitability, and the United States was being called upon to ensure this historic progression. As the European democracies such as Britain, France, and Russia (under its newly democratic regime) were unable by themselves to combat German military power, the United States had to step in. It would have to wage a war against a mighty European power, something it had not done for over one hundred years. The United States would

1 On the Zimmermann telegram, see Friedrich Katz, *The Secret War in Mexico* (Chicago, 1981), 350–5.

now make its military power available to help determine the outcome of the European conflict and, most important, to ensure that the world would be "made safe for democracy." Four days later (April 6), Congress declared war against Germany.

Specifically what difference did American military power make in the war? Initially, it was more psychological than substantive; the news of America's entry into the war compelled the combatants to alter their strategies to take the new development into consideration. True, President Wilson insisted on keeping American forces separate from the allied powers'; instead of joining the latter as allies, the United States would be an "associated" power with its own command structure. Even so, the fact remains that American ships, soldiers, and arms were now added to one side of the war against the other, and this would tip the scale even before American men appeared on European soil.

For instance, Germany would try desperately to bring the enemy to its knees before American reinforcements arrived. To do so, it would be imperative to make maximum use of U-boats to destroy as much British naval power as possible, in the meantime using the ground troops for two principal objectives: to push Russian forces back as far east as possible and to occupy Paris and its environs. Germany was quite successful in the first objective, not least because Russian troops had become demoralized after months of fighting. The March revolution had toppled the unpopular tsarist regime, but the new leaders had trouble appealing to the masses to continue the war effort. Desertions from the armed forces continued, and in the meantime the radical Bolsheviks, who had never accepted the new leadership, actively campaigned among the rank and file to turn them against the war. They denounced the war as an imperialistic exploitation of oppressed peoples. The German high command, eager to exploit the situation, sought to drive Russia out of the war by encouraging such dissent and political instability. In a famous move, they put V. I. Lenin, the leader of the Bolsheviks living in Switzerland, on a train and sent him to Petrograd, with the obvious intention of turning him loose to create further confusion. The strategy worked, and soon the Bolsheviks succeeded in seizing power in Petrograd and a few other cities in November 1917. The

Bolshevik success meant the defection of Russia from the anti-German coalition, precisely what Germany was counting on.

In France, too, Germans were quite successful. They were determined to push on toward Paris before the Americans had a chance to come to the latter's rescue. And in the spring of 1918 German forces advanced to within a few miles of the city. In France as well as in England, Germany also sought to exploit the growing war weariness. The weariness might dissipate once American reinforcements appeared on the scene, and so it was all the more imperative to achieve quick successes in battle. In the meantime, German forces routed Italians in a major battle in October so that, at the end of 1917, it seemed as if German victory were within reach – unless Americans arrived to prevent it.

And arrive they did in impressive ways. Starting in June 1918, altogether two million American troops landed on the French shores, ready to combat the Germans. It would be difficult to say that the Americans were clearly the principal winners in the war, and more correct to note that their role was primarily to stop further German advances. But that was considered sufficient, for in the absence of a clear-cut victory, the German high command realized that time was on the side of the United States. Not only on land but at sea – where America's participation in laying mines and blockading the German coast effectively countered Germany's U-boat campaign – American entry into the conflict demonstrated that the most the Germans would be able to get out of the war would be a draw. In other words, American participation spelled the defeat of German ambitions.

Why were the American forces so successful in fighting against a well-trained, seasoned German military power? A number of factors may be mentioned. American soldiers and sailors were fresh to the war, still in the initial phase of enthusiasm, whereas the Germans had already experienced more than two years of trench warfare. More important, there was an apparently endless supply of American men, whereas German resources had been stretched to the limit. Nor should one forget that Germany's close ally, the Austro-Hungarian Empire, was disintegrating, making it easier for the United States and its "allies" to threaten Germany in the rear by encouraging separatist movements within the Habsburg Empire. For instance, when some Czech leaders established an interim government in Paris, the United States was quick to recognize it. President Wilson even sent a small-scale expedition to Siberia in order to rescue several thousand Czech troops who had apparently been trapped there and were eager to go back to Europe to fight. Washington likewise encouraged the anti-Habsburg sentiments of such other ethnic groups as Serbs and Croatians. All these moves served to weaken Germany's ability to create an effective fighting force to meet the American challenge.

By far the greatest reason for the ultimate success of the American war effort, however, was the nation's economic resources, which it shared generously with its "allies." As noted in the preceding chapter, three years' neutrality had brought enormous riches to the United States as it expanded export trade to the belligerents and lent money to them. Now, the accumulated wealth would be put to use in the form of arms and soldiers. Between April 1917 and the armistice in November 1918, the nation raised (and paid for) an army of four million, a navy of sixteen new warships plus numerous submarines, and an arsenal of formidable arrays of modern weapons. The income tax, which had been enacted just prior to the war, proved to be the most effective way of financing such a military machine, although the government also obtained funds by selling bonds. Altogether the United States lent more than $7.7 billion to the "allies" during the war. Compare this with America's national income of roughly $40 billion in 1917, and it is easy to understand why it must not have been excessively painful for the American people to finance the war.

Nor did the departure of two million American men for Europe deprive the economy of its efficiency or productivity. This is perhaps the most remarkable development of all. To be sure, there were agricultural and other deferments to spare farmers and some others military service. But factories, shops, and offices now had to do with new recruits, many of them women. To replace the work force in the cities, black Americans in large numbers left the South – the "great migration" to the northern cities. They were absorbed into the existing economic system and, it would appear, fitted very nicely into it. This was important as immigration was drastically reduced during the war, both as a reflection of the European war and as a matter of official policy. For it was at this time that the government began tightening restrictions on incoming foreigners, requiring them to take literacy tests before they were admitted. The number of immigrants, who had often exceeded a million a year before the war, now dwindled to a small fraction of that – all the more reason, then, to engage women and southern blacks in northern occupations.

War as a Crusade

The impressive performance of American military power and economic resources was matched – and sustained – by an ideological offensive led by President Wilson. This was not surprising in view of his keen interest, prior to 1917, in shaping the world to come after the war. Now that the United States was in the war, however, the aspirations of a neutral nation's leader developed into official enunciations of principles that were to guide the deliberations of the belligerents as they groped for peace.

As soon as he sent the war message to Congress, the president took steps to ensure that the war would change its character now that the United States was in it. No longer a conventional struggle for power among ambitious countries, it must now be redefined as a crusade – a war to "make the world safe for democracy." The United States would not be interested in merely helping the Europeans restore the prewar status quo. The nation was not fighting for such an old-fashioned goal; rather, it was eager to make a real difference in the shape of the future world, to contribute to defining it. And "democracy" was a key guiding principle precisely in such a context, for it stood for a new political order at home and, therefore, abroad. The underlying assumption was that so long as antidemocratic or nondemocratic governments existed, they would always be interested in wars of conquest, whereas democracies would never engage in such warfare. This was because democracy implied an enlightened citizenry, a responsible public opinion that would reject irrational pursuits of power and yearn for a more rational, orderly, harmonious world. Wilson's conception of "world public opinion" was crucial in this connection. He believed that public opinion worldwide was dedicated to peace, and that when public opinion throughout the world expressed itself – the democratic ideal – peace would prevail. Democracy at home and peace abroad, then, were two sides of the same coin.

There was also an economic basis to the idea. The democratizing crusade implied that individuals should be free to pursue their activities with as little interference as possible. Such activities would be conducive to generating greater wealth at home and to creating a more interdependent world as barriers to economic pursuits came down across national boundaries. Moreover, a more peaceful world meant a world with fewer armaments, in which productive capacities of nations would be devoted less to military preparations than to economic development.

Between April 1917 and the armistice of November 1918, Wilson made numerous statements to spell out his visions, but none was as famous as the Fourteen Points speech of January 1918. In it, he enumerated conditions that would serve as the basis for bringing an end to the fighting. Reflecting his crusading spirit, the Fourteen Points included references to open diplomacy (against secret treaties and alliances), the Open Door, arms control, and a new league of nations to ensure the peace in the future. All these ideas had been around for some time, but Wilson's contribution lay in putting them together in a comprehensive agenda for peace.

The Fourteen Points also included specific proposals concerning national boundaries. This was a rather traditional approach; all wars would result in territorial readjustments. But Wilson sought to redefine postwar boundaries as much as possible in accordance with the principle of "nationality" – what came to be known as "national self-determination." This derived from the Wilsonian notion of democracy, for it implied a people's freedom to determine its own fate, including the establishment of its own nation. The idea that each "nationality" should have its own nation – what may be termed "ethnic nationalism" – had developed since the nineteenth century, and history would show how potent a force it would remain throughout the twentieth. By giving it his blessing, Wilson was identifying with this force, against the idea of a multiethnic national community such as had been exemplified by the Ottoman Empire or the Austro-Hungarian Empire. Thus the Fourteen Points proposed "autonomous development" for the various nationalities composing Austria-Hungary, the independence of Poland (with access to the sea), the reduction of Turkey to areas inhabited by the Turkish people, as well as some readjustment of Italian boundaries along "clearly recognizable lines of nationality." It was much easier to enunciate such principles than to implement them, for it would be rather rare for a nationality group to live only in one area of the world, or for a region to consist only of one nationality. Wilson was not fully aware of these difficulties, but even if he had been, he still would have espoused the principle of self-determination, for without it the idea of a world made safe for democracy would remain an abstraction.[2]

In the rest of his speech, Wilson called on the belligerents to evacuate Russia, Romania, Serbia, and Montenegro, to restore the independence of Belgium, and to reassign Alsace-Lorraine to France. These could also be said to be in accordance with the principle of nationality, although each of these countries and provinces contained complex ethnic relations. Finally, Wilson referred to an equitable adjustment of colonial claims. This, the fifth of the Fourteen Points, was the only reference to the colonial question and may have indicated that at this time Wilson's preoccupation was with European issues. He evidently was not considering the application of self-determination to the European colonies overseas, and in time he and his successors would be compelled to define their attitudes more precisely.

All in all, this was a remarkable enunciation of an agenda for peace, a monument in terms of which the behavior of nations would be judged. Perhaps the key was its universalistic character. It spelled out some basic principles that were to define the postwar world order. Thus it was not meant to be a vindictive statement of peace

2 Much thinking and research on peace terms were carried out by the Inquiry, a group of some 150 academics and other specialists organized in 1918 to assist the president in preparing for the peace conference. See Lawrence Gelfand, *The Inquiry* (New Haven, 1963).

terms to be imposed on Germany. To be sure, the latter would be required to evacuate Belgium and other countries, as well as giving up Alsace-Lorraine. The independence of Poland with access to the sea would deprive Germany of some of its territory. Austria-Hungary and the Ottoman Empire, allied to Germany, would also see their huge dominions broken up. But Britain, France, Italy, and even the United States would be expected to abide by the new rules, some of which might infringe upon their traditional rights.

Wilson presented the proposal in universalistic terms because he believed it was the best way to appeal to the belligerents, especially to the ordinary people in Germany, France, Britain, and elsewhere so that they would decide to put down their arms on honorable terms. Whether the president also had in mind the Chinese, Japanese, and other non-Europeans in the war is not clear, but these latter would soon come to recognize the profound implications of Wilsonianism. (In October 1917, the United States and Japan signed an agreement, the so-called Lansing-Ishii Agreement, to the effect that the former recognized the latter's "special interests in China." This sounded very much like the old diplomacy against which Wilson had crusaded. But the agreement contained a secret protocol, declaring that the two nations would "not take advantage of the present conditions to seek special rights or privileges in China which would abridge the rights of the subjects or citizens of other friendly states." Obviously, this latter was more in accordance with Wilsonian principles. To have had to keep it a secret was ironical and unfortunate, for not being aware of its existence, the Chinese would protest vehemently against the Lansing-Ishii Agreement.)[3]

When the Fourteen Points were announced, most American troops had not yet arrived in Europe, and chances for a speedy peace appeared remote. In fact, in March 1918 Germany succeeded in detaching Russia from the war; as will be seen, the Bolshevik leaders had decided that their priority was to get out of the war, and they were willing to accept even humiliating terms (such as the loss of Poland, Finland, the Baltic states, and the Ukraine) in order to

3 See Burton F. Beers, *Vain Endeavor* (Durham, N.C., 1962), for an interpretation of the Lansing-Ishii Agreement.

obtain the peace. The Treaty of Brest-Litovsk enabled the Germans to concentrate on the western front. The "allies" even feared that Bolshevik Russia might join Germany against them.

In such circumstances, all talk of peace appeared to be premature. Once the tide had turned in the summer, however, Wilson's wartime pronouncements provided the context through which both sides could agree to a cease-fire. At the end of September, the German government approached Wilson to seek a peace on the basis of the Fourteen Points. Wilson welcomed the overture, and after the Germans reformed their government by making it presumably more democratic – the emperor was deposed – he managed to obtain the allies' agreement. By accepting Wilson's initiative, albeit with some reservations (for instance, the European allies wanted reparations from Germany), they were in fact acknowledging American leadership in world affairs. They had been unable to fight the war to its conclusion. American participation had been necessary, but this participation had been far more than military and strategic; it had been even more important in economic and ideological terms. The European war had been fought as an American crusade for peace.

The crusade had its domestic counterpart. Indeed, for Wilson the war effort was inseparable from domestic reforms. He was determined to push the Progressive agenda further through intellectual mobilization. He and his supporters – reformers such as Walter Lippmann, Herbert Croly, and Bernard Baruch – considered the war a rare opportunity to carry on the task, for the war required national unity and mobilization, an ideal condition for reorganizing domestic affairs. They introduced the ideas of economic planning, public service, and public education on international events. This last, what would today be called "public diplomacy," was an innovation. The idea was to acquaint the American people with the significance of the war and about the Wilsonian ideals that would inform America's wartime diplomacy. A new organization, the Committee of Information, was created to undertake the task. Directed by George Creel, a Colorado newspaper man, the committee organized extensive publicity campaigns throughout the country, best illustrated by the activities of "four-minute men," local leaders who would address their neighbors in brief speeches and discuss international problems.

Abroad, the committee sent its own representatives to engage in public relations work – activities that often came into conflict with those carried out by diplomats and consuls.[4]

Such public relations activities in wartime were not unique; Britain, for instance, developed an even more elaborate system of public information at home and abroad through the Foreign Office's Department of Information. But Wilson viewed these activities not merely as serving the immediate needs of the war but also as preparing the ground for the world to come after the fighting stopped. It was ironic that when the war ended, people throughout the globe had become well acquainted with Wilson's visions and that the American people had also acquired an unprecedented appreciation of foreign affairs, but that this very educational process would make foreigners and Americans alike all the more aware of the gaps between ideal and reality, between promise and performance. Moreover, public education would not necessarily make people more internationalist; they might become more nationalistic, even parochial, conscious of their rights as a nationality, an ethnic minority, or an oppressed colonial people. How to reconcile their aspirations with the overall objectives of a peaceful global order was a problem that was only vaguely appreciated during the war but that would present a formidable challenge after the war.

Wilson and Lenin

One aspect of the problem was already becoming clear – the Bolshevik challenge to Wilsonian initiatives. Democratizing international affairs was Wilson's goal as he fought against forces of reaction and autocracy. Ironically, the same appeal to public opinion and to common people was creating, in Russia, a movement vastly at odds with Wilsonianism. The Bolsheviks had come to power in the name of the masses, promising to end their suffering by promptly taking the country out of the war. Whereas Wilson believed he was fighting a war for democracy – and the democratic coalition necessarily included Russia – Lenin, Leon Trotsky, and other Bolshevik leaders

4 Gregg Wolper, "Wilsonian Public Diplomacy," *Diplomatic History* (Winter 1993).

judged, correctly, that the Russian people were tired of fighting, and that the revolutionaries could remain in power only by concluding a separate peace with Germany. In thus deciding on leaving the war, the Bolsheviks were directly challenging Wilson's leadership.

If the Bolsheviks had waited a little longer, the Americans would have arrived in France and ensured the allies' victory, making it perhaps possible for Russia to emerge as one of the victors. But they did not think in those terms then. They were preoccupied with domestic issues, above all with doing everything to consolidate their power. Anti-Bolsheviks, monarchists, and many others were active all over the country, and the Bolsheviks could not suppress them and fight a foreign war at the same time. Besides, they were not convinced that Germany could be defeated so easily. After all, they reasoned, the people in Britain, France, and elsewhere must be as weary of the war as the Russians, and, as Trotsky noted, Russia's example in pulling itself out of the war might inspire them to pressure their own governments to do likewise.[5] If they succeeded, there would soon be a cease-fire, and Russia under the Bolsheviks would be able to claim a leadership role in the peace process. And the peace, if it should come under such circumstances, would be a people's peace, unlike the traditional game of resettling boundaries or obtaining indemnities from defeated nations. This was the second challenge Wilson faced from Bolshevik Russia. Henceforth, wartime diplomacy and strategy would become bound up with the need to cope with the new challenge.

In the meantime, the German-Russian cease-fire had immediate military implications. Not only would the German Army now be able to concentrate on the western front, but the vast resources of the Ukraine and the adjacent areas would be at its disposal. Allied provisions and arms that had been sent to Russia and stored in port cities such as Archangel and Murmansk could fall into German hands. German and Austrian prisoners of war in Russian camps could be released and join the home units. (That some of them, notably the Czech troops, would refuse to do so and instead would join the allies did not significantly alter the picture.) There was,

5 Leon Trotsky, *My Life* (London, 1930), chap. 31.

furthermore, genuine fear that the Bolsheviks might join the Germans in the war. Many in the West believed that the former were actually German agents or in German pay. The combination of German and Russian manpower would present a formidable obstacle to ending the war.

The loss of Russia to the entente powers also had an Asian dimension. For the Bolsheviks did not initially extend their control to Siberia, where "white" Russians remained strong. Skirmishes occurred whenever the radicals sought to replace them in positions of authority. All of Siberia was in civil strife. This was a condition rife with opportunities for separatism – and for foreign, especially Japanese, ambitions. Japan was keenly interested in the developments, and some army leaders began advocating the strategy of detaching at least eastern Siberia from the rest of Russia. Should that happen, Japan would emerge as a formidable Asian power, quite a serious prospect from the point of view of the United States, not to mention China.

For all these reasons, the Bolsheviks' coming to power had important strategic implications. How to deal with them would come increasingly to preoccupy President Woodrow Wilson and his aides.

There was also an economic side to the story. Russia, with the Ukraine, had been one of the leading producers of agricultural produce in the world. But the wartime mobilization of peasants as well as political instability had created severe shortages of grain. Now the loss of the Ukraine would add to the already chaotic economic condition of the country. Then there was the Bolshevik program for nationalizing land, which could add further confusion. Moreover, prewar Russia had accumulated large foreign debts. Foreign, especially French, capital had been invested in its railways, banks, and factories, and the tsarist regime had also sold bonds to pay for the cost of the Japanese war and other expenditures. The Bolsheviks, however, repudiated these debts, saying they had been contracted by a government that had been overthrown and that did not represent the true interests of the Russian people. Such a revolutionary stance would not only make it impossible for the Bolsheviks to borrow money from abroad – even if they wanted to – but antagonize the foreign powers, which would insist on a settlement of the debt issue before they recognized the new regime.

The suffering of the Russian people in such circumstances was severe, but the Bolsheviks apparently reasoned that with the war's end it would become possible to concentrate on domestic economic reconstruction. They would also be able to turn to the humanitarian assistance of sympathetic people elsewhere. This was a rather vacuous hope in that the European belligerents would not be in a position to offer food and supplies when they themselves were having difficulties. The only hope lay in the United States, but it would take time before the Bolsheviks would turn in that direction and the Americans would offer humanitarian relief.[6]

In the meantime, the Bolsheviks launched an ideological offensive to challenge not only traditional European diplomacy but also Wilsonian internationalism. They were ideological heirs to the antiimperialists at the turn of the century – such as John A. Hobson and Rudolf Hilferding – who had assaulted the imperialistic activities of the powers as detrimental to the true interests of the citizens of those powers, especially the working class. It was natural that Lenin, the leading ideologue of the Bolsheviks, should make antiimperialism a central part of his revolutionary doctrine. In 1916 he had argued, in *Imperialism, the Highest Stage of Capitalism,* that capitalist nations were destined to become imperialistic, to seek an outlet for the surplus capital, and that the European war was nothing but an imperialistic war as a result of such a development. It followed that the only way to put an end to war, and also to bring about an end to capitalistic exploitation, was to eradicate imperialism. This could be done, Lenin asserted after the 1917 seizure of power, by espousing the cause of the oppressed peoples in the colonial areas. He, Trotsky, and Leo Karakhan, people's commissar for foreign affairs under the Bolsheviks, repeatedly enunciated the doctrine of antiimperialism. Specifically, they would repudiate all tsarist acts in the colonial areas, denounce colonial agreements with other imperialist powers,

6 On American relief initiatives in Russia, see William Appleman Williams, *American-Russian Relations* (New York, 1952), 193–201.

and call upon the colonial populations to rise up against their Western masters.[7]

Such a stance pitted Bolshevik foreign policy not only against the traditional European power politics but also against the emerging Wilsonian leadership. Lenin ridiculed Wilsonianism as nothing short of bourgeois liberalism, as guilty of capitalist crimes as the more old-fashioned European systems. Wilson, Lenin asserted, was just as interested as the European ruling classes in preserving capitalism, and thus only the Bolsheviks stood for true change, for a radical new order.

Wilson was fully aware of the Leninist challenge, and he consciously formulated the Fourteen Points in order to respond to it. As noted earlier, one of the points was evacuation of Russia, to assure the Russians that no German or other foreign troops would remain in their country after the war. Other points spelled out Wilson's vision of a world guided by the principle of self-determination and the spirit of international cooperation. Unfortunately for him, Lenin dismissed these as capitalist rhetoric that would not reform international relations at all. Self-determination for only European peoples hardly touched the rest of the world, and the proposed league of nations was little more than an assembly of existing powers, which would continue to control world affairs.

There were thus germs of what would soon develop into a gigantic duel between Wilsonianism and Leninism, between American vision and Russian revolution. In 1917–18, however, it would be wrong to suggest that the line was already sharply drawn. For Wilson was trying to distance himself from the European powers even as he joined them in the war effort. He believed the United States had a distinctive role to play during the war and in the postwar world, and to preserve freedom of action it was imperative to keep a distance from the British, French, and other allies. He was hopeful of arousing the masses of Europe to repudiate the Old Diplomacy, and in this regard he was little different from Lenin. Both stood for a new international order. Both saw a clear connection between interna-

7 See Allen S. Whiting, *Soviet Policies in China, 1917–1924* (New York, 1954), for a discussion of Lenin's antiimperialism.

tional order and domestic order. At least as far as Europe was concerned, both Wilson and Lenin supported the breakup of the Habsburg and Ottoman empires. In such a situation, it would not have been altogether beyond the realm of possibility for the two leaders to come together in some fashion to cooperate in restabilizing world affairs.

Unfortunately, relations between the United States and Bolshevik Russia never improved; rather, they definitely worsened when the former, along with Japan, undertook a military expedition to eastern Siberia in the summer of 1918.

The immediate circumstances of the expedition were military and strategic necessities. As noted earlier, there was a genuine fear among the Americans and their allies that Germany might make use of Russian resources and people in the war effort. It seemed imperative, therefore, to prevent this. Both the British and the French governments pressed President Wilson to undertake some sort of military expedition to Russia with this as the aim. Specifically, they argued that an expedition to Siberia would serve to create an eastern front so that German forces and their presumed allies, the Bolsheviks, would be compelled to turn their attention to the region, diverting their forces from the western front. An allied expedition might also embolden anti-Bolshevik Russians who, it was believed, were eager to remain in the war.

Any such intervention, however, would come into conflict with Wilson's stated policy of calling on the powers to evacuate Russia in order to give the Russians the opportunity to develop their own agenda – which would not ultimately mean Bolshevism, he ardently hoped and believed. He was also worried that the allies, in particular the Japanese, might seize the opportunity provided by a military intervention and engage in action for their own selfish purposes, again defeating the lofty war aims Wilson was enunciating.

It was not until the spring of 1918, when Wilson learned about the presence and apparent plight of the Czech legion in Siberia, that he persuaded himself of the urgency of an allied expedition to the area. By then it was becoming evident that the Japanese would send their troops to eastern Siberia no matter what the other powers did. They were intent upon strengthening their position in the region, adjacent to Manchuria where they had consolidated their power by imposing the twenty-one demands on China. Wilson was determined to prevent unilateral action by Japan; the international coalition must be preserved at all cost. Under the circumstances, the best strategy appeared to be to join Japan in an expedition to Siberia. Weeks of frantic negotiations between Tokyo and Washington in the early summer resulted in an agreement that each would send up to eight thousand troops to Vladivostok, to help maintain order in that port city and along the Siberian railway, which had its terminus there, so as to enable the Czech forces to exit Russia safely.[8]

Unfortunately for Wilson, the Siberian expedition was a complete fiasco. For one thing, by the time the American contingents, numbering about eight thousand, arrived in Vladivostok, most of the Czech legion had already made their way safely out of the interior of Siberia, so that there was no need for the Americans to come to their rescue. Moreover, the war in Europe was winding down, and whatever strategic justification might have existed about creating an eastern front also evaporated. American troops really had little to do once they got to Siberia – except perhaps to embroil themselves in quarrels with Japanese troops.

And there were many more Japanese troops. Ignoring the agreement that both nations would send in about eight thousand troops, the Japanese ultimately sent more than eighty thousand, for they were determined to entrench Japanese power in the area. They were sent inland and to some other Siberian cities. Portions of them were diverted to the Chinese Eastern Railway, running northwest to southeast across Manchuria. Their behavior was repugnant to the Americans, and there was open animosity between the two. It is not surprising that Wilson soon came to regret the expedition and began making preparations to get the American forces out as expeditiously as possible once the war ended.

The expedition left a bitter legacy not just in U.S.-Japanese but also in U.S.-Russian relations. The Bolsheviks would long remember the intervention and look upon it as an example of imperialistic meddling with revolutions. It is important to keep in mind that

8 Frederick Calhoun, *Power and Principle* (Kent, Ohio, 1986), 193–210.

when the belligerents met in Paris at the beginning of 1919 to consider peace terms, American and Japanese forces were still in Siberia. As far as Russia was concerned, the German war had long been over (since the Brest-Litovsk peace of March 1918), and it was humiliating to have these foreign troops on their soil. The Bolsheviks were not invited to the peace conference, and they had no intention of joining other countries under the circumstances. Still, there were some attempts on both sides to prevent the situation from getting out of hand. Wilson continued to believe that despite the Siberian expedition, the powers should honor the principle of self-determination of the Russians. He might even intercede on their behalf to see if a representative government might not be established at Petrograd. Lenin, for his part, considered it prudent to retain some connection with the Western nations, in particular the United States, the country that would have the most to offer economically.

There thus might have taken place a meeting of Wilson and Lenin. An invitation was in fact sent from Paris to Lenin, suggesting a meeting at Prinkipo Island where they might discuss the establishment of a representative Russian government.[9] It did not materialize, however, as Lenin insisted that only Bolsheviks be invited, whereas Wilson wanted other factions represented as well. So it would be another twenty-four years before the heads of government of the United States and Bolshevik Russia would confer face-to-face.

9 Williams, *American-Russian Relations,* 164–8.

4. The Versailles Peace

The New Peace

The Paris peace conference was convened on January 18, 1919, and lasted until June 28, when a peace treaty with Germany was signed at the Versailles palace. During these five months, the leaders of the victorious nations sat together and discussed not only the peace terms to be imposed upon the former enemy but also the shape of the postwar world. President Woodrow Wilson personally participated, as did the leaders of the European cobelligerents: David Lloyd George (Britain), Georges Clemenceau (France), Vittorio Orlando (Italy). Two Asian countries that had been involved in the war, China and Japan, were also represented at the Paris Conference, although they did not send their respective heads of government. The participation of these countries as well as the United States in a conference to settle a war that had originated in Europe was a clear indication of the passing of the European-dominated world order.[1]

Each participating nation had its own agenda. The United States had already articulated what it considered to be desirable terms of peace in Wilson's Fourteen Points. The president and his entourage in Paris were determined to define a peace that reflected those terms as much as possible. That was also the German delegation's expectation; having agreed to a cease-fire on the basis of the Fourteen Points, Berlin's representatives believed only a peace along those lines would be acceptable to the nation that was reeling from a post–cease-fire chaos; the military was refusing to admit defeat, while radicals, under Bolshevik influence, were threatening to seize control of government. A peace settlement in accordance with the Fourteen Points would mean some loss of territory but would still

1 The best brief history of the Paris peace conference is still the eyewitness account by Harold Nicolson: *Peacemaking* (London, 1933).

leave Germany with self-respect as the principal power between France and Russia, the main buffer – the Germans argued in Paris – against the spread of Bolshevik radicalism.[2]

The other European governments shared the fear of Bolshevism, but that did not prevent them from seeking a more revengeful and punitive settlement. Britain, France, and Italy were intent upon sharply limiting Germany's armed force so that it would never again be a threat to their security. Territorially, France wanted more than Alsace and Lorraine, insisting on the Saar region rich in coal. The victorious nations also eyed the German colonies, hoping to divide them up among themselves in accordance with their secret wartime agreements. Moreover, they all wanted reparations from the defeated enemy both in order to obtain needed resources for postwar reconstruction and to keep Germany economically weak. Japan, for its part, was determined to keep the German possessions in the Pacific that its troops had occupied and to obtain Germany's rights and concessions in Shantung province in China. The latter naturally opposed such a transfer, and a principal goal of China's diplomacy in Paris was to establish its claim to the former German and Austrian rights in the country.

With such disparate objectives being pursued by the former "allies" of the United States, it is not surprising that the Paris gathering turned into a series of often acrimonious debates among them. Not even Wilson's worldwide prestige and popularity ensured his diplomatic success, and he found himself forced to make concessions to the "allies" in order to salvage the conference and obtain a peace settlement. The Treaty of Versailles, which resulted from their arduous negotiations, was so divergent from the spirit of Wilsonianism that it was with extreme reluctance that the German delegation signed it, and they did so only after it became clear that the alternative would be the absence of any settlement, which would be disastrous for the war-torn nation.

It would be wrong, however, to dismiss the Versailles peace as a

2 The most extensive treatment of the intricate negotiations between Wilson and the Germans in the fall of 1918 is offered in Klaus Schwabe, *The World War, Revolutionary Germany, and Peacemaking* (Chapel Hill, 1985).

complete rejection of Wilsonianism. Actually, it should be seen as a modification rather than a repudiation of the Fourteen Points. Aspects of the peace were extremely harsh toward Germany, but some of the arrangements for the postwar world reflected the Wilsonian vision.

First of all, Germany was to be punished through loss of territory, severe restrictions on its armament, and reparations payments. The once powerful Central European nation was to be shorn of its land to the east and to the west. The newly established nations of Poland and Czechoslovakia would contain some lands formerly belonging to the Reich. Moreover, Poland would be given a strip of land running across Germany, to provide it with access to the North Sea, with Danzig (Gdansk in Polish) being made a free city. The "Polish corridor" thus divided two Germanies even though the ethnic composition of the corridor and Danzig was predominantly German. Although theoretically a violation of the principle of nationality or national self-determination, these decisions were considered just in view of the need to keep Germany in check and to encourage the growth of Poland and Czechoslovakia as viable states. To the west, Germany returned Alsace-Lorraine to France, restoring the situation prevailing before the Franco-Prussian War of 1870–1. Furthermore, Germany was not to station armed forces on the western side of the river Rhine – the areas adjacent to France. This was obviously intended as a way to give France a sense of security, so as to prevent German revanchism against Alsace-Lorraine.

Germany was also to be severely restricted in its postwar armament. True to the spirit of the Fourteen Points, which advocated arms control, although at this time the spirit was applied only to Germany and its erstwhile allies, the Treaty of Versailles limited Germany's armed forces (see the next chapter for specifics) and its arsenal to enumerated lists of items. All such measures would be an infringement on German sovereignty, something the Germans would long remember with bitterness, but for the allies they were crucial steps to bring about a securer world. It was Wilson's intention ultimately to apply some such disarmament formula to other countries as well. In the meantime, however, he, as will be seen, supported further strengthening of the U.S. Navy. At this time, therefore, it must be admitted that disarmament applied only to the defeated nations – even though these latter, certainly Germany, may not have considered themselves to have been defeated.

The Fourteen Points had not mentioned reparations, although, as seen already, the British and French had forced President Wilson to accept the idea in responding to the German overtures for a cease-fire. But he had been basically opposed to reparations, not only because they implied that the war was to be blamed entirely on Germany but also because the vast sums Germany would be forced to pay would be detrimental to its economic recovery, a key to the recovery of Europe on the whole. But the European allies were adamant, and in the end the United States went along. The Versailles treaty did not specify an amount but provided for the establishment of a reparations commission that would fix an appropriate sum for each of the former enemies to pay.

A Germany punished and weakened, then, was to be a key part of the postwar European order. Equally significant was the creation of new states in Central and Eastern Europe. In addition to Poland and Czechoslovakia, there would be Austria, Hungary, and Yugoslavia, all new nations created from the ashes of the Austro-Hungarian Empire. In addition, some Balkan states that had been semi-autonomous, with tenuous ties to either the Ottoman or the Russian Empire, or both, would become full-fledged nations: Romania, Bulgaria, Albania, Greece. It was these states to the east and south-east of Germany that were supposed to contain the latter. Above all, the role of Poland and Czechoslovakia as the immediate neighbors of Germany was critical, and it is not surprising that France, in particular, sought to strengthen these countries or that, twenty years later, Germany's invasion of them automatically meant the coming of another war in Europe.[3]

In the west, the independence of Belgium was restored. Together with the Netherlands, Luxembourg, and France, it would ensure Western European security. By and large, it may be said that these

3 For a contrary interpretation, that the Versailles treaty did not sufficiently weaken Germany, see A. J. P. Taylor, *The Origins of the Second World War* (London, 1961).

arrangements conformed to the spirit, if not the exact letter, of the Fourteen Points. The story was a little different with regard to Italy, which did not change its boundaries much, and for this reason some of its people, believing they had contributed to the allied war effort and therefore should have gotten more territory out of the Habsburg empire, were bitterly opposed to the peace.

Lest such territorial settlements should fail to stabilize postwar Europe or to prevent the resurgence of aggressive German power, the peace conference set up a new world organization, the League of Nations. This, too, had been anticipated in the Fourteen Points. The covenant of the League spelled out in detail how the organization would be structured and how it would function. First of all, it would invite the participation of all sovereign states – although the former enemy countries would, for the time being, be put on probation and allowed to join only after a lapse of time. Also, Russia was not invited in view of its continuing internal turmoil. (It is doubtful if the Russians would have participated in the League even if they had been invited; they dismissed it as little more than an expression of bourgeois internationalism at best, imperialistic deviousness at worst.)[4]

Not all members would count equally, however. A council was to be set up, to consist of representatives of five major powers: the United States, Britain, France, Italy, and Japan. They would be the leaders of the world organization in that they would confer with one another frequently and make recommendations to the larger body. Unlike its successor, the United Nations, however, the council members would not enjoy veto power. Wilson did toy with the idea of the United States, Britain, and France acting together in a mutual security arrangement to keep Germany in check, but he discarded it as contrary to the spirit of the League. The role of the council members would not be military but essentially moral. But that was enough from Wilson's point of view. Ideally, the five powers would set an example of international cooperation through which alone security could be ensured.

4 See John M. Thompson, *Russia, Bolshevism, and the Versailles Peace* (Princeton, 1967).

Article 10 of the League covenant sought to provide for the use of collective force if it should ever become necessary. Should a member nation be seen to have violated the sovereignty and territorial integrity of another, the article said, the League would punish the aggressor state through sanctions, including military force. This meant that any change in national boundaries would henceforth have to be undertaken peacefully, through negotiation, not by force. The principles of "peaceful modification" of boundaries and of "peaceful resolution" of disputes now became the core idea of the new world order.

These principles sounded admirable, but they became targets of severe criticism by opponents of the League of Nations, for they seemed to freeze the territorial status quo in the world. By redrawing the map of Europe – and elsewhere, as will be noted – and combining it with provisions for collective security to enforce the peace, the League covenant could be said to have defined and enshrined a new status quo, to be honored and protected by all the member states. Many of Wilson's American critics rejected the freezing of the status quo, especially since Article 10 implied that the United States would be committed to upholding it. Such an arrangement would embroil the nation in a war that was not of its choosing, a war that might take place far away without touching the security or other vital interests of the United States. Of course, the critics were justified in expressing such fears, but Wilson was also being logical when he reiterated his belief that what was emerging was not a restored old order of armaments and alliances but a new order in which nations would be asked to contribute to the collective defense of one another. He too was justified in holding to his adamant stand that without Article 10 the whole edifice of League internationalism would collapse.

It must also be admitted, however, that as it stood the covenant made it very difficult for a nation to seek to alter its territorial definition. That might not have mattered if national boundaries came to mean less, economically if not politically, and there grew extensive economic transactions among nations. This may have been at the back of Wilson's mind. Indeed, League internationalism would have had a chance to work only if there had also been devised ways to promote economic internationalism. Such, unfortunately, was not the case, at least not until the problem was clearly recognized in the mid-1920s.

The Economics of the New Peace

The economic foundations of the peace were shaky in part because of the German reparations issue. By going beyond the Fourteen Points and deciding to demand reparations payments from Germany, the Versailles signatories were chipping away at one corner of the new peace. For Germany would have to sacrifice its postwar economic well-being to satisfy the vindictiveness of its former enemies, and an economically weakened Germany would be a source of instability in Central Europe. More important, the German people would resent this violation of the Fourteen Points. They would equate the Versailles peace with injustice and hardship, a condition hardly auspicious for the functioning of the League machinery.

This, however, was but one aspect of the larger problem with the League of Nations and its covenant, namely, that they failed to deal with economic issues as thoroughly as they did with territorial questions. Wilson himself, in the Fourteen Points, had insisted on the freedom of the seas and equal access to world markets as prerequisites for a peaceful international order. He was intent on reintegrating Germany and its former allies into the postwar global economy as expeditiously as possible, firmly believing that German economic recovery was particularly crucial for the well-being of Central Europe and, therefore, for European stability after the war. There was little in the League covenant, however, to indicate the powers' interest in this matter.

For one thing, the dispute over German reparations revealed how seriously America's European allies were taking the issue. From their point of view, reparations payments, which were expected to exceed $20 billion at that time, would be of vital importance as they sought to reconstruct their cities, their countryside, and their overall economies. Without some infusion of funds from the defeated nation, the former allies would find it much more difficult to reestablish peacetime economic affairs. They had suffered such huge losses –

scores of billions of dollars of property damage and destruction, and much more in lost production and trade – that they needed external revenue. It could come only from the United States and from Germany.

In the process of economic reconstruction, too, the European governments would be loath to give up quickly wartime restrictions on shipments of gold and on the importation of nonessential foreign products. Exchange and trade control had been instituted during the war, and in the absence of clear signs that reparations funds were forthcoming, there was reluctance to restore the pre-1914 system of international economic transactions.

Wilson, therefore, had to give in to the demands for German reparations. In addition, he was not able to press the Europeans for a swift return to international economic transactions without promising that American funds would assist in the process. But in the United States, the end of the war had brought about a speedy "reconversion" to peacetime affairs, and, while governmental loans to the European nations would continue for the time being – indeed, they amounted to $2.6 billion during 1918–20 – sooner or later all such programs would cease, and foreign financial affairs would revert to private bankers and investors. Under the circumstances, he found it awkward at the Paris peace conference to push for a more vigorous program of economic internationalism.

Actually, even within the United States, there were strong forces for economic nationalism, not internationalism. American businessmen, bankers, officials, and even labor leaders had enjoyed wartime prosperity and believed the best way to maintain this into the postwar period, in the face of the expected return of European competitors in the world arena, was to strengthen America's competitiveness through some policy and legislative initiatives. For instance, Congress had enacted, even before the armistice, the Webb-Pomerance Act, which authorized exporters to combine for export trade purposes without fear of being prosecuted for violation of antitrust laws.[5] This was a way of ensuring continued growth of American trade, but it also signified Wilson's and the American leaders' will-

5 Joan Hoff Wilson, *American Business and Foreign Policy* (Boston, 1971), chap. 1.

ingness to consider national interests even before an international economic framework was redefined. It was not surprising that other nations, too, would establish similar arrangements for protection of industry and expansion of trade.

A somewhat different issue concerned Germany's former colonies, which, too, had economic as well as strategic implications. The Paris conferees had little trouble deciding that Germany should give up its empire, but they had developed conflicting ideas about the disposition of the former German colonies. Britain (including Australia), France, Italy, and Japan had eyed some of them, while the United States had enunciated the principle of self-determination. Although the principle was primarily meant for Central and Eastern Europe, Wilson was hopeful that the former German colonies would not simply be divided up among the victors as spoils of war. In this instance, Wilson was as successful as he could have wished, for he was able to get the participants to agree to a new mandate system, by which the former German colonies would be assigned to one or another of the major powers, which would govern them as their mandates in the name of the League of Nations. In other words, the League would be responsible for the welfare and development of the colonies, but the actual governance would be in the hands of the powers. This was a rather ingenious system, enabling the League to be true to the principle of self-determination in all parts of the world without actually proclaiming the independence of colonial areas.

This system was as much an economic proposition as a political measure, for some of the mandate territories (particularly in the Middle East) were rich in petroleum resources, whose future strategic importance was well recognized, whereas others (such as the Pacific islands) were underdeveloped and would be in need of much infusion of capital and technology. How such a mixture could be integrated into the postwar world economy remained to be seen, but already in Paris Britain and France quarreled over their respective mandate assignments in the Middle East, a harbinger of the difficulties to come in the area of natural resources.[6] In the meantime, Japan, which was assigned former German islands in the Pacific

6 Daniel Yergin, *The Prize* (New York, 1991), chap. 10.

north of the equator, tended to view them as assets primarily in its search for natural resources. But the United States objected to Japan's receiving the island of Yap as a mandate, because this tiny island was situated between Hawaii and the Philippines and could be a useful cable base. Nothing was decided on these disputes at this time, but here was another indication that the economic aspect of the peace was not as fully worked out as the political.

To complicate the situation further, the Chinese and the Japanese delegates at Versailles presented a proposal that the League of Nations Covenant include a reference to racial equality. From their point of view, this seemed to be an excellent opportunity to define a new world order based on justice for all races and peoples. Even an innocuous statement on the "equality of nations" would impress upon the whole world the newness of the postwar order. Neither China nor Japan, of course, expected that a mere enunciation of the principle would change the political realities of the world, but they judged that it would ultimately lead to some restructuring of the global economic system, which they saw as favoring the white nations in terms of space and resources. As Makino Nobuaki, one of the Japanese delegates, noted, if the new peace meant anything, it must be built on a conception of economic equality among nations.[7] Unfortunately, the proposal was not accepted, as the British Commonwealth strenuously objected to it, seeing the principle as a thinly disguised call for unrestricted immigration of Asians into Canada and Australia. President Wilson was sympathetic with the Chinese and Japanese argument, but he apparently was not convinced that this was of sufficiently vital importance to the new peace as to warrant his personal intercession. He ruled that because unanimity was lacking, he could not endorse the idea.

It is strange that, given Wilson's well-known interest in the economic foundations of world order, he gave so little thought to this aspect of the Versailles peace. Perhaps he was too preoccupied with the more immediate political and military issues to give due attention to the economic questions. Even more plausibly, it may be that the powers, having fought a devastating war, were in no mood

7 Dorothy Jones, *Code of Peace* (Chicago, 1991), 41–4.

to be charitable toward one another economically, and that the war had generated a strong sense of economic nationalism. How this would square with the emerging political internationalism would be a major question bequeathed to the postwar world.

Wilsonianism Confirmed – and Betrayed

The Versailles peace had these conflicting aspects, but it would be hard to escape the general conclusion that it reflected to a great extent some of the fundamental tenets of Wilsonian internationalism. Despite its shortcomings and contradictions, the League of Nations Covenant was a Wilsonian document. It proposed an alternative to the conventional international order, which, Wilson was convinced, had been sustained by force. This had created a dangerous arms race and imperialistic activities abroad. Now military power and expansionism were to be replaced by a rule of law in which "world public opinion" rather than alliances and armaments would be the key to international order.

"World public opinion" was a typically Wilsonian concept. It connoted the existence of some moral force emanating from people everywhere. They, rather than their leaders, were the movers of the world, and they were fundamentally moral beings. When they spoke up, they generated a force that was mightier than armed power. Of course, people could be misled, or they could be temporarily captured by irrational desires and sentiments. The Bolshevik success seemed to demonstrate this. But Wilson remained true to his Jeffersonian faith that, left to themselves, human beings acted in such a way as to harmonize their interests; moreover, as they became more aware of their rights, they would ultimately eliminate artificial boundaries that separated them and join together in a quest for the general well-being of mankind. Put this way, the new order built upon "world public opinion" was the best safeguard of peace and stability.[8]

The irony was that his own people, far from embodying "world

8 On the Jeffersonian origins of Wilsonianism, see John Milton Cooper, *The Warrior and the Priest* (New York, 1983).

public opinion," turned against Wilson and rejected the League of Nations, as well as other arrangements for peace worked out at Paris. Of course, the American people themselves were not asked to ratify the German peace treaty and the League Covenant, so Wilson may have believed till the very end that his people were with him. But at least a sufficient number of senators rejected the products of the Paris conference so that they could not be ratified by a two-thirds majority, and the voters in subsequent elections did not reject those senators.

The Senate's deliberations on the treaty lasted between the summer of 1919 and the spring of 1920 – longer than the duration of the Paris conference. This reflected the serious division of views among the senators as well as Wilson's determination to persevere to the bitter end to obtain their endorsement of the new peace. The 1918 elections had resulted in a Republican majority in the Senate (49 Republicans against 47 Democrats), and Henry Cabot Lodge, a bitter political foe of Wilson's, now chaired the critical Foreign Relations Committee, which included 6 "irreconcilables," Republicans who would not accept the Versailles treaty and the League of Nations in any form. Lodge and the irreconcilables were joined by enough others to defeat the treaty.[9]

The opponents of the treaty did not speak with one voice. The irreconcilables – such as William Borah of Idaho and Hiram Johnson of California – were adamantly opposed to the nation's joining any organization such as the League of Nations that would, they believed, compromise America's independence and stain its purity. They were not ignorant traditionalists, however. In their own way they held visions of a world free from scourges of war and aggression, but they did not think the League as it was being proposed was the answer. In their view, the peace settlement and the League established and froze a new status quo, and American membership in the world organization would obligate the nation to defend it, with force if necessary, even if the status quo contained many injustices. The irreconcilables did not like the imperialist powers such as

9 There are many studies of the Senate debate on the Treaty of Versailles. See, for instance, William C. Widenor, *Henry Cabot Lodge and the Search for an American Foreign Policy* (Berkeley, 1980).

Britain and Japan holding sway in the postwar world, and wanted the United States to have nothing to do with perpetuating the situation. In a sense they were being more Wilsonian than Wilson himself.

Others were more explicitly anti-Wilsonian in refusing to believe that a new age had dawned in international relations. They rejected the notion that because the world had changed the United States should be willing to depart from its traditional policy of a free hand. Some argued that the nation's sovereign rights over such matters as the Monroe Doctrine and immigration should never be given up to a new international body. Then there were those who took exception to specific aspects of the peace treaty, such as its failure to coerce Japan to give up Shantung.

Many of these senators, including Lodge, were "reservationists," that is, they did not irreconcilably oppose the peace settlement but insisted on certain reservations before they supported it. They were joined by a number of Democrats who urged Wilson to accept such reservations in order to save the treaty and the League. And the president was ready to offer some compromises. After all, he still perceived the world as consisting of sovereign states, not as one in which they disappeared. He did wish to reduce some of their rights and prerogatives, in particular the use of force for selfish purposes, but he was ready to agree to the excepting of domestic issues (such as immigration) from the League's jurisdiction. Wilson, however, was adamant on Article 10 of the League Covenant, viewing it as the key to the new order of international cooperation. Lodge and others sought to modify America's commitments under the article by requiring congressional authorization for each act that the nation might undertake. This would mean that the implementation of Article 10 was subject to the will of Congress, something the president could not accept in view of the pledge he had made in Paris that the United States would help establish a new international order. The unconditional acceptance of Article 10 was a sacred obligation if the nation were to play a role in the postwar world.

The dispute was real, and the confrontation tragic. In the faith that the American people would support him over the senators, Wilson undertook a tour of the country in September 1919, traveling eight thousand miles in twenty-two days. Before he could measure the effect of the trip, he collapsed, in Colorado, a symbol of an unfulfilled dream. The Senate went on to reject the treaty. (The United States was to negotiate separate peace treaties with Germany, Austria, and Hungary in 1921, all of which would be ratified by the Senate; but they did not include any provision for a League membership.)

If the Senate and, presumably, the American people were not yet ready for a Wilsonian world order, other countries would be even less so. America's failure to join the League of Nations, then, was not quite the same thing as a betrayal; it was more a case of the United States deciding to stay at the level of others. And yet, Wilson's defeat did not mean the demise of Wilsonianism. In many countries, not just in Europe but elsewhere as well, there were emerging Wilsonians who shared his vision, and the world after the peace would be shaped as much by them as by more traditional forces.

Wilsonianism had provided the framework in which the United States redefined its external relations at a time when the age of European dominance was coming to an end. It combined America's military power, economic resources, and cultural initiatives in order to transcend traditional world affairs in which sovereign nations had pursued their interests with little regard for the welfare of the entire globe. War and war preparations had been accepted norms of behavior; and balance-of-power considerations had provided the key conceptual guide to diplomacy. Woodrow Wilson challenged these practices and assumptions. He wanted each nation to serve not only its own interests but those of the world at large. America, he said, should release its energies "for the service of mankind." Other countries should do likewise. The result would be the intermeshing of nationalism and internationalism, sovereign states finding meaning in their relationship to the whole.

"Realists" of the subsequent decades would not be kind to Wilsonian internationalism, castigating it as naïvely idealistic, just as Wilson's opponents in the Senate ridiculed his faith in other countries' commitment to the vision.[10] Much empty debate would be

10 The best example of the realist critique is Robert E. Osgood, *Ideals and Self-Interest in American Foreign Relations* (Chicago, 1953).

carried on between the exponents of realism and of idealism. One should realize that it was not so much idealism as internationalism that informed Wilsonian thought, an internationalism solidly grounded on shared interests of nations and on aspirations of men and women everywhere transcending national boundaries. These are fundamentally cultural forces, so that in a way Wilsonianism was an agenda for putting culture at the center of international relations. Although naked power was to be a crucial determinant of international affairs in the decades after Wilson, who at the end of the twentieth century can deny that culture has reasserted itself time and again? The emergence of the United States as an international player at the beginning of the twentieth century was significant not simply because the nation became the leading military and economic power, but also because it introduced cultural factors into world affairs. Because the globalizing of America has been a major event of the century, Wilsonianism should be seen not as a transient phenomenon, a reflection of some abstract idealism, but as a potent definer of contemporary history.

5. The 1920s: The Security Aspect

Disarmament

The postwar world began in 1919, with the signing of the Versailles peace treaty. Nobody could tell then how stable the new structure of peace would be, or even what the structure meant in different regions of the world. With the U.S. Senate refusing to ratify the treaty, some were already writing off the just begun postwar period as but a brief interlude in otherwise conflict-ridden international affairs, and many were pessimistic about the future of the League of Nations as well as other arrangements the powers had worked out in Paris.

The world during 1919–20 did, indeed, seem very precarious, little different from the situation on the eve of the Great War. Not only did the United States not participate in the League, thus apparently reverting to prewar isolationism, but the peace treaty was proving extremely unpopular in many countries: Germany, Italy, China, and others. In these countries movements were already developing to denounce the peace treaty and what it signified. The Germans condemned the punitive aspects of the peace, the Italians thought they should have gotten more out of it, and the Chinese were disatisfied because the treaty had not forced the Japanese to withdraw from Shantung.

The situation was still unstable in the Soviet Union, and Poland seized the opportunity to invade the revolutionary nation. In Hungary, in the meantime, a radical government established itself, giving rise to fears elsewhere that Bolshevism was spreading. The creation, in 1919, of the Communist International, to coordinate Communist activities throughout the world, conjured up the spectacle of a global movement to challenge the peace. In the colonial areas there grew strong, often radical, antiimperialistic movements inspired by both Woodrow Wilson and V. I. Lenin. Nascent antiimperialism in many parts of the world was disappointed by Wilson's failure to support it at Versailles except through the establishment of the system of League mandates, and its leaders welcomed the Comintern's initiatives to support the movement.[1]

How could such a world find stability? Only those with unusual optimism or foresight could have been sanguine about the postwar international order. And yet, the 1920s were to prove far more stable and oriented to international peace and goodwill than anyone could have dared to hope in 1919. This and the two following chapters explore aspects of the international system of the 1920s and the role played by the United States in its evolution and preservation.

First of all, despite the confusion of the immediate postwar years, the major powers showed remarkable readiness to undertake programs of disarmament. It was, of course, easier to disarm Germany, as stipulated in the peace treaty, than other countries. According to the treaty, Germany was allowed specified numbers of men and weapons; for instance, up to 100,000 men were permitted in the German army, with a maximum of 4,000 officers, 102,000 rifles and carbines, 1,134 light machine guns, and 792 heavy machine guns. The German Navy was restricted to 6 battleships, 6 light cruisers, and 12 destroyers, with a maximum of 15,000 men and 1,500 officers.[2]

Wilson had hoped that arms control would not stop with Germany but that other nations, victors as well as vanquished, would follow suit. In reality, however, the powers, including the United States, kept expanding their navies even after the war. In 1919 Wilson himself endorsed a new naval construction bill calling for the addition of sixteen battleships – if completed, they would make the U.S. Navy the most powerful in the world. For Wilson to support such a plan was patently against his declared principle of disarmament, but he shared the widespread suspicion of Japan – as well as of

1 Akira Iriye, *After Imperialism* (Cambridge, Mass., 1965), 12.

2 See F. L. Carsten, *The Reichswehr and Politics* (Oxford, 1966), for a discussion of German disarmament.

Britain, both of which likewise continued to build warships. The president may have reasoned that only by matching, even surpassing, these countries' naval construction programs would the United States finally be able to induce them to agree to a disarmament proposal. Still, such an arms race was quite destabilizing, coming as it did in the wake of the catastrophic war. And it was not surprising that soon voices should emerge, in America and elsewhere, to stop this mad race and divert the countries' resources to more peaceful ends.

The impetus for a world disarmament conference came from the U.S. Congress, where Senator William E. Borah spearheaded the movement for naval disarmament. Borah had been one of the "irreconcilables" in the peace treaty debate, and his call for global disarmament, a Wilsonian ideal, indicates that while rejecting part of Wilsonianism, he and many others like him had not repudiated it altogether. Many of them came to be known as "peace progressives," those who were opposed to the Versailles peace but who advocated their own schemes for what they ardently believed to be a stabler, juster world order. And one of their major goals at this time was disarmament. They argued that the world would never be spared another conflagration until the major military powers, including the United States, undertook arms reductions. Many of these senators also believed that the nation should end the occupation of foreign countries, recognize the Soviet Union, and support movements for colonial self-determination. These views were not isolationist; on the contrary, they anticipated what the nation would espouse in the decades to come. Others were less willing to go that far, but at least on the disarmament question there was developing a strong consensus in and out of Congress. Henry Cabot Lodge, another opponent of the Wilsonian peace, was to become one of the American delegates to the naval disarmament conference that would be convened in Washington in November 1921.[3]

Of course, it took more than some senators' efforts to convene an arms reduction conference, and a disarmament agreement would not

3 Roger Dingman, *Power in the Pacific* (Chicago, 1976), is still the best work on the Washington Conference.

have been achieved unless other nations had shared the same belief in the need to put an end to the naval race. It so happened that in Britain and Japan, too, voices grew in favor of arms limitation. The reasoning was both economic (the folly of spending so much money on armaments when it was needed for postwar recovery and reconstruction) and political (the need not to antagonize the United States). Although naval officials in these two countries were initially reluctant to see their respective navies cut down in size, civilian authorities in London and Tokyo early on decided to accept the American initiative. The result was the Washington Conference of 1921–2, attended by political leaders and naval officials of the United States, Britain, Japan, France, and Italy. (Several other countries were also represented, to discuss questions dealing with China, as will be noted.)

Disarmament, however, could not be separated from other questions of Asian-Pacific security, in particular the future of the Anglo-Japanese alliance and the fortification of the powers' bases in the Pacific Ocean. The alliance, first signed in 1902 and extended in 1911 for ten years, was up for another renewal in 1921, but the United States was vehemently opposed to it. Washington was adamant that the alliance be abolished, not only as contradictory to the principle of open diplomacy (i.e., the rejection of particularistic arrangements such as military alliances) that sustained the new peace – another indication that the Americans continued to adhere to the spirit of Wilsonianism – but also because the alliance, if renewed, would have strategic implications for the United States, which would be forced to augment its own fleet to match the combined force of the British and Japanese navies. The latter two, for their part, would try to keep up with such increases, thus inviting a naval race among the three that would be as dangerous to world peace as the British-German naval rivalry had been prior to 1914. British and Japanese officials understood this, and although many of them were loath to give up an association that seemed to have served the two countries' respective interests well, they were in no position to recommend challenging the United States.

The resulting decision to abrogate the Anglo-Japanese alliance made it easier for the three powers to undertake a program of naval disarmament. In Washington their representatives readily agreed on a formula for multilateral naval disarmament. According to it, the United States and Britain would scuttle some of the existing warships and refrain from completing the construction of some others, so that the total capital-ship tonnage of each ("capital ships" referred to warships displacing more than 10,000 tons of water and equipped with eight-inch guns) would not exceed 525,000 tons. As the existing tonnages were far greater, the naval agreement would result in America's destroying 30 of its 48 ships (in being or under construction). Britain would reduce its navy from 45 to 20 warships. Japan, on its part, would be limited to 315,000 tons and would destroy 17 of its 27 warships. This was the famous 5-5-3 ratio, giving Japan the equivalent of 60 percent of each of the navies of the United States and Britain. Some Japanese naval leaders denounced the inferior naval ratio as a disgrace and warned that with a reduced navy it would be impossible to defend the empire. Some of them would never reconcile themselves to the Washington formula, but many were persuaded to accept it when the three naval powers agreed to maintain the status quo in fortifications in their possessions in the Pacific, except for Pearl Harbor and Singapore. (Australia and New Zealand were not covered by the agreement.) This nonfortification agreement was as much part of the disarmament package as the abrogation of the Anglo-Japanese alliance.

If some Japanese were upset by their inferior naval ratio, still more so were the French and Italians, whose navies were given 175,000 tons each, or one-third the size of the U.S. and British navies. However, the civilian authorities in Paris and Rome ultimately accepted the new formula for much the same reason as the British and Japanese: They could not afford a costly arms race. The result was that within a little over two years after the signing of the Versailles treaty, one of the unfulfilled promises of Wilsonianism had become a reality.

Because the Washington naval agreement covered only capital ships, the powers were free to develop other types of ships, the so-called auxiliary craft, such as light cruisers, destroyers, and submarines. Moreover, they, not least the United States, were quite interested in the concept of air power. Airplanes were in their infancy, but they appeared much less expensive than warships, and air war more "humane" than land war in which soldiers confronted one another to kill, or be killed.[4] Even some of the staunchest advocates of disarmament supported the development of air power, and there was to be no international agreement on this newest type of military force. In 1927, however, the United States took another initiative for naval arms limitation, this time focusing on the auxiliary craft. The United States, Britain, and Japan sent delegates to a meeting in Geneva, but France and Italy refused to participate. Moreover, the United States and Britain had divergent views on the cruiser question; the latter needed a larger number of light cruisers to defend its far-flung empire than the latter was willing to concede. The United States, for its part, wished to have many heavier cruisers. The Japanese tried to mediate the two positions, without success. So nothing came of the Geneva meeting. It would be another three years before a more successful naval disarmament conference was to be held.

Although there were such failures, the fact remains that until the 1980s, when nuclear disarmament agreements were to be concluded, the 1920s was the only decade in recent history when arms reductions actually took place. It is true that the German Army sought to build beyond the Versailles treaty limits through clandestine arrangements with the Soviet Union, but it would still be correct to say that there was in the world less armament in 1929 than in 1919.[5] The nations were spending proportionally less of their incomes on arms, and munitions factories and shipyards were increasingly manufacturing nonmilitary, consumer goods.

Were these developments conducive to stabilizing international relations? Or did they create a false sense of security in the world? In retrospect, one can argue that arms control, at least the restrictions on American and British naval power, was a mistake because it led to the downgrading of military power in international affairs. Somehow it seemed wrong to build up arms, an attitude that would

4 On the development of American air power, the best history is Michael S. Sherry, *The Rise of American Air Power* (New Haven, 1989).

5 Harold J. Gordon, *The Reichswehr and the German Republic* (Princeton, 1957), 188–9.

persist into the 1930s when military strengthening actually became necessary. In such a perspective, the United States should never have destroyed its superior naval power.[6]

On the other hand, it would be wrong to judge the 1920s solely in the framework of what was to happen in the 1930s, or to attribute the breakdown of the peace in the 1930s simply to the disarmament arrangements of the preceding decade. One needs to see these arrangements for what they signified at that time, as a symbol of the new peace. If nothing else, they are a monument to the Wilsonian formulation. The very fact that the United States took the lead is important. The Republican administrations that followed Wilson's presidency were just as committed to Wilsonian internationalism as he himself, at least insofar as disarmament was concerned. To reduce arms, thereby removing restrictions on peacetime economic development, and to do so through international cooperation, were significant achievements, indicating a widespread determination not to repeat the mistakes of pre-1914 Europe. There was a clear, shared perception that the world had changed, that history had entered a new phase, to be characterized more by peace than by war.

Peace in Europe and Asia – and Elsewhere

The peace of the 1920s was built on more than just disarmament agreements. It was sustained through various other arrangements, including the League of Nations, the Locarno Conference treaties in Europe, and the Washington Conference treaties for Asia, all of which were expressions of hope and determination that the world should never have to face another major war.

The League of Nations, it is true, had to do without the participation of the United States, the one country on whose willingness to support the peace much depended. Still, Britain, France, Japan, and Italy – the four permanent members of the council – along with other members were determined to make use of the new institution for stabilizing international affairs. The council consisted of repre-

6 See Robert E. Osgood, *Ideals and Self-Interest in American Foreign Relations* (Chicago, 1953).

sentatives from seven nations – the four permanent and three other members – and its endorsement was required for all decisions taken by the general assembly. This was the largest organization of its kind in history – initially consisting of forty-one member states – and embodied the idea that henceforth interstate disputes should be brought before the organization rather than be settled locally through recourse to force. In reality, very few disputes were brought to the League's attention, the 1925 territorial quarrel between Greece and Bulgaria being one such case. Still, the League's very existence stood as a symbol of the new age.

Even more important, there were established several international organizations as part of the League's activities, for instance the International Labor Organization and the World Health Organization. The titles of these organizations revealed that the League was to be concerned with much more than territorial or political questions; it would also deal with economic, social, and medical problems in the postwar world. There was a clear recognition that these problems were of global importance, and that only an international effort would suffice to deal with them. In addition, the League established a committee on intellectual cooperation, designed to promote scholarly and artistic interchanges among individuals of various countries. Together with the Permanent Court of International Justice, or the so-called World Court, which was established at The Hague (but not the same institution as The Hague Permanent Court of Arbitration, founded in 1901), these international bodies, even more than the League itself, promoted the idea of cooperation across national boundaries. The assumption, of course, was that through such cooperation the nations of the world would learn to live in peace and harmony with one another. Internationalism thus implemented would be the backbone of the postwar peace.

Although the United States was not a member of the League of Nations, it was represented in the ILO, the WHO, and the committee on intellectual cooperation. Individual Americans were active on behalf of the activities of these organizations. Unfortunately, the United States chose not to adhere to the World Court's protocol, which would have meant that the nation might seek its opinion concerning some cases, or that an American judge might be called upon to pass on some disputes. The Republican administrations throughout the 1920s were supportive of the idea, but the Senate was opposed, fearing that the court might provide a back door through which the nation might find itself a member of the League. In retrospect, however, it would seem that the role of the court in promoting internationalism was much less than that of the ILO and other bodies, so that the United States – or at least individual Americans – had an ample opportunity to serve the cause of international cooperation and peace.

In the meantime, in Europe the postwar peace remained fragile in the immediate aftermath of the Versailles conference. In 1920 the League's reparations commission set the figure of $33 billion as the sum Germany was to pay its former enemies as reparations. But the Germans refused, considering the figure exorbitant and resorting to printing money to sabotage reparations payments. In anger, in 1923 French and Belgian troops occupied the Ruhr Valley, an industrial center, and started taking payments in kind. This in turn provoked a German strike. These events coincided with Adolf Hitler's coup attempt in Munich, which was applauded by those in Germany who had remained bitterly opposed to the peace settlement. It seemed as if the French-German antagonism might deal a fatal blow to the postwar peace.

Fortunately, the crisis abated once the United States stepped in, not through formal diplomacy but, as will be described in the next chapter, through "the diplomacy of the dollar." The upshot was that in 1925 the governments of Germany, France, and Belgium signed treaties at Locarno to freeze and mutually guarantee their respective frontiers. This paved the way for Germany's admission into the League, which came in 1926. Within Germany, Hitler was imprisoned, and those, principally in the army, who remained adamant about getting rid of the Versailles restrictions were replaced by men more willing to accept the new status quo. Although the role of the United States in this settlement was financial rather than political, Washington welcomed the Locarno agreements and hailed German reintegration into the European order. The Weimar Republic's policy of economic recovery and political reconciliation fitted nicely into American conceptions of postwar international order, as did France's willingness, under Foreign Minister Aristide Briand, to build its security on a solid understanding with Germany.

In Asia, in the meantime, the Washington Conference of 1921–2 established a framework for cooperation and stability. Besides the naval disarmament treaty, the United States took the initiative in bringing about the drafting and signing of various other agreements designed to stabilize Asian-Pacific affairs. For instance, the four-power pact among the United States, Britain, France, and Japan provided for mutual consultation with regard to regional security issues, and several nine-power agreements (signed by China and these four plus four other European states) established the principle of consultation and cooperation in China and stipulated specific steps to be taken to effect a revision of the "unequal treaties."

As will be seen, these agreements did not immediately produce a peaceful environment in Asia; Chinese nationalists sought a more rapid and radical change in the treaties, and the Soviet Union encouraged their assault on the Washington treaties. Nevertheless, "the Washington system" worked as well as "the Locarno system" in giving definition to the postwar regional order. A good indication of this was that Japanese diplomacy became much more cooperative during the 1920s than earlier, and that there were few acts of overt military aggression on the part of the Japanese Army against China. The Chinese, on their part, in the end accepted the Washington treaties as the basis for their diplomacy. When the Nationalists came to power in Nanking in 1928, the United States quickly recognized the new regime and began negotiations for treaty revision, steps that were followed by other countries.[7]

The spirit of cooperation, rather than coercion and unilateralism, also came to characterize Latin American affairs. During the war, it will be recalled, American relations with Mexico had worsened, and United States forces were sent to Haiti and Santo Domingo. American troops also remained in Nicaragua. After the war, however, much changed. The United States now showed willingness to redefine Latin American policy in light of its changed world status and of the impact of Wilsonianism upon official thinking.

7 Iriye, *After Imperialism,* chap. 3.

To be sure, the United States still upheld the Monroe Doctrine as the key to its policy in the region, but its meaning underwent significant changes. Rather than safeguarding the tenet of the Roosevelt Corollary to the doctrine that had justified military intervention and fiscal tutelage of some Caribbean states, officials in Washington came to view the Monroe Doctrine as an expression of pan-American solidarity and cooperation. Thus the United States convened a meeting of Central American states in Washington during 1922–3 so as to promote general disarmament and arbitration. Secretary of State Charles Evans Hughes declared that the Monroe Doctrine did not mean the establishment of protectorates or overlordships in American republics. And in 1928, J. Reuben Clark, under secretary of state, wrote a memorandum arguing that intervention under the cloak of the Monroe Doctrine was wrong. He asserted that the doctrine must go back to the pre–Roosevelt Corollary days. That same year, after he won the presidential election, Herbert Hoover toured Latin America and stressed the concept of "the good neighbor." He voiced his opposition to the policy of intervention itself, and in fact there was to be no military intervention in Latin America under his presidency.[8]

The steady building up of systems of international cooperation and peace in various regions of the world was given a symbolic reaffirmation when thirty-three countries, including the United States and even the Soviet Union, signed the Kellogg-Briand Pact (the so-called Pact of Paris) in 1928. Secretary of State Frank B. Kellogg and French Foreign Minister Briand drafted the document as a statement of hope that war could be outlawed. It declared that the signatories "condemn recourse to war for the solution of international controversies, and renounce it as an instrument of national policy in their relations with one another." In addition, they agreed that "the settlement or solution of all disputes or conflicts . . . shall never be sought except by pacific means." These words sounded too idealistic even for that period, and many American observers noted that such a paper peace was dangerous as it could lead people to

8 On the development of the inter-American system, see Gordon Connell-Smith, *The Inter-American System* (London, 1966).

think they no longer needed to be militarily armed. But others, notably Senator Borah, were quite serious and believed this sort of internationalism was even more realistic and just than the League-defined world order. In time the Kellogg-Briand Pact would become codified in international law in that it would be cited as one of the key documents with which to condemn the aggressors in World War II. There is little doubt, in any event, that the Pact of Paris was another reflection of the earnest efforts made during the 1920s to solidify the structure of the new peace.

Coping with Revolutionary Nationalism

By signing the Kellogg-Briand Pact, the Soviet Union could be said to have joined the world community at long last. It had refused to associate itself with other nations, least of all with the United States. Only a few years earlier the Soviet leaders would have sneered at something like the outlawry of war as bourgeois sentimentalism and asserted that world peace would come only when capitalism had been replaced by socialism, imperialism by colonial independence.

What had happened? There certainly had been little change in American policy toward the Bolsheviks. Although some Republican leaders, notably Senator Borah, favored a change in Wilson's anti-Bolshevik stand, the successive Republican administrations during the 1920s adhered to the policy that the Soviet Union would not be recognized unless certain essential conditions were met: agreement on repayment of outstanding debts, compensation for nationalized enterprises, and a pledge not to engage in propaganda activities in the United States. Such a rigid stance all but ensured that there would be no establishment of diplomatic relations between Washington and Moscow. Neither side took the initiative to alter the situation.

On the other hand, the absence of diplomatic relations did not prevent other types of interaction between the two countries. During 1921–3 the American Relief Administration provided the Russians with food totaling more than 900,000 tons and valued at $66 million. It was said that the shipment of such food – and the ARA supplied 90 percent of all relief goods going to Russia – saved more than ten million Russians from starvation.[9] It would be hard to document such an assertion, but at least the episode indicates that Americans saw few serious obstacles in the way of approaching the Soviet Union, should they decide to do so. Likewise, as will be noted, trade between the two countries went on, albeit on a much smaller scale than American trade with other European countries. The point is that neither Washington nor Moscow believed the establishment of formal diplomatic ties was urgently needed; they could deal with one another irrespective of such ties.

Still, Russian foreign policy and Comintern activities during most of the 1920s were such that the Soviet Union clearly stood outside the generally accepted postwar peace structure. To be sure, most countries, including Britain, France, and Japan, one by one came to recognize the Bolshevik regime, but such a development did not prevent Moscow from engaging in anticapitalist, antiimperialistic activities through the Communist parties of other countries, and through the nationalistic movements in the colonial areas.

This latter phenomenon was particularly notable in China, where the Soviet Union successfully established ties to various centers of power: the government in Peking, various warlords controlling the provinces, the Kuomintang (Nationalists) in the Canton area, and the nascent Chinese Communist party. The upshot was the radicalization of Chinese nationalism, turning China's leaders and public opinion against the Washington Conference treaties that had provided the framework for international cooperation in China. Chinese officials, students, merchants, and other groups condemned the Washington treaties as totally inadequate, and the Nationalists and Communists combined their forces to launch a massive antiimperialistic campaign in the mid-1920s. They attacked American, European, and Japanese personnel and property in China, forcing a large-scale evacuation of foreign merchants and missionaries from the interior of the country.

Although more limited in scale, equally serious for the United States was what the State Department termed, in a 1927 report, "Bolshevik aims and policies in Mexico and Central America." Be-

9 Frederick L. Schuman, *American Policy Toward Russia* (New York, 1928), 203–7.

cause the Mexican constitution of 1917 had stipulated that all rights to the country's subsoil resources belonged to the state, there continued a bitter dispute between Mexico and the United States over American property rights and concessions in the country, particularly the mining and refining of petroleum. Neither Alvaro Obregón, coming to power in 1920, nor Plutarco Elias Calles, who succeeded him in 1924, was willing to accept the American contention that the principle of nationalization should not be applied retroactively, to rights Americans had held prior to 1917. Such an adamant stand the State Department was prone to attribute to Bolshevik influence, which certainly did exist, though not to the same extent as in China. Moreover, the United States suspected that Communist agents from Russia and North America were behind Mexico's support of a faction in Nicaragua against the established regime.

Such exaggerated fears of radical nationalism, however, did not last long, nor were they so pervasive as to prevent the development of an alternative approach by Washington. By the late 1920s, American officials had come to recognize that rather than maintaining an antagonistic relationship with radical forces in China, Mexico, and elsewhere, a relationship that might conceivably lead to war, it would be much better if some compromise could be worked out through close economic ties. It so happened that in these countries forces looking to some accommodation with the United States and other capitalist powers steadily gained influence. Known as the "national development wing" in Mexico, these forces were first and foremost intent upon economic development and ready to moderate their nationalism in order to obtain goods, capital, and technology from the advanced countries, above all the United States.[10] Representing this new development, Calles was ready for a reconciliation with Washington, and the latter eagerly obliged, President Calvin Coolidge sending a Wall Street banker, Dwight W. Morrow, as a new ambassador to Mexico in 1927 to work out a compromise settlement of the petroleum question. He was quite successful, a

10 Robert Freeman Smith, *The United States and Revolutionary Nationalism in Mexico* (Chicago, 1972), 245.

good indication of the shared interests between Mexican nationalists and American businessmen. Similarly, in China, when the Nationalists unified the country in 1928, their leader, Chiang Kai-shek, quickly took steps to conciliate the United States in order to entice American financiers and engineers to invest in the country's modernization. Americans were eager to reciprocate such overtures, and indeed the United States was the first among the principal capitalist nations to extend recognition to the new regime in Nanking and signal its willingness to modify the existing treaties.

Against such a background, the Soviet Union's joining other countries in signing the Pact of Paris was symbolic of the changing state of relations between that country and the rest of the world. It was as if the Soviets were now less intent on revolutionizing the globe than in consolidating their gains and stabilizing their foreign relations. That was in essence what Joseph Stalin implied when he began talking about "socialism in one country." Rather than trying to turn all countries in the direction of socialism – a strategy still being advocated by Leon Trotsky, Stalin's arch rival in the struggle for power after Lenin's death in 1924 – Russia would be content with its own survival as the sole socialist state. Stalin's own survival became bound up with this, more modest goal. In any event, henceforth the Soviet Union, too, would focus on its domestic economic modernization rather than engaging in global revolutionary missions. It followed that Moscow now would be willing, indeed eager, to repair its relations with other countries. The result was that in this connection, too, stability returned to the international arena. Coupled with the successful conclusion of disarmament agreements and various other treaty arrangements for solidifying the new status quo, the Soviet Union was, by the end of the 1920s, willy-nilly playing a role in the consolidation of the postwar order.

6. *The 1920s: The Economic Aspect*

The Diplomacy of the Dollar

Any stable system of international relations must be built on economic foundations, and the situation in the 1920s was no exception. Indeed, given the devastation brought upon the European economies, no postwar order could be conceived that did not include an economic agenda. How to restore the European economies and, through them, reestablish stable international economic relations was a key issue of the postwar period, the more so since, as noted earlier, the Versailles peace treaty had failed to address the issue squarely.

The Great War had cost Europe dearly; 9 million of its youths had died in war, another 20 million had been wounded, and more than $400 billion had been expended on battle. Inevitably, the European countries, victors and vanquished alike, suffered from a decline in industrial and agricultural production, which, combined with a severe inflation, caused social and political instability. Moreover, foreign exchange mechanisms remained confused. The system of multilateral trade and investment that had functioned before the war had been based on the gold standard and the principle of currency convertibility, both of which had been given up during the war and could not be automatically restored when the peace came. (Only the United States lifted the ban on gold shipments right after the war.)

Added to the chaotic picture were the issues of German reparations and the allied war debts to the United States. As seen earlier, Germany was called upon to pay reparations totaling as much as $33 billion, which its leaders and people alike considered an outrageous sum. The British, the French, and the Italians, for their part, were adamant on the reparations question because their postwar economic recovery appeared to hinge on such payments. At the same time, these countries had borrowed much from the United States after 1917. As noted earlier, their indebtedness during 1917–20 had exceeded $10 billion. These loans had been extended at 5 percent interest. The Americans expected interest payments to continue, as well as the eventual repayment of all debts. The Europeans, however, insisted that they could not do so unless the interest rate were lowered and, more important, until they received reparations moneys from Germany.

Thus developed one of the most serious disputes in postwar U.S.-European relations. The United States was opposed to coupling the reparations and debt issues, asserting that the former had to do with Germany's war guilt, whereas the latter was a purely commercial transaction. The Americans, to be sure, would be willing to lower the interest rates, and as a result of long negotiations throughout the decade, the United States and its wartime allies did come to some understanding, lowering the interest rate on British loans to 3.3 percent, French to 1.6 percent, and Italian to 0.4 percent. These concessions were not sufficient from the Europeans' point of view, however, for they still had to come up with the money, which they expected to obtain, at least in part, from the German reparations. Given the French-German crisis over the question, the formula of Britain, France, and Italy receiving funds from Germany and then using them to pay back the American debts did not work. With Americans continuing to insist that the wartime allies honor their obligations, there developed severe strains in U.S.-European relations. The French felt particularly hurt as they had suffered most from the war and believed they had sacrificed themselves for three years before the Americans bestirred themselves to come to their aid. The French, they said, had paid with their blood, whereas Americans were talking about money. Moreover, some in France calculated that the country had lent money to the Americans during the latter's war for independence that had not been paid back.[1] The dispute became very tense, and the Commerce Department in Washington even sought to forbid American private loans to France while the crisis lasted.

1 Jean-Baptiste Duroselle, *France and the United States* (Chicago, 1976), 124–6.

Things reached a critical stage during 1923–4, with French and Belgian troops occupying the Ruhr Valley, Germans refusing to budge, Americans bitter over the European failure to honor wartime obligations, and no restoration of the system of currency convertibility having been effected. It was at this point that the U.S. government chose to step in and help alleviate the tensions. It would not act directly, for it judged that the reparations question did not concern the government, which had not signed the Versailles treaty, although the nation did intend to ask for some payment from Germany for war damages. The best approach, Washington officials believed, was to work through private bankers and businessmen, to let them take the initiative, with the government staying in the background, and approach their counterparts in Europe.[2]

This arrangement, an early example of "corporatism" or a system of state-business cooperation, worked very well. In 1924 three bankers – Charles G. Dawes, Henry M. Robinson, and Owen D. Young – were asked by President Calvin Coolidge to organize themselves as a commission to investigate German finances. They went to Europe and proposed a revised schedule of German reparations payments, which in effect would reduce the total amount Germany would be expected to pay. To enable the country to start reparations payments, the former allies would supervise plans for stabilizing German currency, including an immediate advance of foreign loans, of which the major portion consisted of a $110 million loan to be raised in the United States. American bankers had little difficulty making the loan, and thus the reparations settlement, known as the Dawes Plan, paved the way for stabilizing European financial as well as diplomatic affairs. Together with the settlement of the allied debt question, which was completed by 1926, the United States and the European nations were able to resume normal economic relations for the first time since the war.

As if to commemorate the occasion, more than twenty nations decided to reestablish the gold standard. More correctly known as "the gold exchange standard," the system lifted the wartime ban on

2 The best study of U.S. policies toward the reparations and debt questions is Melvin Leffler, *The Elusive Quest* (Chapel Hill, 1979).

shipments of gold, thereby restoring convertibility among different currencies. Their rates of exchange were more or less fixed through the medium of gold. That is to say, the value of a currency was determined by the price of gold in that currency, and its ratio of exchange with another currency would be the same as the comparative values of the two currencies in terms of gold. For instance, one ounce of gold was fixed at $20.67. In pounds sterling, one ounce would cost around 4.13 pounds. In other words, a pound was worth $5. This was the same as the prewar rate of exchange; both currencies were relinked to gold at "prewar par," as it is sometimes written. Such a decision did not take into consideration wartime and postwar inflations. Because dollars or pounds bought less than before the war, their respective values in terms of gold might also have declined. To restore the gold standard at prewar par meant, therefore, to try to combat inflation by making money dearer, and prices of commodities lower. This could produce a recessionary trend, resulting in shortages of capital and also higher unemployment. But in the mid-1920s such a policy appeared to be a better alternative to inflation. Exchange stability, it seemed, had to be restored if normal international economic transactions were to be resumed, and such stability appeared to depend on maintaining the value of each currency as much as possible.

For the United States such a policy did not bring about economic retrenchment since there was sufficient demand at home and abroad to keep factories in full operation, even though there was a chronic agricultural depression. And to the extent that the domestic economy did not grow fast enough, surplus capital could readily be invested abroad.

Indeed, American capital was the main sustainer of the international economic system during the 1920s, in particular after 1924. The role of American financial resources has sometimes been referred to as "the diplomacy of the dollar."[3] The term signifies the fact that whereas the government in Washington refrained from active participation in world political affairs and was particularly sensitive about domestic opposition to working with the League of Nations, private

3 Herbert Feis, *The Diplomacy of the Dollar* (Baltimore, 1950).

bankers, speculators, and others were anxious to make use of the opportunities presented for expanding their roles in economic transactions abroad. Starting with the 1924 loan of $110 million to Germany, American loans and investment overseas grew rapidly.

Foreign investments are usually divided into two categories: direct and indirect. The former refers to doing business abroad, for example by establishing factories and manufacturing commodities with capital one has brought; the latter alludes to the purchase of bonds, debentures, and securities, in other words, public loans and private investment in foreign countries. Both categories of investment grew in the 1920s so that, for instance, in 1929 alone American direct investment in Europe amounted to $1,352 million, and indirect investment to $3,030 million. Altogether, American funds totaling more than $10 billion were being sent abroad – this at a time when the nation's national income was about $80 billion. Given the size of the economy, the Americans could easily afford to engage in such investment activities.[4]

Whether, for the recipients of such funds, the continuous inflow of American capital in large amounts was a desirable development was seriously debated, but they really had little alternative, given the shortage of capital in war-devastated Europe and the fact that as late as 1929 the United States accounted for nearly 50 percent of the world's income. Clearly, as the countries of Europe as well as elsewhere sought to recover and develop economically, it was much easier to turn to the one source of capital rather than to generate funds internally.

In some such fashion, a relationship of financial interdependence was developing between the United States and Europe – and indeed the rest of the world as well. Europe was particularly important as the inflow of American funds enabled Germany to pay reparations to Britain, France, and Italy, and the latter, in turn, paid back portions of their wartime debts to the United States. The mechanism depended on the continued flow of American capital and on the understanding among these countries of the essential interdependence. It was not surprising that in 1929 a new arrangement was worked out

4 Charles P. Kindleberger, *The World in Depression* (Berkeley, 1973), 56, 71.

for German reparations. Known as the Young Plan, after the American banker, Owen Young, who helped arrange it, the plan reduced the reparations to about $9 billion, to be paid in fifty-nine years with an interest rate of 5.5 percent. Combined with the various debt settlements the United States and the wartime allies had by then negotiated, the 1929 arrangement epitomized the spirit of cooperation and the pivotal role played by the dollar in international affairs.

American financial involvement in the Western Hemisphere was also extensive. In 1929, American direct investment in Canada amounted to $1,960 million, in Cuba and the West Indies to $1,054 million, in Mexico to $913 million, and in South America to $1,548 million. Nearly equal amounts were sent to these countries as indirect investments and governmental loans. Some of these were risky investments; in Argentina, for instance, there were so many business failures that the Commerce Department in Washington cautioned bankers against investing more money there.[5] Still, these countries, too, could not have undertaken economic development programs without the massive infusion of American capital.

Although smaller in scale than American investments in Europe or the Western Hemisphere, there was also an impressive outflow of capital to Asia and the Middle East. American funds sent to Japan were instrumental in enabling the country to recover from the devastating earthquake of 1923, which destroyed much of Tokyo and caused property damage upward of $1 billion. The Ford Motor Company built factories and manufactured the first automobiles in Japan, and Americans also invested in Japanese companies in chemical, electronic, and other enterprises that were fast industrializing and urbanizing the country. In China, in the meantime, American investment was particularly notable in providing utilities and telephone systems in the larger cities. The Standard Vacuum Oil Company engaged in the refinery business in the Dutch East Indies as well as on the continent of Asia. Altogether, close to $1 billion was being invested in that part of the world on the eve of the Great Depression.

The 1920s were also notable because American business interests,

5 Joseph Tulchin, *Aftermath of War* (New York, 1971), 174.

with the strong backing of the State and the Commerce Departments, energetically entered the Middle Eastern oil fields. The region's rich petroleum resources had been mostly divided up into British, French, and Dutch concessions, but the Americans, sensing an urgent need to supplement domestic with imported oil (the development of the automobile made this a clear requirement), energetically entered the field. Supported by the government, they succeeded in getting the Europeans to agree to a redrawing of the oil concessions map so as to make room for American companies. The so-called red-line agreement of 1928 defined where these four countries would have primary rights for the development of oil fields.[6]

Outside these regions, Liberia and the Soviet Union may be mentioned as significant examples of American economic activities during the 1920s. In the African republic with close historical ties to the United States, the main target was rubber plantations. Rubber was needed for automobile tires, but its production and pricing tended to be controlled by Britain, which possessed rich rubber resources within its Asian empire, especially Malaya. The Firestone Rubber Company kept in close touch with the Commerce Department as it developed rubber production facilities in Liberia. In the meantime, the Soviet Union, despite its antiimperialistic ideology, did not hesitate to turn to the United States for much needed capital. Although the absence of a diplomatic relationship meant binding legal contracts could not be worked out, this did not prevent American entrepreneurs and Soviet officials from concluding several business agreements. For instance, the Sinclair Oil Company obtained a concession to develop oil fields on northern Sakhalin; W. Averell Harriman invested in manganese mines; and, most famous of all, Henry Ford built tractor factories. Altogether, more than a hundred proposals for concessions in the Soviet Union were made by Americans from 1926 to 1929; in 1928 and 1929, there were fifty-four proposals, amounting to 26.1 percent of all foreign proposals during those years.[7]

6 Daniel Yergin, *The Prize* (New York, 1991), 204–5.

7 William Appleman Williams, *American-Russian Relations* (New York, 1952), 208–25.

If America's foreign investment was a major international activity of the 1920s, one that undoubtedly contributed to world economic recovery and development, trade also played a pivotal role. World trade had suffered an overall decline during the European war, and it did not recover the prewar level till the second half of the 1920s. This was due to several factors: the devastations the war brought the European countries; their loss of millions of productive workers (and consumers); the chaotic state of foreign exchange in the absence of a gold exchange standard prior to 1925; the development of "import substituting" manufactures in many parts of the world that would encourage domestic production and discourage foreign imports. In the overall picture of trade stagnancy, however, the United States was almost always an exception. Its export trade, which expanded spectacularly during the war, slowed down somewhat after 1919, but the nation was still the principal exporter in the world, providing Europe with much of the necessities of life as well as industrial equipment and less tangible items like Hollywood movies.

Although the United States also imported from Europe, trade balances were always in the former's favor. This reversed the situation that had existed before the turn of the century. What was remarkable about the postwar years was the declining importance of Europe as America's trading partner. Whereas during 1910–14 the European countries together had accounted for 62 percent of total American export trade and 49 percent of import, after the war the average annual rate fell to 45 percent and 30 percent, respectively. This last figure, indicating that less than one-third of American purchases now originated in Europe, had serious implications for the European nations. If they were to resume and expand their trade, as they had to in order to reconstruct their economies and pay for American loans, and if they could no longer count on as close a commercial relationship with the United States as before the war, they would have to try exporting aggressively to other parts of the world, such as the Middle East and Southeast Asia, areas of their colonial control, parts of which were now governed as League mandates. In such regions, too, however, Americans were keen on stepping in. The Open Door policy that had earlier been enunciated in connection with the China market was now energetically applied elsewhere, the Commerce Department taking the initiative for opening up what it considered to be closed doors.

American trade in the formerly European enclaves of the Middle East, Africa, and Southeast Asia was still limited, but that in East Asia and the Western Hemisphere grew rapidly. Asia's share in American export trade increased from 6 percent before the war to twice that proportion after the war, and in America's imports, from 15 percent to 29 percent. Fully one-third of American exports were going to the countries of the Western Hemisphere at the end of the 1920s. These figures indicate that in trade relations, too, the United States was fast globalizing itself. World trade, on the whole, increased by only 13 percent between 1913 and 1929, whereas American trade more than doubled, and so one may well speculate as to whether global commerce would have expanded further if the prewar patterns of close U.S.-European trade links had been preserved. What is indisputable is that the penetration of world markets by American goods as well as capital and technology was providing a basis, the economic foundation, for the postwar international order.

Business Civilization

These economic activities, moreover, were sustained by an ethos, a mentality that played a unique role in the postwar world, in particular in the United States. At a League-sponsored world economic conference held in Geneva in 1927, for instance, the delegates recognized that international peace now depended on economic underpinnings. They set up a committee of experts to inquire into the commercial and financial arrangements best suited for achieving "understanding and harmony" among nations.[8] Although the U.S. government did not participate in these activities, Americans certainly shared such a perspective. They developed what may be termed an idea of business civilization as the key to national and international affairs. To a nation weary of both geopolitics and an ideological crusade, the emphasis on economics was most welcome. Production, distribution, banking, and related business endeavors as a model of rational action and an inspiration to the whole nation and

8 Quincy Wright, *A Study of War* (Chicago, 1965), 417–18.

indeed the entire world – such was the philosophy of business civilization that underlay American foreign relations during the 1920s.

Herbert Hoover, Henry Ford, Walter Lippmann, and Reinhold Niebuhr, representing divergent backgrounds and engaged in different professions, may be taken as examples representing, each in his own way, this business philosophy. Hoover, secretary of commerce for eight years before becoming president in 1929, was a strong believer in private American initiatives – economic and humanitarian – that would contribute to a stabler and more prosperous world. What he termed "American individualism" relied not on governmental authority but on the self-interest and civic spirit of citizens who collectively would increase national wealth and make use of it for similar purposes elsewhere.[9] Henry Ford preached the gospel of the new age of machinery, which he believed was promoting the cause of world progress. As he wrote, "Rightness in mechanics, rightness in morals are basically the same thing. . . . Just as a clean factory, clean tools, accurate gauges, and precise methods of manufacture produce a smooth-working, efficient machine, so clear thinking, clear living, square dealing make of an individual or domestic life a successful one, smooth-running and efficient to everyone concerned." Like Hoover, Ford believed that the United States had much to show other countries. Taylorism – after Frederick Taylor, who had disseminated ideas about efficient systems of production and of labor-management relations – symbolized the American way, but this was eminently exportable. As the industrialist noted, "foreign lands are feeling the benefit of American progress, our American right thinking. Both Russia's and China's problems are fundamentally industrial and will be solved by the application of the right methods of thinking, practically applied." It followed that "political boundaries and political opinions don't really make much difference. It is the economic condition which really forces change and compels progress."[10]

Lippmann and Niebuhr, among the most influential commenta-

9 Herbert Hoover, *American Individualism* (New York, 1922), 71.

10 Henry Ford, *My Philosophy of Industry* (New York, 1929), 35, 37–9, 45. On Taylorism, see Frederick W. Taylor, *Principles of Scientific Management* (New York, 1911).

tors on foreign affairs, likewise argued that a country like the United States, extremely powerful economically but reluctant to employ military force, was in the best position to define international order. Lippmann, who had been disillusioned by Woodrow Wilson's failure to bring his visions of peace to fruition, now accepted the business orientation of American foreign relations and believed the nation's economic ties to other countries might prove to be the glue that held the world together. Niebuhr, a young theologian with a keen interest in social issues, was more critical of corporate capitalism, but he too believed that the age of armament expansion and empire building had been replaced by a new "economic age" in which the "legates of our empire are not admirals or proconsuls, but bankers." If, he wrote, "we do not support our economic power by extraordinary military force, then [we] shall learn to live in a world community and make those adjustments to the desires and needs of others which are prompted by prudence and conscience."[11]

All these comments reflected the widespread perception that economics, as opposed to traditional geopolitics, was becoming the dominant force in national and international affairs, and that the United States, as the leading economic power, was playing the most influential role in the postwar world. The idea that economic interactions brought about a more peaceful international order was not new; both Presidents William Howard Taft and Woodrow Wilson had espoused the same thing. Now, however, ideal and reality appeared to be coming closer through the diplomacy of the dollar.

Whether the "economic age" would really make the Versailles peace more durable would depend in part on the continued economic strength of the United States and in part on the latter's willingness to heed "the desires and needs of others," in Niebuhr's words. Until the onset of the Depression in 1929, the first condition was clearly present, so the crucial question was the second, whether American economic policies served the interests of the world community. Did the United States pursue policies that tended to promote the further interdependence of the world economy, besides contributing to the nation's own enrichment? Did it make use of the

11 *Harper's* 149 (Jan. 1932): 90, 92, 95.

accumulated wealth on behalf of a harmonious, orderly international community?

Here the picture was mixed, and throughout the decade of the 1920s there was a tension between economic internationalism and economic nationalism. Historical judgment has not been very generous and tended to depict America's economic policy then as having been self-centered, parochial, and shortsighted. As evidence, commentators have noted the wide gap existing between the nation's professed Open Door policy and its protectionist tariff system. One may also add its restrictionist immigration policy in this connection. Both these policies made the United States less open to foreign goods and people than it might have been, given its dominating position in the world economy.

Protectionism was a Republican article of faith during the 1920s, as it had been before the war. The Fordney-McCumber Tariff of 1922 revised upward the Wilson administration's low rates on most imports, both manufactured and agricultural. It would be difficult to determine if this sort of protectionism caused world trade to grow rather slowly during the 1920s, but it is possible that America's particularly large trade surpluses with regard to Europe were achieved because of the policy and that the high tariffs made the nation a net exporter both of capital and of goods.

To take a typical example, in 1928 America's balance of trade was $880 million in its favor, and Americans sent some $970 million abroad as loans and investments, as if to help other countries pay for their trade deficits toward the United States.[12] This situation was different from Britain's before the war. Prior to 1914, London had been the financial capital of the world, lending and investing its funds in the United States and elsewhere. The recipient countries of these funds had been able to make payments on them through building up trade surpluses vis-à-vis Britain, which practiced a liberal commercial policy and tended to develop trade deficits with the borrowers. This was how Britain functioned as the economic hegemon and contributed to world stability, at least in the commercial and financial realm. After the war, however, the United States

12 Walter Lippmann, *Interpretations, 1931–1932* (New York, 1932), 46.

became a different sort of hegemon because of its protectionist tariffs. European critics, as well as those Americans who shared their views, argued that this was an untenable situation, making other countries, especially those in Europe, so much more dependent on the United States. The image of America as self-centered and insufficiently concerned with the larger picture emerged.

Defenders of the system, on their part, pointed out that there was nothing wrong with the arrangement; so long as Americans continued to send funds abroad, other countries could balance their books. Of course, these latter would have to pay interest and dividends on American loans and investments; in 1928, such payments amounted to $800 million. Was this not impoverishing America's debtors? Americans would counter by noting that they were also spending money abroad as tourists (this came to $660 million in 1928), and recent immigrants from Europe were remitting substantial portions of their savings to the mother countries ($220 million). If these financial arrangements could have been made to continue, one might well have argued that this system was as effective an instrument of orderly international business transactions as the prewar British-centered system.

American protectionism was also justified by Herbert Hoover and other leaders in its own terms, as necessary both for the nation and for the world. They argued that global economic development depended on a strong American economy; and a high-tariff policy would stimulate domestic production, bring in additional revenue, reinforce the value of the dollar, and enable the country to function as the world's banker. All this should be a welcome development not just for the nation but for the rest of the world. To such an argument, critics responded that America's protectionism gave the impression to the world that, despite the evident lead the United States was taking in establishing an economically more interdependent world order, the nation was not yet fully committed to internationalism, at least not to the extent of paying attention to the "desires and needs" of other countries. By not adopting a more liberal trade policy, the United States, it was sometimes noted, failed to set an example to others. For they, too, instituted protectionist tariffs, with rates going much beyond the levels prevailing before the war. The result was fierce trade competition that did not promote the cause of economic internationalism.

Such criticism seems justified at least insofar as American trade with Europe was concerned. It must, however, be put alongside the generous debt settlements with Britain, France, and Italy, as well as the support of German economic reintegration through American loans and investments. It would be best to say that, as the postwar economic hegemon, the United States acted to promote European reconstruction but that there was a limit to its commitment to commercial internationalism.

The picture becomes even more complex when we consider the non-European parts of the world. Through its exportation of goods, capital, and technology, the United States played a key role in bringing them into the global economy. Countries beginning their modernization effort, such as Mexico and China, accepted, if they did not uncritically welcome, the American role. Their powerful antiimperialist rhetoric turned the nationalistic leaders in these countries against the infusion of American funds, but by the end of the decade most of them had come to recognize that they could not do without them.

It is interesting to observe, in this connection, that even Joseph Stalin came grudgingly to admire American capitalism. In a pamphlet he published in 1924 (*Foundations of Leninism*), he repeated the standard Leninist argument that "colonial and dependent countries" must "wage a struggle for liberation" from "a world system of financial enslavement and colonial oppression . . . by a handful of 'advanced countries.'" At the same time, Stalin wrote, separate national economies and national territories had been integrated to create "a single chain called world economy," out of which "true internationalism" might emerge, an internationalism of "national liberation movements." Before the oppressed peoples of the world achieved such a goal, however, they should learn to combine "Russian revolutionary sweep" and "American efficiency." This latter, he explained, was "that indomitable force which neither knows nor recognizes obstacles; which with its businesslike perseverance brushes aside all obstacles; which continues at a task once started until it is finished, even if it is a minor task; and without which serious constructive work is inconceivable."[13] Such a statement in a sense accommodated revolutionary nationalism with the American business ethos and could, if needed, have provided justification to leaders in non-Western parts of the world for accepting goods, capital, technology, and management skills from the United States.

If, then, American economic influence was linking different parts of the world closer together, thereby creating a greater sense of global interdependence, there was a contrary trend as well: the new immigration policy of the United States. Both the 1921 and the 1924 immigration laws established a quota system on the basis of nationality. Henceforth only those from Western and Central Europe would be welcomed, and even they could not exceed the total combined figure of 150,000 annually. Immigrants from Eastern Europe would be severely restricted. Asians were excluded entirely. (The quota system, however, did not apply to Canada or to Latin America.) Such legislation, enacted by a nation that was the richest in the world, could not but impress other countries as narrow-minded and self-centered, an unfortunate impression given America's active promotion of international economic interchanges on many fronts. For the countries of Asia, Africa, and the Middle East, in particular, the near-total exclusion of their people from the United States was in sharp contrast to their growing commercial ties with the latter, as good an example as any of the tension between nationalism and internationalism in American foreign affairs.

13 Josef Stalin, *Foundations of Leninism* (New York, 1939), 27, 79, 81, 122–4.

7. The 1920s: The Cultural Aspect

Peace as an Ideology

Peace as a dominant idea was a distinctive feature of the postwar decade. This is not to say that there had been no forceful movements for peace or effective presentations of ideas of peace before then. Before the Great War, there had developed various strands of pacifism, ranging from traditional Christian conceptions to the more recent socialist formulations. In the United States, scores of peace societies had been established to organize the international community better to promote a stable, interdependent world order. And then, during the war, Woodrow Wilson and V. I. Lenin had emerged as spokesmen for two contrasting ideas about international affairs and propounded their respective visions of a world without war.

It was after 1919, however, that the idea of peace, of whatever shade of meaning, came to hold center stage in discussions about international affairs. We have already seen how potent were the drives for disarmament, outlawry of war, economic stabilization, and American capital movements, which together created an environment more conducive to peaceful interconnections among nations than to war and military preparedness. But the phenomenon had deep cultural roots as well and was sustained by intellectual developments in the 1920s. One might think of the ideology of peace at that time as a "hegemonic ideology" – the term Antonio Gramsci, the Italian Marxist, began to use as he penned his thoughts in prison.[1] According to him, a society was held together through a set of ideas produced, refined, and manipulated by its elites in order to maintain some sort of order and cohesiveness. These ideas were so pervasive that even those opposed to the elites

1 Antonio Gramsci, *Letters from Prison* (New York, 1989).

employed them consciously or unconsciously. An ideology, therefore, was more than a product of a class, an expression of its interests; at the same time, it was far more precise than people's collective ethos vaguely defined. An ideology had specific origins and objectives, expressing power relationships in society; it was also comprehensive so that even those without power would embrace it as a way of ordering social, national, or international events.

Peace was such an ideology in the 1920s. Its origins, to be sure, were diverse, but to the extent that one can speak of elites in the more advanced countries of Europe, North America, or Asia, it would seem that they established the idea of peace as the overarching framework in terms of which national and international affairs were to be discussed. Peace, in other words, was elevated to the position of a privileged concept so that a world existing in peace was considered to be the normal and normative – of course, these were by no means identical – state of affairs, and war an aberration.

Peace as a privileged concept had various connotations, strategic and economic, as has been discussed. It served the needs and interests of countries eager to devote their energies to reconstruction, as in Europe, to industrialization and development, as in Japan, or to enhanced levels of prosperity, as in the United States. These countries' leaders equated peace with economic well-being, political stability, and social cohesiveness. Domestic order, in other words, was considered to be dependent on a peaceful world order, and vice versa – hence the cardinal importance of international organizations and activities that were expected to solidify international community.

All this is quite clear, but how did the masses relate themselves to such an ideology? How were they incorporated into the hegemonic ideological system? Of course, some were not; militant nationalists in France and Germany in the immediate postwar years, or radical antiimperialists in China, Mexico, and elsewhere, were exceptions. Even they, however, would in time come under the strong influence of the peace ideology, at least to the extent that they would feel themselves to be on the defensive, in need of justifying their opposition to the idea of peace as a normal state of affairs. By the time the Locarno treaties were signed in Europe, and certainly by 1928 when the Soviet Union joined thirty-two capitalist and developing nations in signing the Kellogg-Briand Pact, it may be said that peace had become the most dominant global ideology.

It is not surprising, in such a situation, that studies about peace – or, more broadly, about international relations – became a major concern of nations everywhere. For the first time in modern history, peace became an object of serious intellectual inquiry, and international relations a subject taught at academic centers. As James T. Shotwell, the Columbia University historian and a major figure in the postwar peace movement, pointed out, the search for peace was at bottom an intellectual enterprise, requiring a conscious effort to turn from "the narrower conceptions of the past to a worldwide view."[2] Many shared his view, as evidenced by the initiation of study groups and research organizations throughout the world devoted to the examination of international relations. Among the most famous were the Royal Institute of International Affairs in London and the Council on Foreign Relations in New York, both established in the immediate aftermath of the war for the promotion of specialized research in the field. The League of Nations, on its part, took the initiative to encourage the teaching of international affairs at schools and universities in various parts of the world.

Nowhere was the subject more widely and enthusiastically taught than in the United States – a clear indication that its official abstention from the League of Nations did not mean the nation was not part of the intellectual climate of the time. On the contrary, through their scholarly and professional efforts, Americans may be said to have retained the intellectual leadership of the worldwide peace movement. A good example of this was the project undertaken by Quincy Wright and his colleagues at the University of Chicago for a massive study of war and peace. At that university a graduate program in international relations was launched in 1923, said to be the first of its kind in the United States (perhaps in the world as well). Wright directed the program, which brought together specialists in history, political science, anthropology, economics, sociology, and other disciplines. In 1926 they launched an ambitious project, to

2 Shotwell memorandum, May 31, 1932, ED25/25, Board of Education Archives, Public Record Office, London.

examine all past wars, inquire into their immediate causes and broader circumstances, and list conditions that would ensure peace. The project was so open-ended that by the time it was completed, in 1942, the realities of world affairs had changed drastically from the more optimistic days of the mid-1920s. Nevertheless, such an enterprise was not an isolated phenomenon but was part of a global trend toward an intellectual understanding of war and peace.[3]

The postwar decade also gave the traditional term "international understanding" a far more intellectual and educational connotation than in the past. It was believed that chances for world peace would be enhanced if peoples understood each other better and if they refrained from chauvinistic excesses in their school curricula. Here again, the United States was very much part of the global trend. During the 1920s a steadily increasing number of colleges and universities began offering courses in the histories and languages of Russia, China, Japan, and other non-Western countries. Newly created foundations for support of scholarly research, such as the Social Science Research Council and the American Council of Learned Societies, pooled their resources to encourage the initiation of "area studies" at selected centers of learning.

Curricular revision, in particular the rewriting of school textbooks so as to minimize distorted statements about other countries, was more difficult to achieve in America because of the decentralized nature of its educational administration. But while the League of Nations called upon such countries as France and Germany to revise history textbooks to promote mutual understanding, in America comparable efforts were made to develop a more dispassionate understanding of recent history, in particular the origins of the Great War. Many "revisionist" writings were published, questioning the accepted views about the causes of the war (with an emphasis on German militarism and war guilt) and about the reasons for U.S. entry into the conflict. Writers like Harry Elmer Barnes attacked those who had, he asserted, uncritically accepted British perspectives and become unwitting agents of pro-British propaganda.[4] Al-

3 Quincy Wright, *A Study of War* (Chicago, 1965).

4 Warren I. Cohen, *The American Revisionists* (Chicago, 1967), chap. 3.

though few went that far, such revisionism was in line with the climate of the age when textbook revision in the spirit of internationalism was seen as an important path to peace.

Peace Through Cultural Exchange

The proposition that peace was an intellectual engagement led to a major contribution of the postwar period: the idea that cultural and intellectual cooperation among nations was an effective way of promoting peace. We may term this idea "cultural internationalism" – the view that cultural communication, understanding, and cooperation were fundamental preconditions of international peace and order. The League of Nations endorsed the idea at its very inception when its council declared in 1921, "no association of nations can hope to exist without the spirit of reciprocal intellectual activity between its members."[5]

What did the council mean by "reciprocal intellectual activity"? First and foremost, the term suggested associative and cooperative activities by intellectuals across national boundaries. Paul Valéry, the French poet, asserted that a league of nations implied "a league of human intellects." A British scholar agreed, saying that "men and women of knowledge and ideas" in many lands had the responsibility to promote "mutual understanding between the peoples . . . independently of national or racial boundaries."[6] To implement what these men were advocating, the League of Nations established a committee on intellectual cooperation to organize scholarly, literary, and artistic exchanges among the cultural and intellectual leaders of various countries.

The idea was unquestionably elitist, but we must remember that the world had just come through a war in which scholars, artists, journalists, and other intellectuals – supposedly men and women of culture – had dedicated themselves to the war efforts of their respective countries, giving higher priority to patriotism than to interna-

5 League of Nations, "Moral Disarmament," Feb. 24, 1932, ED25/25, Public Record Office, London.

6 Heath memorandum, May 25, 1929, ED25/25, Public Record Office, London.

tionalism. Deeply embarrassed about the experience, many writers in Europe, joined by several in the United States, issued a declaration of intellectual independence, drafted by Romain Rolland, the French novelist.[7] It was a ringing assertion of intellectuals who recognized, belatedly, that their primary role should have been to overcome national differences and to strive for peace or, if this was impossible, at least to mitigate the effects of war by maintaining international communication at the cultural level even when their nations were taking up arms against one another. As the declaration said, "we do not know peoples. We know the People . . . the People of all men, all equally our brothers"; people did not recognize the artificial political boundaries into which they had been categorized. Much more united than divided them, and therefore it would be – it had been – wrong for their intellectual leaders to bestir them with patriotic rhetoric so that they would come to hate their counterparts elsewhere. Now that the tragedy had passed, the intellectuals of all nations had a responsibility to teach the masses how not to be caught up in chauvinistic frenzy but instead to become even more aware of their shared destiny throughout the world.

This stress on the role of intellectuals as shapers of national and international affairs was a common theme running through the 1920s. The intellectuals enjoyed what Gramsci called "social hegemony"; in other words, they mediated between the power of the state and the masses composing the society. He distinguished between the state and "civil society," the latter consisting of private individuals and groups not permeated by the power of the state. As intermediaries between the two, the intellectuals were in a position to narrow or widen the distance between them. And in the postwar world, it is not surprising that many writers believed that the state had grown too powerful, and that in order to prevent another disastrous war, this trend must be reversed. The sovereign authority of the state must somehow be checked through an assertion of the rights of individuals, or civil society, through what G. Jellinek, a distinguished German jurist, called the "common consciousness of the community."[8] Only through curbing state sovereignty could

7 Jean Francois Sinirelli, *Intellectuels et passions françaises* (Paris, 1990), 41–2.
8 Joshua Fogel, *Nakae Ushikichi in China* (Cambridge, Mass., 1988), 33–8.

there be international understanding and peace. The intellectuals must seize the moment to further the movement.

Such views on intellectual cosmopolitanism, arguing for a new world order through curbing state power and nationalistic excesses, did not go unchallenged. In France, where the debate was particularly intense, nationalists insisted that the world was still divided into countries, and that the primary responsibility of French intellectuals, at least, was to the French nation.[9] In Germany, Carl Schmitt, among others, continued to argue that national power remained the key in a world defined by power.[10] Of course, that was precisely why so many sought to redefine world affairs by curbing the authority of the state. The debate between traditional nationalists and postwar internationalists was inconclusive, but at least it would appear that by 1929, ten years after the conclusion of the war, cosmopolitan ideas had established a firm foothold and had to be taken seriously in any discussion of national and international affairs. Contrary views continued to be expressed, but the relatively small number of publications exalting the heroism of dying for one's country – as, for example, René Quinton did in his book *Maxims on War* (1930), or Alfred Rosenberg in his *The Myth of the Twentieth Century* (1930) – suggests a tone of defensiveness against the prevailing intellectual climate of the time.

That climate was exemplified by the League's committee on intellectual cooperation, which served throughout the interwar period as the headquarters for promoting cultural interchanges. A typical example of the committee's activity was its sponsorship of open exchanges of views by some of the world's leading intellectual and artistic figures. The best-known instance of this was the open exchange of letters between Albert Einstein and Sigmund Freud in 1932 on war and peace. Although the exchange took place after the stability of international order had begun to be threatened by the Depression, the ideas the two expressed were typical of the optimism and faith of the 1920s. Both Einstein and Freud agreed that only through the active cooperation of internationalist-minded individuals and through the cultural enterprises they pro-

9 Sinirelli, *Intellectuels,* 43–7.

10 Joseph W. Bendersky, *Carl Schmitt* (Princeton, 1983), 87–92.

moted would it be possible for humanity to rid itself of the scourge of war.

Lesser minds than they were similarly active. In scores of countries leading scholars, artists, musicians, and others organized their respective national committees on intellectual cooperation to serve as liaisons between the League committee and the cultural communities of nations. And in Paris an international institute for intellectual cooperation was established and held numerous exhibits and symposia. (Out of these organizations and activities the United Nations Educational, Scientific, and Cultural Organization was to be created in 1945.) There existed, moreover, a large number of international associations, the bulk of which were organized in the immediate aftermath of the war, that cemented ties among the world's cultural figures: the International Office of Museums, the International Congress on Popular Arts, the International Society of Contemporary Music, to cite but a few examples. The philosophy behind all such bodies was the idea that "internationalizing" (a word that had been in the English language since the late nineteenth century but acquired its modern meaning in the 1920s) cultural affairs through collaborative endeavors was the surest way for achieving international understanding and hence a durable peace.

Americans were very much part of this cultural internationalism. Raymond Fosdick of the Rockefeller Foundation represented the United States on the League's committee on intellectual cooperation, and even after the Senate's rejection of the Treaty of Versailles, Americans regularly attended the committee's meetings. They also established a national committee on intellectual cooperation, of which James Shotwell long served as chairman. Besides participating in various international organizations, Americans organized some 350 associations devoted to furthering scholarly communication and international dialogue. Typical was the Institute of Pacific Relations, established initially in Honolulu but then moved to New York. It was an association of Americans, Canadians, Europeans, and Asians interested in Pacific issues, designed to facilitate their dialogue in a nonpartisan setting. The IPR drew the participation of distinguished scholars, journalists, and businessmen from the

United States and elsewhere, conducted research on current affairs affecting the region, and held biannual meetings for the exchange of opinions. Another important organization established in the 1920s, the Guggenheim Foundation, which awarded grants to scholars and artists, actively solicited research proposals from Latin American intellectuals.

Perhaps the major contribution of the United States to intellectual cooperation at this time was through student exchanges. Before the war, a number of foreign youths had come to study in American schools and colleges. Most notable had been Chinese students who had been brought over as "Boxer indemnity students" (with funds the United States had remitted China from the Boxer indemnity payments). But it was in the wake of the Great War that American foundations and educational institutions became keenly interested in educating foreign men and women. The Institute of International Education actively engaged in fund-raising for bringing foreign students and placing them in colleges and universities. Although most of the students came from Asia and, increasingly, from Latin America, there was also a transatlantic traffic of exchange students and teachers, some of whom were sponsored by the British national committee for interchange.

Cultural and intellectual cooperation, then, represented an earnest activity by the world's leaders to contribute to internationalism and peace, and Americans were very much part of the movement. Of course, one may wonder to what extent such endeavors actually furthered the cause of peace. Certainly, all the efforts by scholars, writers, and other men and women of education could not prevent the coming of yet another period of international crises. Cultural internationalists of the interwar years were undoubtedly naïve to think that if only they could transcend parochial concerns and chauvinistic excesses, international tensions could somehow be surmounted. In retrospect, their idealism may be said to have made them less sensitive than warranted to the continued existence of traditional loci of loyalty, especially ethnic and national entities. Nevertheless, many of their ideas were to survive another world war and to contribute enormously to enriching human communities in the second half of the twentieth century.

The Americanization of the World

Had efforts at cultural communication and cooperation been limited to intellectuals and artists, their impact on world affairs might not have been substantial. A major characteristic of the 1920s was that cross-national interchange went much beyond interelite endeavors and touched the lives of common people throughout the world. This was fundamentally because of the pervasive impact of American popular and material culture.

The Americanization of the world in terms of material and popular culture was not a new phenomenon, even in the 1920s. As Emily Rosenberg, Jacques Portes, and others have noted, already at the turn of the century foreign observers were remarking how pervasive the impact of American goods and ways of life had been throughout the world.[11] The American people, who were already then enjoying the highest standard of living among all nations, were the object of envy elsewhere; they seemed to represent material prosperity, comfort, and a certain life-style free from Old World complications. Such products of modern technology as electricity, automobiles, and telephones, which for most countries did not arrive in large quantities till after the Great War, had become commonplace in America before the war. (There were, in the United States, 18 million light bulbs in 1902, 902,000 registered automobiles in 1912, and 10 million telephones in 1914.)

What was notable after 1919 was that these developments accelerated and that American influence now became undisputed because of the decline of European prestige. The so-called decline of the West, made popular through the publication of Oswald Spengler's book of that title in 1918, really meant the decline of Europe. Because of the war-related devastations and the partially successful attempts by non-Europeans to catch up with them in industrialization and trade, the Europeans felt themselves to be on the defensive, no longer the unquestioned center of civilization or foundation of wisdom. Indeed, it seemed that Europe had little to offer the world as it

11 Emily Rosenberg, *Spreading the American Dream* (New York, 1982); Jacques Portes, *Un fascination reticente* (Nancy, 1990).

sought to reconstruct itself. The task of defining the peace – not just geopolitically but economically and culturally – would have to be entrusted to others, above all the United States.

And America, virtually unscathed by the war, was more than ever before the symbol of the new material and popular culture. In a pathbreaking study of a "typical" American community (actually Muncie, Indiana), the sociologists Robert and Helen Lynd noted, in the mid-1920s, the growing influence of "inventions imported from without – automobile, motion picture, and radio."[12] Imported from "without" (i.e., from other parts of the nation), these inventions were linking small towns to the outside world, making local citizens conscious of their interrelationships with people elsewhere. Although the Lynds were commenting on the homogenization of American culture, the same phenomenon could also be observed globally.

The automobile, the motion picture, and the radio – these three artifacts that were linking together Americans in different parts of the country – were also serving the same function in the wider world. Because all three were overwhelmingly products of American civilization, and because they spread to all corners of the globe in the years immediately following the war, we may speak of the cultural Americanization of the world during the 1920s.

Just to cite one example, the motion picture, another American sociologist, Robert Park, traveled extensively and was deeply impressed with the cinema's impact on international affairs. The cinema, he wrote, "may be regarded as the symbol of a new dimension of our international and racial relations which is neither economic nor political, but cultural." The spread of the motion picture as well as the radio was affecting "men's minds and . . . their intimate personal experiences," and bringing "the ends of the earth into an intimacy unimaginable a few years ago." The result, Park was convinced, was that "all the peoples of the earth" were being brought "measurably within the limits of a common culture and a common historical life."[13]

12 Robert Lynd and Helen Lynd, *Middletown* (New York, 1929).
13 Robert Park, *Race and Culture* (Boston, 1940), 149.

In retrospect, it is clear that such a view vastly exaggerated the effect of technological innovations in obliterating national differences. The subsequent decade was to show that even a culturally Americanized world did not necessarily guarantee international understanding and peace. Nevertheless, there is little doubt about the phenomenon of Americanization itself. People in even the remotest corners of India or Brazil saw the same movies as the Americans and Europeans. Well-to-do Asians as well as Europeans owned radios and automobiles and sensed that they were sharing a common experience with the Americans.

Even those who were appalled at such a phenomenon unwittingly acknowledged the unmistakable influence of American culture when they denounced it as detrimental to maintaining the cultural integrity of their own countries. To cite but one example, two French writers published a book entitled *The American Cancer* in 1930 and asserted that France was being colonized by the United States through the ideas of productivity and efficiency. The "new feudalism," they argued, of bankers, commerce, and industry with their emphasis on mechanization was stifling the true spirit of the French Revolution, embodied in the principles of individuality and human rights. "The principal means of the American conquest whose menace weighs over Europe and the whole world is not so much brute force as the American spirit, its cult of blind reason and rational construction." France, the authors concluded, was now under the tutelage of "Yankee inspiration and direction" where the people were demoralized and lay at the service of a cosmopolitan plutocracy.[14]

The very extremeness of such language testified to the extensive influence of American commercial culture, in a sense corroborating what Park was writing about. All these observers were noticing the spread of American cultural influence, which, combined with its economic power, was redefining national and international affairs. Ultimately, what was happening was the construction of an international order, the postwar peace, that was founded as much on economic and cultural factors as it was on military factors. This was a peace that was being sustained through economic and cultural inter-

14 Robert Aron and A. Dandieu, *La cancer américaine* (Paris, 1931), 14–16.

changes, one in which nonmilitary means were replacing arms as the key to world affairs. The United States exemplified this new age. Just as the postwar world was defined, at one level, through the peace treaties and naval disarmament, and, at another, by the movement of goods and capital across national boundaries, so it was also developing a global cultural order. And because America had always (and particularly under Wilson) sought to give international affairs a cultural definition, it was not surprising that the age of cultural internationalism was also the age of Americanization.

8. *The Collapse of International Order*

The World Economy in Disarray

One would never know if the collapse of the American economy and, as a consequence, of the world economic order in the years following 1929 was more or less preordained by the very structure of economic affairs during the 1920s, or whether the prosperity and peace of the postwar decade could somehow have been maintained if the United States and other nations had taken more forceful measures to cope with the economic crisis at its inception. One thing is certain, however. The world economy of the 1920s had been so intertwined with American economic resources and performance that whether the relative stability and prosperity of the postwar decade could have been perpetuated hinged to a considerable extent on action taken by American officials, bankers, and others. Their inaction or passivity, by the same token, would have profound implications for world affairs of the 1930s.

As of 1929, the United States still accounted for 40 percent of the world's industrial production, 50 percent of the world gold reserve, and 16 percent of international trade. Should something happen to the American economy, therefore, it would have a severe impact on other countries. And, indeed, something drastic did take place; after the stock market crash of October 1929, production was cut by 50 percent by 1932, export trade fell by 60 percent, and unemployment rose from 1.5 million to 12 million in the same period. Industrial and agricultural prices fell, wages for those still employed declined, personal and business bankruptcies were legion, and the cult of productivity and efficiency as the prevailing ethos of the first postwar decade was replaced by severe attacks on capitalism.

Much of this, though not its scale, could have been foreseen. The speculative boom preceding the crash had been fed by low interest rates, which banks adopted to make it easier for individuals and factories to borrow money; the policy attracted American capital away from foreign investment markets and fueled the boom. Had the banks retained higher interest rates, some of this might not have happened, although if the rates had been noticeably higher than the returns on investments abroad, this, too, might have brought American capital home and created a speculative atmosphere. Even more serious was the fact that during the 1920s, despite the overall growth of the American economy, the average purchasing power had not kept pace, and that in some sectors, especially agricultural, there had been overproduction, depressing farm income. Farmers, factory workers, and shopkeepers had tended to spend more than they earned, and were thus chronically in debt. The 1920s had ushered in a period of installment purchases, where consumers borrowed money in order to buy goods. But toward the end of the decade, many of them also borrowed to speculate in the stock market. All these combined not only to create the panic of 1929 but also to bring about not just a temporary readjustment of the stock market but wholesale bankruptcies and disequilibriums at all levels of the economy.

In the context of American foreign relations, the Depression could not have come at a worse moment. As noted in Chapter 6, the United States and the European countries had just concluded an agreement through their banking representatives (the Young Plan) for a debt and reparations settlement. The way seemed to have been opened for further stabilization of European affairs. Now, however, even such a funding arrangement lost much of its value because American funds, which were at the core of postwar international economic relations, suddenly became unavailable. The recall of American capital had started before the stock market crash, but was accelerated by the panic that accompanied the crash and did not swiftly go away. With confidence shaken in their own economy, Americans might have turned to overseas markets for investment, but they now had much less capital to play with. Falling stock market and commodity prices, business bankruptcies, and unemployment meant there was little excess capital available for foreign investment. This naturally caused a chain reaction in other countries; with a drastic reduction in American funds, not only their reparations and debt payment but also their productive activities as well would be jeopardized. These countries, too, would experience business failures, the closing of factories, and unemployment. With reductions in output and in personal income, trade would suffer, and the decline in export trade would further entail reduced production and more unemployment.

The postwar international system that had been based on multilateral trade, currency convertibility, and the free flow of capital from one country to another now became unhinged. World trade shrank from $30.3 billion in 1929 to $20.3 billion in 1931; Germany's capital imports fell from $967 million in 1928 to only $482 million in 1929, and further to $129 million in 1930. By 1932 the United States, the major provider of capital not only to Germany but to most other countries, had virtually stopped investing its funds overseas. The dwindling trade and capital movement severely strained the gold exchange standard, the mainstay of postwar multilateralism. Nations were now unwilling or incapable of making their payments in gold – unwilling because they feared the draining of gold out of the country would cause further loss of confidence in the economy, incapable because in some countries (Austria, then Britain) central banks lost their gold holdings because of panic "runs" on gold. The result was that by 1932 several nations (including Germany and Japan – the latter had readopted the gold standard only in 1930 – in addition to Austria and Britain) had abandoned the gold exchange standard; international transactions would no longer be conducted in terms of gold-defined fixed rates of exchange among different currencies, but would be subject to fluctuating rates of exchange. Governments would be under pressure to inflate their currencies in order to make their respective commodities comparatively cheaper in the world market. "Managed currencies," as the practice was called, would be one way of augmenting exports and reducing imports. For the same reason, governments would be tempted to legislate higher tariff rates so as to maintain a favorable balance of trade.

Another aspect of the collapse of multilateralism was the emergence of economic regionalism, or autarky. Autarkies were blocs or associations of certain countries that would be bound together closely through certain economic arrangements, such as mutual reductions of tariffs, but that would adopt a more exclusive policy toward the outsiders. One of the earliest manifestations of this trend was the abortive establishment of a German-Austrian customs union which would have tied the two countries economically closer together. It had to be given up when it met strong opposition from other countries, but in the very same year representatives from Britain and the members of the Commonwealth met at Ottawa and adopted a preferential customs agreement through which they would impose lower tariff rates on each other's goods than those imposed on imports from other countries.[1]

These trends – managed currencies, protectionism, autarkies – signaled the demise of the multilateral economic system that had prevailed during the postwar decade. Although, as noted earlier, that system had not been free from economic nationalism, the basic rules of multilateralism, symbolized by the gold exchange standard, had been accepted by all. Now that linchpin was gone, and so the urgent question was whether the old system should be revived and, if so, how to accomplish the task. Alternatively, if it was impossible, or undesirable, to resuscitate multilateralism, what new arrangements were to take its place? Or was the world about to enter a period of rampant economic nationalism without any shared rules of the game, so that each country would see its own interests without concern for the global picture? What would be the likely consequences of such a development?

It was clear that responses of the United States to these questions would be of critical importance. The world had become so accustomed to depending on American financial resources that it would be faced with a threat of total collapse unless the United States now did something to alleviate the situation. What would be Washington's position regarding such issues as German reparations, Eu-

1 For a discussion of the world economic crisis, see Charles P. Kindleberger, *The World in Depression* (Berkeley, 1973).

ropean debts, currency devaluations, high tariffs, and trading blocs? Would the United States take the initiative to restore some stability in international monetary transactions and trade?

These were the questions that confronted President Herbert Hoover almost as soon as he entered the White House. He, his secretary of state (Henry L. Stimson), and other officials spent the entire four-year term trying to cope with the economic crisis. Unfortunately, little that they did worked, and there was much that they wished to carry out but could not because of domestic and international circumstances.

Hoover was, as seen earlier, an economic internationalist, albeit at the same time a high-tariff advocate. He strongly believed in the role of the United States in the world economy. And his initial reaction to the Depression suggested he had not changed his views. He sought to persuade the American people not to lose confidence in their economy, asserting that it was fundamentally in good shape. When unemployment nevertheless continued to grow, he initiated a modest program of public works. He also supported a high-tariff policy. Even before the Wall Street crash, Congress had discussed raising tariffs, and in June 1930 a new schedule of import duties, the Smoot-Hawley Tariff, was enacted. It raised rates on most commodities, especially sugar and textiles. The tariff had Hoover's support, as he believed that it should protect domestic production, curtail imports, and contribute to expanding exports.[2]

In the meantime, the United States was called upon to do something about the reparations and debt question and about the growing chaos in international monetary transactions. Here Hoover's response, while sensitive to economic interests at home, was designed to restore the system of postwar international economic relations, which, he believed, had served the nation and the world so well. In June 1931, he proposed a one-year moratorium on all intergovernmental debts and reparations. The moratorium went into effect in July, by which time German banks had been closed, followed in September by Britain's decision to go off the gold stan-

2 On Hoover's response to the Depression, see Albert U. Romasco, *Poverty of Abundance* (New York, 1965).

dard. Clearly the Hoover moratorium was not sufficient to moderate the crisis, but at least it showed America's willingness to cooperate with other countries to cope with the situation. Unilateral action was eschewed, and the governments tried desperately to save the basic structure of international economic transactions.

The moratorium, in any event, was a temporary palliative, and the European nations convened a meeting in Lausanne in June 1932 to discuss the reparations and debt question. They agreed in reducing Germany's reparations – if the United States likewise consented to renegotiate the allied debts. Hoover, however, refused to take precipitous action and agreed only to a six-month extension of the moratorium. When it expired in December 1932, he insisted that the former allies resume debt payments, and some did: Britain, Italy, Finland, and others, but not France. Hoover's adamant position was in part based on his view that the debt payments would help balance the U.S. budget and bring about business recovery, but it was also part of his comprehensive strategy, to deal with the reparations and debt questions in a larger framework of international cooperation in support of multilateralism.[3]

Much to his disappointment, Hoover lost the presidential election of November 1932 (even some of the outspoken internationalists deserted him), so that henceforth America's economic policy would be shaped by his successor, Franklin D. Roosevelt. Hoover, however, did not lose his confidence in the multinational approach and sought to persuade the incoming president to prepare seriously for an international economic conference that was being planned for mid-1933 in London where trade, foreign exchange, reparations, debt, and other questions were to be discussed. Above all, he wanted to make sure that the gold exchange standard would be restored as the key to economic recovery and restabilization. The nations of the world, he continued to argue, would have to agree to give up restrictive trade practices and regional arrangements, and to readopt some system of fixed rates of exchange. It is to Hoover's credit that, although none of these recommendations was initially adopted by Roosevelt, in time many of them would be accepted by

3 Melvin Leffler, *The Elusive Quest* (Chapel Hill, 1979), 234–45.

the United States as well as other countries, and form a basis of a new global economic system that would be set up after another world war.

Japan's Challenge to World Order

President Hoover had another idea about controlling the economic crisis: to encourage further disarmament. As noted in Chapter 5, the United States, Britain, and Japan had failed to come to terms on enlarging the scope of their disarmament agreement to cover the so-called auxiliary craft – light cruisers, destroyers, and submarines. As soon as he became president, Hoover was determined to try again, and the third naval disarmament conference in ten years was convened in London in January 1930. Although initially unrelated to the Depression, Hoover became convinced of the connection, believing that disarmament would enable governments to reduce public spending; balanced budgets were considered desirable if nations were to put an end to economic chaos, restore business confidence, and preserve the value of their currencies. Hoover was also beginning to make a connection between the settlement of the reparations and debt question and disarmament; he would be willing to consider reducing, even canceling, those payments only if the amounts thus saved would not go into armament. Thus, both in the naval disarmament conference of 1930 and in the general disarmament conference that the League of Nations convened in Geneva in 1932, Hoover showed an unusual interest. They were all part of his strategy for economic recovery through international cooperation.

In the 1930 naval conference, he could at least take pride, for it was a successful instance of cooperation – albeit with unforeseen consequences. The American, British, and Japanese delegations resolved their differences over the three navies' respective sizes in different categories of ships. The Japanese Navy had insisted on a 10:7 ratio in auxiliary craft, arguing that the 10:6 ratio adopted at the Washington Conference with regard to capital ships had already compromised national security. The American and British representatives believed that to grant Japan's request would jeopardize *their* Pacific possessions' security. Besides, they had not resolved their differences over cruiser tonnages, which had brought about the failure of the 1927 Geneva Conference.

It may well have been the world economic crisis that prodded the three governments to work extra hard to arrive at a compromise settlement. All three governments desperately needed to avoid a costly naval arms race, and they also believed that a failure on the naval issue, at a time when nations were driven by unilateralist forces, would deal a fatal blow to the structure of international relations built upon mutual cooperation and consultation. The London compromise was an ingenious arrangement: Japan's relative naval tonnage would be equal to 6.975 as against America's 10. This average was worked out by applying a 10:6 ratio on large cruisers, parity on submarines, and a 10:7 ratio on other categories of auxiliary craft. In addition, it was agreed that the Washington formula of the 10:6 ratio regarding capital ships would be maintained.[4]

The London compromise was a triumph of common sense and evidence that at this time there was enough determination in the three principal capitalist countries to retain the framework of cooperation. Unfortunately, this proved to be the last such occasion. These three powers would never again act together on naval issues or, for that matter, on any issue for many years to come.

For this the Japanese Navy was much to blame. Although the navy representatives on Japan's delegation in London accepted the compromise, most of the naval leaders in Tokyo refused to do so, attacking the new treaty as detrimental to national security and honor. They seized the opportunity to mount a publicity campaign to embarrass the civilian government, which they accused of having violated "the right of supreme command" – the right of the sovereign emperor to decide on strategic questions in consultation with the military. By maneuvering to persuade the emperor to accept the London treaty despite naval objections, the opponents argued, the government had in effect violated national sovereignty. Public opinion became incensed, and a right-wing youth physically assaulted the prime minister, leading to the latter's death. Japan's civilian

4 On the London naval conference, see James B. Crowley, *Japan's Quest for Autonomy* (Princeton, 1966).

government, which had been identified with the diplomacy of international cooperation, was deeply shaken.

As if this were not enough, an even graver crisis confronted the Japanese government as well as the international community in 1931. On September 18, the Japanese military force in Manchuria, the Kwantung Army, blew up a few feet of rail on the South Manchuria Railway near Mukden (Feng-t'ien) Station, seized the moment to create confusion in the city, and fought skirmishes with the Chinese contingents guarding the government offices. (Japanese forces had been stationed in Mukden since 1905 when, as a result of Japan's victory over Russia, it took over the rights the latter had enjoyed in southern Manchuria since the late 1890s.) Thus began the Mukden incident, which quickly developed into a Manchurian crisis. The crisis entailed Chinese-Japanese clashes throughout Manchuria and ended in an almost complete Japanese victory, as the Chinese forces in the region were too weak to put up resistance without support from those under the Nanking regime's control, but the latter decided early on not to become militarily involved in the areas north of the Great Wall.[5]

In the middle of the international economic crisis, there was little the United States and other nations could do to influence events in faraway Manchuria. Put another way, the Japanese Army's timing was well calculated to take advantage of the situation. The naval opposition to the London treaty had already weakened the civilian government, and the army had decided to vie with the navy for greater power and to add another blow to the party politicians, bureaucrats, businessmen, and intellectuals who had stood for a liberal political order at home and international cooperation abroad. It is no accident that, while planning for military action in Manchuria, some army and navy personnel were involved in a scheme – which proved abortive – to overthrow the government and to establish a military dictatorship. From the conspirators' point of view, 1931 was as good a year as would ever present itself for such action. International cooperation, though achieved at the London Confer-

5 The best study of the Manchurian incident in English is Sadako Ogata, *Defiance in Manchuria* (Berkeley, 1964).

ence in 1930, had not been easy to maintain as the economic crisis worsened, and the world's capitals were desperately trying to cope with the banking crises in Germany and Austria. (The Bank of England, it is to be noted, went off the gold standard on September 21.) The Japanese activists correctly judged that other powers would be little inclined to become involved in the Manchurian conflict so long as they presented their action as a case of self-defense against Chinese attacks on the treaty rights.

The Chinese, on their part, desperately turned to the League of Nations and to the United States for help. From their point of view, here was a blatant violation of the postwar principles of peace and order, and therefore a test case for collective security. And they, too, were successful, to a point. The League of Nations, to which China appealed immediately after the Japanese attack on Mukden, could not ignore such pleas. In Geneva a council meeting was quickly convened and urged the two combatants to cease fighting. But before the League went farther, it turned to the United States for assistance.[6]

And so the United States, too, found itself being compelled to take a stand. Should it support the League and therefore China in the name of collective security? What would such support entail? Would the American people stand for such a policy? Or, should the United States remain aloof; if so, how should it explain its position, which would surely be interpreted as an abandonment of international cooperation? What should America's attitude toward Japan be? What would be the consequences of Japan's successful conquest of Manchuria for American security and interests? These were serious questions, and the United States government did its best to respond to them. Unfortunately, both because the international community was in disarray due to the economic crisis, and because the Japanese Army was intent on holding on to the fruits of conquest, no matter at what cost, American action made little immediate difference.

The initial reaction of Secretary of State Stimson, which was

6 On China's response to Japanese aggression, see Parks Coble, *Facing Japan* (Cambridge, Mass., 1991).

shared by most officials in Washington, was that the unilateral acts by the Kwantung Army would be checked by Tokyo's civilian leaders. They had been quite cooperative during the 1920s, and Stimson could not believe that they would want to sanction any action that would undermine the framework of the Washington Conference treaties. But the Americans overestimated the Japanese government's ability and willingness to rein in the military. For the civilian leaders in Tokyo had been badly shaken by the London naval treaty episode. With public opinion expressing deep satisfaction with the military action to "punish China," and with the opposition parties attacking the cabinet for its weak-kneed diplomacy, there was little inclination to heed Stimson's wishes. Japan even sought to prevent the League of Nations from meeting to discuss the Mukden incident, preferring to settle the affair bilaterally with China. When the League nevertheless met and called on the two nations to agree to an immediate cease-fire, the Kwantung Army responded by extending the hostilities to the Chinchow area, that is, along the southern border of Manchuria. Japan, as well as China, did agree to the establishment of a League commission of inquiry in December, each believing that its findings would be favorable to its own side.

An American, General Frank R. McCoy, was appointed to serve on the commission, which was headed by Lord Lytton. This showed a deep U.S. involvement in the international efforts to contain the crisis. Stimson had earlier sent an American consul at Geneva, Prentiss B. Gilbert, to participate in League discussions on the Manchurian crisis, indicating a rare willingness to work closely with the world organization. And when, in early January 1932, the Japanese Army completed the conquest of southern Manchuria, Secretary Stimson issued a statement declaring that the United States would not recognize any agreement China and Japan might enter into that violated the principles of China's territorial and administrative integrity or of the Open Door. These instances indicate that the Hoover administration was desperately trying to preserve the structure of international affairs that had been established after the war. If it took joining the League's efforts, America would do so. Implemented at a time when President Hoover was acting in similar fashion regarding world financial issues, American policy during the Manchurian crisis gave strong evidence of a determination to retain a framework of international cooperation.[7]

The same thing could be said of America's role in a 59-nation general disarmament conference, convened under League auspices in Geneva in February 1932. Here again, the United States was ready to be associated with a League undertaking, and President Hoover at one point even suggested that all nations might cut one-third of their respective armaments. Although nothing came of the suggestion, Britain, France, and other countries turned to the United States for support in any disarmament program; they would agree to reduce arms provided the United States promised to come to their assistance if they should be attacked (presumably by a rearmed Germany). America could not give such a pledge, but at least it would be willing to be consulted. As seen earlier, American policymakers sought to combine the issues of arms reduction and of reparations and debts in an overall framework of restoring world order.

That, however, was as far as the United States would go. When Japan defied the Lytton Commission's report blaming it for the Manchurian crisis and urging the two Asian countries to return to the status quo of September 1931, the United States did little to prevent Japan's withdrawal from the League, even though this was a serious blow to the world organization. Likewise, the Hoover administration was helpless when German voters in 1932 gave massive support to both the National Socialists and the Communists, two opponents of the postwar order. Thus by the time Hoover left the White House in March 1933, the international system, despite all his and his colleagues' efforts and good intentions, had been seriously undermined. Whether it was still worth preserving would be the key question bequeathed to the next administration.

Liberalism Under Attack

The economic and diplomatic crises of the Hoover years also witnessed a severe challenge to the ideological foundations of American foreign policy and of the postwar international order. As seen in the

7 See Gary Ostrower, *Collective Insecurity* (Lewisburg, Pa., 1979).

preceding chapter, both had been based on a new conception of peace, more specifically a view of world affairs that gave primacy to economic and cultural interrelations over arms and military strategies.

Capitalism and democracy at home, and economic interdependence and cultural exchange abroad, had been visualized as the keys to international order and stability. Now, however, these assumptions came under attack as the seemingly unending economic crisis gave rise to serious questioning about capitalism and liberalism. Already by 1932 an increasing number of commentators were talking of the demise of these systems and their replacement by radical alternatives from the right and the left. The American way of life, which only a few years earlier had seemed destined to transform the whole world, now began to look bankrupt. Far from being able to influence other countries in their own image, Americans began to wonder if foreign nations might not have a better solution to cope with the economic crisis. As they watched the Soviet Union successfully completing its first five-year plan (1928–32) or the increasing influence of Nazis and Communists in Germany, Americans wondered if socialism, collectivism, and even a dictatorship might not work better than an essentially laissez-faire system of capitalist activities. Politically, too, American politics appeared incapable of addressing the crisis, and many saw little difference between the two major parties. Some began to call for an alternative party, one that was less geared to business interests.[8]

It is not surprising that in this growing critique of the liberal capitalist system, many observers explicitly rejected the kind of internationalism that had prevailed during the 1920s, seeing it as a reflection of the capitalism that failed. It was argued that the international order that matched the domestic order of free enterprise, speculation, and acquisitive instincts had only enriched the already rich but had not brought visible benefits to the country as a whole. Wall Street bankers, speculators, and investors had been notable for their eagerness to promote economic internationalism. Now that they were being discredited, economic internationalism, too, be-

8 See Alan Brinkley, *Voices of Protest* (New York, 1982).

came suspect. Whereas President Hoover sought desperately to revive it, his critics wanted to have nothing to do with it, instead pushing for a radical redefinition of American foreign policy, one that minimized extensive international economic connections in favor of domestic economic pursuits. This was what Charles Beard meant by "the open door at home" in a book of that title published in 1934.[9] The idea was to seek to bring about recovery through focusing attention on the home front, not by bringing back multilateralism. In order to prevent the economic crisis from growing worse, it seemed imperative to reduce foreign commitments and ties as much as possible.

What about cultural internationalism? Was it also a victim of the Depression? It most certainly was, in the sense that the reaction against economic internationalism contained within it the rejection of the principles and values that had envisaged the emergence of a world community of interdependence and mutual cooperation. In an atmosphere where domestic, national interests took precedence over concerns for the larger community, the kind of international consciousness that had been a notable feature of the 1920s was bound to suffer. Thus the intellectual leadership in America passed from the Frederick Taylors and Henry Fords, those who spoke the language of universally valid principles, to the Charles Beards and others emphasizing domestic needs, even to men like Charles E. Coughlin, the Detroit priest who began bitterly attacking financiers, intellectuals, and other internationally oriented people for having misled the country. Even Walter Lippmann, who had exemplified one strand of postwar internationalism, now accused the American political leaders of having promoted "the ideal of acquisitiveness" to the detriment of "those things which make a people self-respecting, serene, and confident."[10] In the context of the economic crisis, this was the language of national, not international, salvation. It was no accident that Lippmann joined many other editorial writers in opposing American intervention to help China defend itself in Manchuria. There were more pressing needs at home.

9 Charles A. Beard, *The Open Door at Home* (New York, 1934).
10 Walter Lippmann, *Interpretations, 1931–1932* (New York, 1932), 28–9.

On the other hand, internationalism did not just disappear. Because of the very resurgence of nationalism and often narrow-minded chauvinism in many parts of the globe, there were heroic, albeit ultimately frustrating, efforts by committed cultural internationalists to keep the fire ablaze. If anything, the Paris-based International Institute of Cultural Cooperation became even more active in the early 1930s than earlier, and Germany and Japan continued to send delegates to the League's periodic gatherings to further cultural interchanges. Perhaps most notably, the League's committee of scientific advisers succeeded in having "moral disarmament" included in the agenda of the Geneva disarmament conference. The idea was that no technical limitation on the size of armed forces would ensure peace unless it were backed up by a habit of mind that was broad-minded and cosmopolitan.

In the United States, too, organizations like the Foreign Policy Association and the Council on Foreign Relations never let up their activities during the Depression. Although handicapped by the fact that corporate and individual donations significantly diminished, these associations continued to recruit new members and sought to combat the rising tide of antiinternationalism. Some of the most important meetings of the Institute of Pacific Relations took place during 1929–32, where Chinese and Japanese intellectuals joined their colleagues from America and Europe and tried earnestly to resolve the Manchurian dispute. The fact that all these efforts proved unavailing does not detract from their historical significance, for the idea of intellectual communication and cooperation would be kept alive during the dark years of the 1930s and reemerge as one of the potent principles for constructing another postwar world order.

9. Totalitarianism and the Survival of Democracy

Totalitarianism and War

The statement by Walter Lippmann quoted earlier suggests that even in the United States influential commentators were recognizing the need for a fundamental reorientation, even restructuring, of politics and society if the severe economic crisis were to be overcome. Lippmann was so much concerned with the crisis that at one point he went so far as to admit that only a dictatorship might save the nation.[1] That even someone as committed to democracy and liberalism as Lippmann had been should feel this way reveals the profound despair felt in America about the ability of the existing institutions to cope with the crisis.

If some Americans responded in such fashion, it is not surprising that in other countries, less rooted in democracy, forces would develop that would transform their political systems into dictatorships.

The rise of modern totalitarianism should not, it is true, all be attributed to the Depression. Both the totaliarianism of the right (fascism) and of the left (communism) had existed before 1929. Even if we confine our discussion to the twentieth century, it is to be noted that fascism (which may be defined as a dictatorship of the state) had developed in Italy, Germany, Hungary, and elsewhere in the wake of the Great War, where movements emerged that would challenge party politics, parliamentary democracy, and pluralistic ideologies and substitute for them a centralized system of political, economic, and social control under the state. Discontent with the results of the war, postwar inflation and unemployment, dissatisfaction with the mood of internationalism – all these played a role. Outside of Italy, however, the movement had been unable to seize power and establish its domination over national politics. After

1 See Ronald Steel, *Walter Lippmann and His America* (Boston, 1980).

1929, however, fascism increased its appeal because of the Depression and the climate of uncertainty in national and international affairs.

Typically, a fascist movement would gain power both through parliamentary politics (elections) and through mass demonstrations and violence, and once in power enter into an alliance with the armed forces and the business community to stamp out opposition and centralize decision making. The masses would be incorporated into the new regime through cultural and educational policies that attacked liberalism and "bourgeois decadance," through public works projects that created new jobs, through youth organizations, through parades and fireworks – and through intimidation. Dissidents would be silenced, imprisoned, expelled, even assassinated. In all fascist countries, the key institutional apparatus was the state, and the dominating ideology was national culture, the devotion to and exaltation of one's cultural heritage defined, however, narrowly in terms of the state or of race. Particularism, in other words, was placed above universalism in political, economic, and cultural affairs.[2]

Communism, in the meantime, had emerged in Russia out of the Bolshevik Revolution of 1917. It had always insisted on a dictatorship of the proletariat in which the Communist party would wield ultimate power as the embodiment of proletarian interests. Eventually, the state was supposed to "wither away," and when all countries reached that stage – that is, after they had gone through a proletarian revolution – there would be no separate state entities but only one world. But in the late 1920s, when Joseph Stalin established himself as the undisputed leader, he reoriented the revolutionary agenda so that the preservation and expansion of the interests of the Soviet Union took primacy over considerations of the worldwide solidarity of the proletariat. The Communist party remained the key organization, but the state, whose leaders were all members of the party, developed its own system of power – above all, police and intelligence agencies – and established virtually total control over individual citizens. Although this tendency had emerged before

2 See F. L. Carsten, *The Rise of Fascism* (Berkeley, 1967).

1929, and although the Depression did not affect the Soviet economy as severely as the capitalist ones, it was nevertheless confirmed in the late 1920s and the early 1930s when the Soviet Union launched its first five-year plan. Here the stress was on self-sufficiency and the development of heavy industry. With American and European capital drying up, it was inevitable that funds and manpower for industrialization had to be sought at home, a process that confirmed the policy of collectivization – and the further growth of state power.

Although fascism and communism differed in origin, they thus shared many common features: the undisputed power of the state, rejection of democracy and pluralism, particularistic nationalism. The differences between the totalitarianism of right and left were less significant than the fact that they both assaulted democracy and liberalism, the prevailing orientations of postwar national and international affairs. And in the early 1930s more and more countries were abandoning, or at least weakening their commitment to, democratic politics, liberal economics, and free cultural expression. In Europe, Austria, Romania, Finland, and others saw the erosion of democratic government; in Asia, Japanese political parties became steadily weaker, powerless to stem the growing power of the military to control decisions, while in China the Nationalists turned to Germany and Italy for inspiration even as they fought against the Communist insurgents; and in Latin America fascination with totalitarianism was spreading, typically embodied in Juan Perón's fascist movement in Argentina.

One key question at that time was what implications such a trend toward totalitarianism would have for international affairs. Would there be a connection between a domestic dictatorship and a foreign aggression? Would a world in which democratic politics was under attack and totalitarianism was on the rise be more prone to war? What should be done to preserve international order and peace? Could the nations, deeply involved as they were in trying to solve their economic crises, turn their attention outward and develop an effective foreign policy?

These were extremely important questions, and to pose them revealed how different the world environment had become from the

1920s. In this chapter these questions will be discussed primarily for the years 1933–7, the first four years of Franklin D. Roosevelt's presidency, but it will be useful first of all to examine the conceptions of world affairs, of war and peace, held by the dictatorships.

War, Ernst Röhm, commander of the SA (storm troopers), asserted, "is an internal necessity for a people which desires to remain on this earth and to conquer. For the soldier war is the foundation of youth, hope, and fulfillment."[3] Such an expression, which was repeated regularly in the fascist states, was a clear rejection of the prevailing peace sentiments of the 1920s. Instead of looking upon peace as a normal and normative state of affairs, now war came to symbolize what was good and noble in human societies, at least in fascist communities. In such communities the state was to be the embodiment of the will to war, of the self-sacrifice and willingness to die for the collective good. Peace, on the other hand, suggested a passivity, a mundane existence, doldrums that gave no meaning to the collectivities. "In all other countries," an American observer noted in 1934, "future wars are regarded, except by small groups personally interested in war and war profits, as a possible evil for which one must be fully prepared. In Nationalist Socialist Germany, war is the national ideal and the end of all political and social aspirations. . . . It . . . is the end of statecraft itself."[4] He might have added Italy and Japan to the list. For those and other countries that were joining the ranks of fascist states, war was taken as a perpetual condition of national and international affairs. The Communist leaders in the Soviet Union may not have necessarily shared such a view of war, but they too perceived the world as an arena for struggle for power where war was a constant possibility threatening the domestic regime. As Alan Milward has pointed out, none of these countries was at this time making plans for a long-drawn-out war.[5] But at least the fascist states of Europe considered the use of force as a plausible national policy not only for specific ends but for the effect it had on national discipline and glory.

3 See William Shirer, *The Nightmare Years* (New York, 1984).

4 *Harper's*, 168 (April 1934): 517.

5 Alan Milward, *War, Economy, and Society* (Berkeley, 1979).

This was not just a return to the Hobbesian conception in which sovereign states were in a constant state of war or war preparedness. In the 1930s, the totalitarian countries were making a far more explicit connection between domestic order and foreign affairs than had ever been made before the Great War. For the fascist nations, and for the Soviet Union under Stalin's dictatorship, war was inseparable from the very being of the state; memories of wars connected the present to the past, and the thought of war to come established the legitimacy of the domestic order. Totalitarianism, then, was a system of political control that gave priority to internal unity, discipline, and self-sacrifice in the name of national power and glory. Even when there was no actual war, war as a state of mind always existed; the political system was built on and further confirmed it.

Specific instances of wars started by totalitarian states will be mentioned, but it is important to recognize that the rise of fascism had an immediate, unsettling impact on international affairs. The question was whether this turn of events totally disrupted the international system. The answer would hinge increasingly on the responses of the democracies.

The Democracies and War

How were the democracies going to cope with the growing influence of totalitarianism throughout the world? In March 1933 Lippmann was writing that "the peoples that knew democracy in the nineteenth century, the peoples that have lived under the heritage of liberalism, have not fallen into disorder and have not surrendered to dictators."[6] He had in mind the democracies of Scandinavia, Switzerland, France, Britain and the Dominions, and the United States. These appeared to be the only democracies left, and Lippmann confidently asserted that they had been "able to fortify democracy" despite the spread of totalitarianism because in those countries "popular government was inherently strong." He would soon become less confident of this, and would indeed attack the presidency of Franklin D. Roosevelt as taking the country down the path of

6 Walter Lippmann, *Interpretations, 1933–1935* (New York, 1935), 297.

fascism. And in other democracies, too, there were forces (such as the Union movement in Britain) that were growing impatient with the slow pace of democratic government in the face of a severe economic crisis. Voices were everywhere calling for some type of authoritarian control at least until the crisis passed. They asserted that traditional democratic politics, characterized by squabbling among party politicians beholden to interest groups, was not capable of dealing with the issues of massive unemployment, mortgage foreclosures, and widespread hunger, nor could ordinary business mechanisms be trusted to alleviate the crisis. What was needed was a new system where a central regime would act forcefully to create jobs, redistribute income, and otherwise satisfy the minimum needs of the people.

During the first half of the 1930s the democracies were thus confronted with an unprecedented challenge to their legitimacy. They were being called upon to meet the challenge without transforming themselves into something alien to the democratic tradition. This was the task Franklin D. Roosevelt, along with the leaders of other democracies, sought to perform as he entered the White House in March 1933. His New Deal programs need not be described in detail here, as we are more concerned with U.S. foreign affairs. But no discussion of international relations in the early 1930s will be adequate without some mention of the momentous experiment being undertaken in the United States, for many contemporary observers agreed that if democratic government disappeared in the world's biggest democracy, it would have grave implications for the other democracies, and as a consequence international affairs would significantly alter their character, given the proclivities of fascist states for war.

The New Deal revealed an experimental agenda that went much beyond past reform measures but stopped short of the statism characteristic of fascist countries. The key was the initiation of government-directed, -planned, and -sponsored programs for creating jobs, increasing prices and wages so as to encourage production and consumption, redistributing private wealth, insuring bank deposits, and otherwise guaranteeing minimum social security for the American people. All these would necessitate the strengthening and centralizing of government; and the mushrooming of federal agencies administering diverse programs set in motion one of the principal features of recent American history, the growth of the bureaucracy. But the bureaucrats did not eclipse but worked through party politicians, more specifically Democratic party leaders who devised New Deal programs. More important, politicians and bureaucrats cooperated with the private sector – in particular, business people (although many bankers and industrialists were bitterly opposed to Roosevelt, at least initially), lawyers and other professionals, and labor union leaders who were brought together in various consultative bodies and contributed to economic and social planning. Those who refused to cooperate would be penalized, although, unlike some other countries, there was no severe repression of dissidents.

Because such an arrangement fortified national unity, and because there was now a greater degree of collaboration between state and society (as represented by business, labor, and the professions), American politics during the New Deal fell somewhere between the traditional liberal state and the fascist state. But the New Deal struck many contemporary observers as a program carrying the nation farther and farther away from liberalism and moving it toward fascism. Benito Mussolini, for one, congratulated Franklin D. Roosevelt for emulating Italy's fascism in transforming American government.[7] Walter Lippmann, too, came to characterize the New Deal as totalitarian. It cannot be denied that the United States was now becoming more centralized and bureaucratized, and that in that process traditional conceptions of democracy, liberalism, and free enterprise were being significantly redefined. Writing in 1934, a contributor to *Harper's* magazine noted, "To attempt a defence of democracy these days is a little like defending paganism in 313 or the divine right of kings in 1793. It is taken for granted that democracy is bad and that it is dying. . . . One notices a certain shame among liberals and democrats of today, as if they dared not avow their beliefs. They are like pariahs, satisfied to be allowed to vegetate."[8] Nevertheless, the same author asserted, correctly, that so long as there remained freedom – the freedom of expression, assem-

7 John P. Diggins, *Mussolini and Fascism: The View from America* (Princeton, 1972), 280–1.

8 *Harper's*, 169 (Sept. 1931): 418, 426.

bly, politics – the nation would not go the way of Germany, Italy, or the Soviet Union. And indeed, in the United States the growth of federal planning and bureaucracy did not result in the suppression of freedoms. If anything, it might even be argued that more people than ever were now given an opportunity to express themselves; they were being incorporated into the political system, not through totalitarian manipulation from above or through massive indoctrination to glorify the state but through economic and social measures that gave the population a stake in the New Deal and enabled them to be active participants in the political process.

It may well be that Mussolini was at least partially right in his assertion that Roosevelt was emulating him in that the United States was developing a corporatist system – an arrangement for the collaboration of state and society, in particular the government, business, and labor. But, as noted in a previous chapter, such an arrangement had emerged in the 1920s, if not earlier, and has been known by the term "corporatism." Whether the New Deal can be characterized as a corporatist arrangement may, however, be questioned. At its inception, in any event, there was a great deal of government supervision of the economy rather than the kind of voluntary cooperation between government and business that had existed in the 1920s. Indeed, in sharp contrast to the business civilization of the preceding decade, the early 1930s saw the capitalists and industrialists being placed on the defensive, blamed for the economic disasters. The prevailing ethos of the country was strongly antibusiness, and various protest movements, such as those led by Huey Long of Louisiana and Francis E. Townsend of California, were seeking to redistribute America's wealth through political action. Under the circumstances, the New Deal offered a less radical agenda without, however, going to the other extreme of creating a fascist-type alliance of the state and business.

On the other hand, it may be noted that American labor gained power and influence during the New Deal. It actively participated in New Deal programs and benefited from them. To be sure, some radical labor leaders and intellectuals thought the New Deal was not moving fast enough, that it was merely designed to save capitalism from certain collapse, and that what the country needed was a much more far-reaching structural reform.[9] They pointed to the Soviet Union as a model, just as a few extremists on the right turned to fascism or Nazism for ideological inspiration. By and large, however, the extremism of right and left did not succeed in converting public opinion, the bulk of which opted for the type of reformism that the New Deal exemplified.

In any event, in the United States, as in the European democracies, there was no resurgence of warlike sentiments as a consequence of the Depression. People were preoccupied with domestic affairs, and only a tiny segment of them turned to a radical departure in foreign policy as the key to the national crisis. There certainly was no rediscovery of the gloriousness of war, and no abandonment of pacifism. At a time when in many other countries such a trend was becoming noticeable, the fact the democracies did not share the trend had important implications; they would tend to eschew foreign entanglement even as the totalitarian regimes were resorting to the use of force to undermine international order.

The Isolationist Impulse

That was the background against which the phenomenon known as isolationism became a major force in America in the mid-1930s. Isolationism of the decade in essence meant the nation was not going to depart from its basic orientation to peace and instead was going to avoid any involvement in external complications. Because external complications were inevitable, given the totalitarian regimes' proclivities toward war and an activist foreign policy, the continued adherence to pacifism and abhorrence of war suggested that the United States would become more isolated, and therefore less relevant, in world affairs than it had been during the first decade after the war.

The isolationist sentiment was abetted by the failure of the Hoover administration to contribute to restoring some order in international affairs after the world had been shaken by the unilateral action of Japan and by the independent economic measures undertaken by

9 Malcolm Cowley, *The Dream of the Golden Mountains* (New York, 1980).

various European nations. Because the American efforts to support the League of Nations in stopping Japanese aggression and to promote worldwide disarmament and economic cooperation had not succeeded, public opinion, as well as official thinking, after 1933 came to be much less willing to endorse repetition of these attempts. Both were convinced that the first priorities of the new administration should be to restore confidence in the domestic economy and to do something about the Depression to stem the tide; as a result, foreign complications had to be avoided. The time seemed to have passed when some international cooperative action would bring about economic recovery, especially since so few countries now seemed willing to cooperate. Rather, the time had come, many argued, when the Americans must stop worrying about world events and turn their energies inward. A typical example of their isolationist sentiment was the Neutrality Act of 1935, which forbade arms shipments to all belligerents involved in a war. This completely reversed the traditional U.S. position on neutral rights, including the right to sell arms to belligerents. Now it was considered best not to insist on such rights, as had been done during 1914–17, but to restrict them so as to minimize risks of becoming involved in foreign complications.

American foreign affairs during the first Roosevelt administration reflected such isolationism. The new president did, it seems, appreciate the potential danger the rise of Hitler in Germany posed to the world and to the United States. Initially, however, he shared the American people's distaste for foreign involvement and their sense that international affairs were of secondary importance to domestic recovery – and these two appeared less and less connected. Under the circumstances, Roosevelt felt justified in persisting in a rather passive stance toward foreign affairs.

Yet because vast changes were taking place in the international sphere during these years, America's passivity and isolationism in effect amounted to abrogating its role as world leader. The United States would stand by as others sought to redefine world order, even if such redefinition was not to its own liking. There was little American resistance to forces abroad that were fast conspiring to undermine, if not completely destroy, the system of international relations that had been built with so much time and effort.

Some specific examples can illustrate the point. Concerning the chaotic state of international economic transactions, Roosevelt, unlike Hoover, was little inclined to play an assertive role at the London economic conference, which had been prepared while Hoover was still president but was not convened till June 1933. The conference was an opportunity – as it turned out, the last opportunity – for the world's industrial nations to see if they could coordinate their foreign economic policies on such thorny issues as debts and reparations, protectionism, and managed currencies. And the outcome depended to a great extent on the United States; for, despite the Depression, it was still seen as the linchpin of the international economic order.

But American performance at London was not such as to inspire confidence in the future of that order. If some American officials, notably Secretary of State Cordell Hull, were genuinely desirous of preserving a framework of economic internationalism, others were much less committed. The American delegation included, besides Hull, Senator Key Pittman of Nevada whose main interest was in remonetizing silver (i.e., in having nations adopt silver as an additional medium of exchange), and Raymond Moley, one of the "brain trusters" who advocated drastic measures such as protectionism and dollar devaluation to expand American export trade. There was no agreement among them on the key questions discussed at London, nor did President Roosevelt offer well-defined leadership.

The success of the London economic conference depended on whether the United States would actively cooperate with Britain, France, and others in stabilizing foreign exchange rates – through a restored gold standard – so as to avoid further chaos in international trade. Exchange stability was becoming a hotly debated issue in all countries, above all the United States, for it was a principle for preserving economic internationalism at a time when more and more nations were abandoning it in favor of economic nationalism. For Americans, who would have to play a leading role if economic internationalism was to be sustained, exchange stability implied a high value of the dollar vis-à-vis other currencies, which would mean not only making American goods comparatively more expensive abroad but also having to support the value of other currencies through the shipment of gold out of the country, which could stifle domestic recovery. Even if the value of the U.S. currency remained stable in the world market, its domestic value (i.e., prices of commodities) could fluctuate drastically, exacerbating economic instability at home. Roosevelt was sensitive to these fears and shared the view that a hasty return to an international gold standard would put the national economy at the mercy of foreign currencies. It would be better to have a dollar currency with the same purchasing power domestically year after year, to prevent prices from falling drastically at home. Because Roosevelt felt this latter objective was incompatible with exchange stability, he opposed any agreement on the question at London, thus causing the economic conference to fail. This was a good example of the Roosevelt administration's decision during its first years to give priority to domestic over external considerations.

The same general attitude was evident in America's responses to other international crises at that time. Perhaps the most obvious – and unfortunate – example of this was the Silver Purchase Act of 1934, a product of pressures by congressmen representing silver and farming interests. The act in effect nationalized silver; President Roosevelt ordered the Treasury Department to purchase all silver in the United States at fifty cents an ounce, which was considerably higher than current prices. The intent was to remonetize silver and increase its circulation, particularly in the western states. But the policy had the effect of attracting silver in other parts of the world to the United States. China, a silver-monetized economy, was particularly hard hit as quantities of silver were drained out of the country, attracted by higher prices in the United States. The Japanese Army occupying Manchuria and parts of northern China was not above manipulating the operation to create further confusion in the Chinese economy. The severe impact of American silver purchases on China was not an intended result of Roosevelt's policy, but the episode was characteristic of American-Asian relations at that time.

These relations would no longer be put in the framework of collective security, as they had been under the Hoover-Stimson policy. Rather, the United States would abandon efforts at a collective solution of the Sino-Japanese conflict and deal with the situation in a pragmatic fashion as events unfolded. Not that the United States would recognize the fruits of Japanese aggression. There was no question of extending recognition to the puppet state of Manchukuo, which the Japanese had proclaimed in occupied Manchuria in 1932, or altering the professed policies of the Open Door or the territorial integrity of China. When the Japanese Foreign Ministry announced, in 1934, that the nation would look with disfavor upon third countries' separate dealings with China, Washington immediately protested against such an infringement upon these principles. The United States likewise refused to consider Japan's offer of a new Pacific condominium, each side defining its own spheres of influence in the region and both pledging to abide by the new status quo. The Roosevelt administration would not reward Japanese expansion, but neither would it undertake any significant step to push it back. The passing, in 1934, of the Tydings-McDuffie Act, promising independence to the Philippines in twelve years, fitted into the overall picture. The United States was ready to withdraw from the western Pacific as a colonial power. But this was more in response to domestic pressures – various interest groups feared the rising competition of Filipino goods unless the Philippines became severed from the United States – than a product of strategic rethinking about that part of the world.

The drift and indecisiveness in America's Asian policy was also evident in the failure to renew naval disarmament agreements with Japan and Britain. The Washington and London naval agreements were both to expire in 1936 unless renewed, and preliminary discussions were held by representatives of the three navies throughout 1934 and 1935, but they came to nothing as Japan insisted on parity in all categories of ships, something the United States and Britain refused to accept. For the Japanese the principle of parity would recognize the new status quo in the Pacific, whereas for the Americans parity would only lead to an arms race; they instead called for a

20 percent across-the-board reduction in all categories of ships, a proposal neither Japan nor Britain accepted. There was no agreement, and the Japanese took the lapse of the disarmament agreements seriously, immediately beginning to work on a new naval strategy aimed ultimately at controlling the southwestern Pacific. No such reorientation took place in the United States, where naval construction tended to be viewed more in connection with creating jobs for the unemployed than in the framework of power rivalry across the Pacific.

Similarly, in Europe, U.S. policy lacked precise definition other than that of trying to keep out of trouble spots. When Italian troops invaded Ethiopia in 1934, the first overt challenge hurled at international order since the Japanese conquest of Manchuria, Roosevelt explicitly condemned Italy as the aggressor but mitigated its impact by invoking neutrality. American citizens were prohibited not only from selling arms to the belligerents but also from traveling in their vessels. Of course, because Ethiopia would not have the cash or ships to tempt Americans, the effect of neutrality was to penalize Italy. Still, this policy was intended more to avoid becoming involved in foreign complications, as happened during the Great War, than to try to change the outcome of the conflict. When the League of Nations voted to impose economic sanctions on Italy – significantly, oil was exempted from sanctions – the president called on the American people to abide by the resolution. The result was a moral embargo, without the force of law, and American shipments of oil and other goods to Italy did not significantly abate.[10]

Regarding Hitler's Germany, American policy was, if anything, even less decisive. To be sure there was moral reprehension in much of the country against Germany's race policies, especially the persecution of Jews. Some Americans spoke out in favor of instituting a boycott of German trade, others publicly denounced Nazi practices, and still others held rallies against the Nazis. But government action did not amount to much. The State Department, for instance, refused to increase immigration quotas to accommodate

10 Diggins, *Mussolini,* 290–2.

German Jews wishing to enter the country, fearing that they would become public charges as the German authorities would not permit them to take money with them.[11] President Roosevelt did toy with the idea of a trade embargo against Germany in case the latter undertook aggressive action, but there were practical difficulties, such as defining "aggression," and little came of it at this time.

Indeed, compared with those of Japan and Italy, Germany's immediate goals were modest, to get rid of the restrictions imposed upon it by the peace treaty of 1919. Rearmament was the major issue, with Hitler intent on eliminating the restrictions on the size of Germany's armed forces and on their stationing in the Rhineland. Thus in 1933 he denounced the Geneva disarmament conference and withdrew Germany from the League of Nations; two years later he entered into a naval agreement with the British in which German naval power would be limited to 35 percent of Britain's (still a considerable increase over what had been granted Germany in 1919); and in 1936 German troops marched into the Rhineland to reoccupy the hitherto demilitarized area.

Against these acts in violation of the Versailles arrangements, the powers did very little or nothing, and the United States was no exception. Officials in Washington felt there was very little the United States could do without seeming to take sides. International cooperation through the League of Nations appeared to have vanished, nor was there much hope that Germany could be persuaded to rejoin the organization. If the European nations could somehow work out a way for dealing with remilitarized Germany, that was fine, but that would be basically their business, and the United States should not become involved. That was the overall attitude of the Roosevelt administration, reflecting the sense that the postwar international system was now beyond repair and that there was very little the United States could do to help redefine world order. When German troops reoccupied the Rhineland, America's response was tame; the State Department declined intervention because, as Hull said, the sections of the Treaty of Versailles pertaining to the Rhine-

11 A. A. Offner, *American Appeasement* (Cambridge, Mass., 1969), 105.

land were not included in the American peace treaty with Germany, signed separately in 1921.[12]

So the overall picture of American foreign policy during Roosevelt's first administration echoed the isolationist sentiment of the public and emphasized avoidance of trouble, a far cry from the Hoover administration's serious efforts to prevent the total collapse of international order. The world was becoming unhinged, and America was not assigning itself the task of resuscitating it.

This does not mean, however, that the United States undertook no diplomatic initiatives during these years. Two instances of American foreign policy decisions revealed that things were not exactly at a standstill, and that within the overall framework of passivity, small steps were being taken that would have much future significance.

Of the two, the first, recognition of the Soviet Union, did not yield immediate results but was pregnant with important implications for international relations. The decision to recognize the socialist nation was not a product of mature deliberation on world affairs in which the implications of the rising power and unilateralism of Japan and Germany were fully discussed. Rather, Roosevelt responded to Soviet overtures for normalizing relations – and as far as the Russians were concerned, there was little doubt that they were becoming worried about the developments in Europe and Asia – as a modest diplomatic achievement and, moreover, something that would please farmers, industrialists, and traders who were keen on expanding the Soviet markets. Formal recognition came in November 1933, but that was not followed up by any significant measure that would bring the U.S.-Soviet connection into the equation of world politics. William C. Bullitt, whose interest in reaching out to the Soviets went back to the Paris peace conference days, was named first ambassador to Moscow, but he soon became disillusioned about establishing close ties with the Soviet Union.

The lack of interest in making use of the Soviet diplomatic connection in international relations could be seen in America's indifference, even aversion, to the Comintern congress of August 1935

12 Ibid., 141–2.

which called for the formation of a global popular front against fascism. If the United States had been even minimally interested in influencing international relations, it might have taken more interest in the Soviet initiative, but instead it viewed the affair as another instance of Comintern propaganda. Only a handful of American radicals seized the opportunity and began what proved to be a long and often frustrating effort to refocus national attention away from domestic to external crises.[13]

Initiated with greater fanfare was the Roosevelt administration's Latin American policy, which came to be known as the Good Neighbor policy. As noted earlier, the decision to reverse U.S. interventionism – of the type exemplified by Theodore Roosevelt's Corollary and by the occupation of Haiti and Santo Domingo during the Wilson presidency – had been made by President Hoover. What the Franklin D. Roosevelt administration did was to expand the scope and to espouse openly the policy of nonintervention. When Secretary of State Hull went to Montevideo, Uruguay, in December 1933 to attend the seventh international conference of American states – such conferences had been held since before the war – he supported the declaration to the effect that "no state has the right to intervene in the internal or external affairs of another."[14] As if to put the principle into practice, Washington proceeded to abrogate the Platt Amendment with respect to Cuba (1901) through which the United States had retained the right of intervention in that country. Now Cuban sovereignty was fully recognized. United States troops in Haiti, sent there in 1916, were withdrawn in 1934, making American forces in the Canal Zone the only military presence in the Western Hemisphere outside U.S. territory.

These steps fitted in with the overall direction of American foreign policy, away from activism toward isolationism and passivity. For the first time since the turn of the century, the United States would not take upon itself the task of ensuring political or economic stability in the Caribbean. It would not again intervene in the domestic affairs of another American state. In retrospect, of course,

13 Cowley, *Dream of the Golden Mountains.*

14 Irwin F. Gellman, *Good Neighbor Diplomacy* (Baltimore, 1979), 23–6.

it is clear that this aspect of the Good Neighbor policy lasted for only a short while. Within less than ten years, American military power would once again involve itself in Latin America, albeit under different circumstances. It should be noted, however, that the Good Neighbor policy also formed part of an emerging approach to the Western Hemisphere in the framework of regionalism, that is, as part of the global trend toward regional, as opposed to global, arrangements. Although not quite the same thing as the British Commonwealth's imperial preference system or Japan's Asian autarky, the Good Neighbor policy sought to bind the American republics together politically and economically. Thus the Reciprocal Trade Agreements Act of 1934, authorizing the president to negotiate with foreign governments for raising or lowering tariffs, resulted in a series of trade agreements with Latin American countries. Although there was no immediate expansion of hemispheric trade, these negotiations did serve to cement the emerging regional ties, enabling the American nations to withstand the tensions caused by developments elsewhere. In a sense, then, the Good Neighbor policy was designed to isolate the Western Hemisphere from Asia and Europe. In that way, too, it was an aspect of American isolationism. It reflected the determination that, in a world being buffeted by increased armaments and their aggressive use on the part of some nations, the United States would remain underarmed and eschew military engagement abroad. Without a decision to increase arms, and without a willingness to undertake an ideological offensive of the kind the Comintern was pursuing, isolationism seemed the only feasible alternative.

10. The Emergence of Geopolitics

Wars in Asia and Europe

Until 1936, totalitarianism in Asia and Europe had not been directly connected. Japanese militarism had developed its own agenda on the Asian continent, while Italian fascism and German Nazism had pursued their respective strategies, the former seeking to conquer Ethiopia and the latter focusing on asserting the right to rearm and to repudiate the Versailles restrictions. The three offered piecemeal challenges to the world order, but their interests and orientations were sufficiently divergent that their separate actions had not added up to a combined threat to global peace and security.

The picture began to change in 1936. In July a civil war broke out in Spain, the Fascists led by General Francisco Franco challenging the authority of the republican government in Madrid. Almost immediately, Germany and Italy began assisting the insurgents, while the Soviet Union took sides with the Republic. Britain and France desperately sought to prevent the civil war from turning into an international war and succeeded, at least on paper, in establishing an international committee of nonintervention. But the civil war continued, and during 1937–9 Franco's forces steadily gained ground with the help of German arms, particularly aircraft as well as aviators.

In November 1936 Germany, Italy, and Japan signed an anti-Comintern pact. Ostensibly an agreement to cooperate in order to combat Comintern-led subversive activities in the wake of the newly promulgated popular-front strategy, the pact contained a secret clause in which the signatories pledged to come to each other's aid should one of them become involved in a war against the Soviet Union. Thus for the first time the three totalitarian states on the right became pitted against the dictatorship of the left, giving rise to the possibility that the world's antidemocratic forces might turn upon one another.

In the meantime, there were equally momentous developments in China. In December, as Nationalist forces commanded by Chiang Kai-shek surrounded the Communist insurgents in Sian, the ancient capital in the western interior of the country, troops loyal to Chang Hsüeh-liang, the erstwhile Manchurian warlord, captured Chiang in order to force him to stop his anti-Communist campaigns and instead to lead the nation in a unified resistance against Japanese aggression. Chang had the support of the Chinese Communists and many others who had accepted the Comintern's call for a popular front. Chiang agreed to the terms for his release, returned to the capital, Nanking, and announced the formation of a united front. This amounted to nothing less than a major turning point in modern Chinese history; the Nationalists, instead of almost annihilating the Communists, now joined forces with them, even amalgamating the respective armies into one, to fight against the Japanese. Chiang Kai-shek's prestige soared, but at the same time the Communists were saved from a possible defeat and elimination from Chinese politics.[1]

The coming together of totalitarian states, and the formation of the second united front in China, were sure indications that events in Europe and Asia were impacting on one another. Slowly but steadily, the entire world was moving along the path of violence and war, forcing nontotalitarian states, as well as the Soviet Union, to respond with a greater sense of urgency than earlier.

If there was any doubt that the totalitarian states would refrain from aggressive war, it disappeared in 1937 and 1938, the years in which Japan and Germany proved willing to use force at the expense of neighboring countries.

In July 1937 China and Japan began a war that was to last eight years. Although the origins of the initial clash in Peking on the night of July 7 are still disputed, there is no question that the military conflict was a direct result of the confrontation between the

1 The best study of the Sian incident is in Parks Coble, *Facing Japan* (Cambridge, Mass., 1991).

newly aroused Chinese nationalism and the Japanese Army seeking to preserve and extend its influence in northern China. The latter successfully pushed Chinese forces out of the area and pursued them to central China, where the capital fell in December. The fighting in the Nanking area resulted in huge Chinese civilian casualties, said to have numbered over 300,000 according to Chinese studies. The brutal mass slaughter was a harbinger of things to come.

Throughout 1938 the Japanese Army kept pushing south and west in an attempt to capture and control most of China. But the Chinese continued their resistance, removing their capital first to Hankow and then to the remote southwestern city of Chungking. And so, after two years of fighting, the end was nowhere in sight. In order to improve the situation, Japan tried to set up a pro-Japanese government in Nanking, persuading Wang Ching-wei, a prominent Nationalist, to leave Chungking for Hanoi and then for the capital under Japanese occupation. In the meantime, in November 1938 the Japanese government issued a declaration for the establishment of a "new order" in East Asia, asserting that the old order was forever gone and that Japan was calling upon other countries in Asia to cooperate together to define a new regional system. That system would be characterized by Asian values and principles, rather than by Western ones that had dominated the region – although no one could quite understand how the two sets of values and principles would differ.

As Japan was trying to construct a new order in East Asia, Germany moved to establish its hegemony in "Mitteleuropa" – Central European lands with substantially German populations, such as Austria, Sudetenland in Czechoslovakia, and Danzig. This was an objective that many before Hitler had advocated: to unite all ethnically German peoples who had been forcefully dispersed by the creation of Austria, Czechoslovakia, and Poland. But Hitler was willing to use force to attain the objective, whereas others had hesitated.

The annexation of Austria (the so-called *Anschluss*), which came in March 1938, was carried out with little bloodshed and without much protest on the part of other powers, basically because Austria was ethnically overwhelmingly German and its independent status had been suspect all through the postwar years. Czechoslovakia and Poland were different cases, however. These states had symbolized Europe's postwar order, existing between Germany and Russia and tied to France through security arrangements. Any infringement on their independence would undermine the Versailles system, so the other countries could not but be concerned.

Yet that was precisely why Hitler wanted to act against the two new states, to deal a death blow to the system. Whether in this period he also had more far-reaching ambitions is not entirely clear. After destroying Czechoslovak and Polish sovereignty, he may have intended to continue pushing eastward to obtain the space and grains of the Ukraine; he may have visualized an ultimate race war against Slavic peoples, including those in the Soviet Union; he also may have had in mind controlling all of Europe as well as challenging the British Empire overseas. He may have entertained all such visions, but apparently he did not have a systematic war plan against any major European power prior to 1939. Rather, he would first go after Czechoslovakia and Poland and then, depending on circumstances, plan for the next step.[2]

The initial step turned out to be a diplomatic one. The British and the French governments were willing to negotiate with Hitler so as to avoid a premature war. Their policy was called "appeasement" and was derived from the idea that while those nations built up arms, it would be prudent to try negotiation. Some compromise settlement, even if it might mean a further erosion of the Versailles arrangements, would be preferable to a destructive war for which the democracies were not prepared. One prominent example of the appeasement policy was the Munich agreement of September 1938 by which Sudetenland was annexed to Germany with the blessing of Britain and France. When this was followed in March 1939 by Hitler's annexation of most of the rest of Czechoslovakia, however, British and French reaction was swift. They immediately declared that they would no longer acquiesce in acts of German aggression

2 On Hitler's possible war aims, see two conflicting interpretations in A. J. P. Taylor, *The Origins of the Second World War* (London, 1961), and Gerhard Weinberg, *The Foreign Policy of Hitler's Germany,* 2 vols. (Chicago, 1970, 1980).

and that if Hitler should move against Polish independence they would honor their commitment to the latter, implying that they would even use force to stop Germany.[3]

By the spring of 1939, then, the lines dividing Germany from Britain and France were being drawn more sharply than heretofore, and the appeasement strategy was being abandoned by London and Paris. At the same time, the British and French governments approached the Soviet Union for possible agreement on strategic cooperation against Germany. The picture became complicated, however, when Moscow and Berlin also began negotiations looking toward some sort of a deal that would prevent war between the two. For both nations such a deal made sense; Germany would not have to worry about a two-front war, and the Soviet Union would also be able to avoid a premature conflict with Germany at a time when it was concerned with the Japanese menace in the East. (Soviet and Japanese troops clashed in Nomonhan, along the Siberian-Mongolian-Manchurian border, throughout the summer.) The upshot was a German-Soviet nonaggression pact on August 23, 1939. The pact not only undermined the antifascist global popular front the Comintern had been seeking to erect, it also brought two major totalitarian states together, at least for the time being.

The Western democracies were put on the defensive. They not only faced the prospect of war against Germany, but were also confronted with the spectacle of a worldwide coalition of antidemocratic powers. To Germany, Italy, and Japan, now the Soviet Union seemed to have been added. To make matters worse, the Spanish civil war ended in Franco's victory in 1939, so that the world fascist camp now had one additional member. It might have seemed that the democracies were in greater danger than ever before.

America Reenters the International Arena

It was in such a context that the United States resumed an active role in international affairs. For some time after 1933 it had eschewed

3 On the coming of war within a year after the Munich conference, the best account is D. C. Watt, *How War Came* (London, 1989).

assertive diplomacy (except, perhaps, in the Western Hemisphere, but even there the emphasis had been on reciprocal trade). Steadily after 1937, however, the Roosevelt administration began showing signs of a willingness to reenter the international arena. Not that it worked out a carefully crafted, comprehensive response to the rising crises in Asia and Europe. Rather, these crises gradually compelled rethinking and reorientation of U.S. foreign affairs.

There was a significant lag between challenge and response. Throughout 1936, the isolationist thrust of American foreign policy did not change, reconfirmed by the Neutrality Act of that year which extended mandatory neutrality to the extension of loans and credits to belligerents. When the Spanish civil war broke out, the State Department instituted a moral embargo, exhorting Americans not to ship arms to either side. This was in a sense the application of the Montevideo policy of nonintervention to Spain, but it was tame even in comparison with the European powers' nonintervention committee (not joined by the United States).

Perhaps the only visible indication that something new was happening was President Roosevelt's trip to Buenos Aires, the Argentinean capital, in late November to open an inter-American "conference for the maintenance of peace." He had just won the election for a second term and felt the American people were solidly behind his domestic programs. He may now have decided to make use of the trip to reassert America's role in world affairs. The role, to be sure, was for now to be focused on developing a sense of hemispheric solidarity, but even that would have clear implications for world affairs. As he told the delegates, outside nations that sought to commit acts of aggression "will find a Hemisphere wholly prepared to consult together for our mutual safety and our mutual good." He was serving notice to any outside state (Germany was obviously implied) that sought to extend its power across the Atlantic that the United States and other American republics would be determined and capable of resisting such a challenge. After Roosevelt left Buenos Aires, the conferees spent the rest of December discussing and adopting various agreements, including one for voluntary consultation to cope with threats to the hemisphere. This was a rather modest achievement, indicating that the hemispheric nations were not quite ready to act in unison to defend their collective security, but for the United States, at least, it signaled a willingness to make its voice heard, and not just in Latin America but elsewhere as well.

The Buenos Aires Conference also adopted a program for an exchange of graduate students and teachers on government fellowships between the United States and other American nations, the first such program officially sponsored by Washington.[4] This was an important indication that cultural cooperation was being taken seriously as an official concern of the United States. It is interesting to note that during the 1930s several governments actively promoted cultural exchange and propaganda activities. Britain, Germany, Italy, Japan, and others established governmental or semiofficial agencies to carry out such work, attesting to the importance they attached to influencing other countries through exchange and informational programs with a view to creating pockets of favorable foreign opinion. In the United States cultural exchange had been carried out by private foundations and educational institutions, but now Washington officially adopted the view that foreign policy entailed more than the protection of security and economic interests. Of course, culture had been a major factor in international relations during the 1920s, but at that time the stress had been on cultural internationalism, the promotion of a sense of worldwide interconnectedness and human unity. In the 1930s, in contrast, there was a particularistic tendency, cultural exchange being frankly envisaged as an instrument of official policy. This was understandable in view of the emergence of conflicting ideologies and political movements that were being put to the service of state power. World affairs, now more than ever before, had a cultural dimension, albeit in a subordinate position to power. It is therefore not surprising that the United States, too, belatedly began emphasizing cultural diplomacy.

The time was none too soon, for in the wake of the Buenos Aires conference the American people were confronted with a crisis of their neutrality and compelled to recognize that in a world so sharply divided between forces of democracy and totalitarianism, the policy of neutrality was not something to be innocently indulged in

4 Irwin F. Gellman, *Good Neighbor Diplomacy* (Baltimore, 1979), 64–5.

but would have serious implications for the struggle between these forces. This was as much a cultural as a conventional foreign policy issue, and the American people had to grapple with the question of how to avoid involvement in another war while at the same time not assisting, through their action or inaction, forces of totalitarianism and aggression.

In January 1937, Congress enacted another neutrality law, extending an arms embargo to any foreign country engaged in a civil war, and thus forbidding the shipment of arms to either side in the Spanish civil war. (There was the fear that the moral embargo might be defied by some Americans.) At first this appeared to be the right policy, to avoid American involvement in external complications, but it soon became clear that American neutrality was actually helping Franco's forces because they were obtaining arms from Germany, and the latter was not being prevented by neutrality legislation from purchasing weapons from the United States. This and the reported instances of the insurgents' brutal assault on the republic in time gave rise to serious soul-searching among American isolationists. The question was whether the nation could long remain uninvolved when there were wars and civil wars abroad in which there were clear differences between aggressors and victims. Neutrality did not make a distinction between them, so it could end up further victimizing the victims by not coming to their assistance. On the other hand, to do anything to help resist forces of aggression would by definition be a nonneutral act and might bring war closer home when the people and the government neither wanted nor were prepared for war.

The dilemma might still not have produced significant new thinking about foreign affairs if there had been no further international crises. But the outbreak of the Sino-Japanese War in July 1937 ensured that the Americans would not enjoy a respite from foreign crises. Although the war was called an "incident" and so did not entail American neutrality, the United States was extremely careful not to become involved in the cross fire. The State Department encouraged Americans to evacuate from the interior of China and discouraged ships carrying aircraft and other arms for China from reaching their destination lest they should be intercepted by the Japanese Navy.

Despite such caution, American leaders were beginning to establish connections between developments in Europe and Asia and grope for ways to cope with them as related phenomena, as essentially one global crisis. One early indication of this was President Roosevelt's proposal, in late July, to Prime Minister Neville Chamberlain to visit the United States to discuss cooperation in international affairs. Chamberlain turned down the invitation, uttering the famous words: "It is always best and safest to count on nothing from the Americans but words."[5] Although the prime minister has been held up to posterity's ridicule for such a statement, it is perhaps not difficult to understand why he felt that way. After all, the United States under President Roosevelt had eschewed collective action (save in Latin America and that, too, had been mostly "words"), so why should Britain now take seriously an offer of transatlantic cooperation?

On the other hand, it might also be noted that during Roosevelt's first administration he was virtually immobilized in foreign affairs because of his preoccupation with domestic economic problems, whereas after winning a second term in the election of 1936, he may have felt ready to undertake some foreign policy initiatives. The country's economic indexes (national income, production, foreign trade, etc.) had not quite recovered the levels prevailing prior to 1929, but the worst was clearly over; unemployment, farm foreclosures, and business failures had declined considerably. Although Roosevelt had several new items on his agenda – such as the "packing" of the Supreme Court so as to have more justices on the bench who were supportive of his domestic programs – he evidently believed he could now be more assertive in foreign affairs. The invitation to Chamberlain was his first attempt – and his first failure.

But the failure did not daunt him, for he returned to the theme of cooperation again and again. Quite clearly, he was groping for ways to tie the United States once again to some other countries in defense

5 A. A. Offner, *American Appeasement* (Cambridge, Mass., 1969), 189.

of peace and order in the world. That this gesture primarily was a verbal one does not detract from its significance, for ultimately American cooperativeness, rather than isolation or unilateralism, would make a major difference in global developments.

Roosevelt's next initiative came in October when he made a speech in Chicago calling for international cooperation to isolate – or "quarantine" – aggressive states. As he said, when an epidemic breaks out in a community, "the community approves and joins in a quarantine of the patients in order to protect the health of the community against the spread of the disease." Likewise, in the international community, those with a disease (the disease of aggressiveness) must be quarantined by the rest.

The "quarantine speech" was barely noticed abroad, and at home the president kept saying that no new departure in foreign policy was being contemplated. Nevertheless, in retrospect the speech is significant for it, combined with other, albeit disparate, initiatives by the administration, indicated a willingness on the part of the United States to assert once again a voice in world affairs. For instance, the speech was immediately followed by a proposal by Under Secretary of State Sumner Welles for a world conference to enunciate fundamental principles of international relations. Nothing came of it as Secretary of State Hull thought the time was inopportune for such an effort. But both Roosevelt and Hull supported the League of Nations when it called for a conference to discuss the Sino-Japanese War. The conference, convened in Brussels, was boycotted by Japan and Germany but was attended by the United States as well as the European signatories of the Nine-Power Treaty and by the Soviet Union. Although little came of it except for a condemnation of Japanese aggression, the gathering was another milestone in America's reemergence in the global scene.

Even more drastic developments came at the end of 1937, when Japanese military aircraft fired at and sank an American gunboat, the *Panay,* on the Yangtze as it was evacuating embassy personnel and others from Nanking toward Shanghai. Two American lives were lost, and thirty were wounded. This was a shocking event, suggesting that even when the United States maintained neutrality in a foreign war the lives of its citizens could be jeopardized. Short of completely withdrawing all Americans from areas of conflict, the nation would have to be prepared for similar incidents in the future. And should they continue, the country might have to use military force, however reluctantly, in order to protect its nationals.

In this instance, Japan, not wishing to provoke the United States further, offered an immediate apology as well as indemnities, so outwardly things returned to normal. President Roosevelt, however, became so alarmed that he sent Captain Royal Ingersoll, chief of the U.S. Navy's intelligence division, to London for secret talks with his British counterpart for a possible joint strategy against Japan. This was, of course, a very unusual step, but for that very reason it suggests Roosevelt's growing concern with the Asian crisis and willingness to take action, however secretively. Ingersoll arrived in London toward the end of the year and initiated what proved to be the first of binational discussions on cooperative military action. The action contemplated even included, at Roosevelt's behest, a blockade of Japan by U.S. and British ships. Although nothing came of this, it showed how far the president had traveled in a brief span of time toward defending world order.[6]

The momentum, once developed, would not be reversed. To be sure, Roosevelt did not want to go too far ahead of public opinion, and in official pronouncements he continued to profess his determination to keep the country out of foreign complications. But there was much that he thought the nation could and should do short of direct involvement in overseas conflicts. Thus in January 1938 he resurrected Welles's idea of an international conference, for which he proposed Washington as the site. Again Chamberlain resisted, not wishing to identify Britain too closely with the United States at a time when he was engaged in a delicate diplomacy to detach Italy from Germany (by recognizing the Italian conquest of Ethiopia). When Germany went ahead with the *Anschluss,* the United States took no action but announced that it would step up its rearmament program. Roosevelt was particularly eager to strengthen American naval power and fully endorsed the Vinson Naval Expansion Act of

6 See James R. Leutze, *Bargaining for Supremacy* (Chapel Hill, 1977), for a discussion of the Ingersoll mission.

May, providing for a new program of naval rearmament, including the augmentation of capital ships to a strength of 660,000 tons – for the first time going beyond the "treaty limits" imposed by the earlier naval disarmament agreements (nullified since 1936).

At that time, however, it was felt that to increase naval power even to this modest extent would take ten years. Besides, the naval bases at Pearl Harbor and Subic Bay in the Philippines badly needed repair, and a new one had to be built on the island of Guam. In the meantime, the United States would revise its war plan "orange" (for a hypothetical war against Japan) to take account of Japan's growing power in the western Pacific. Hitherto, the idea had been to move the U.S. fleet across the Pacific and engage the Japanese fleet in an offensive assault near the Japanese homeland, but now a defensive strategy was adopted; the United States would have to concede the Philippines to Japan in the initial phase of a war and then subsequently try to launch a counterattack. In any event, war with Japan no longer appeared like a remote possibility.[7]

In the meantime, in Europe, the president was extremely interested in playing a role during the Sudetenland crisis. On September 26, three days before the fateful Munich agreement was signed by the German, British, and French leaders to reincorporate Sudetenland into Germany, Roosevelt sent an appeal to the European governments to resolve the difficulties peacefully. A similar appeal was sent to Mussolini on September 27, and to Hitler on September 28. When the Munich conference seemed to have succeeded in preventing war, he expressed his satisfaction. His thinking was probably reflected in Under Secretary Welles's hopeful assertion that "a new world order based upon justice and upon law" was emerging.[8] This may have been a self-deceiving exaggeration, but the episode at least revealed that the American government was now more willing to express its views on international affairs.

That the United States was prepared to go beyond issuing statements and appealing to the European governments to avoid war

7 An interesting recent study of American strategy toward Japan is William Honan, *Visions of Infamy* (New York, 1991).

8 Offner, *American Appeasement,* 269.

became clear soon after Munich. First, outraged by the "night of the broken glass" – attacks on Jewish businesses in Germany in November – President Roosevelt withdrew Hugh Wilson, chargé d'affaires in Berlin after the resignation of the ambassador, William Dodd, in late 1937 in disgust at Nazi race policies. Hitler responded by withdrawing the German ambassador from Washington, and thus the two embassies were to be without their chiefs for the duration of the prewar period.

Second, in December another conference of American states was held in Lima. A resolution against Nazi race doctrines was adopted, and the conferees also agreed to improve the existing consultative procedures to safeguard against any threat to the "peace, security, or territorial integrity" of an American state. This reaffirmation of inter-American solidarity was a major achievement if only because U.S. relations with Mexico were at a breaking point in 1938. The accommodation between Mexican nationalism and American economic interests, which had been tentatively worked out through the efforts of Dwight Morrow and others (see Chapter 6), had once again been undermined after Lazaro Cárdenas became president in 1934. He was more radical than Calles in his economic and social programs, and in March 1938 his government issued an oil expropriation decree, nationalizing the properties of British and American oil companies. The United States retaliated by stopping the practice of purchasing Mexican silver above world prices and boycotting Mexican oil, whereupon Mexico sought to sell it to Germany and Japan. Even such a serious crisis, however, did not prevent the issuing of the Lima declaration, and soon, in 1939, Mexico and the United States were able to come to agreement on fair compensation to the oil companies.[9]

Third, at the end of the year President Roosevelt decided on the sale of military aircraft to Britain and France, to strengthen their defenses for a possible war against Germany. Treasury Secretary Henry Morgenthau was instructed to coordinate such sales, and soon representatives appeared from those countries – including Jean Monnet of future fame as a founding father of European integration

9 Gellman, *Good Neighbor,* 50–4.

– to obtain U.S. planes. Such sales were not a violation of neutrality legislation, as there was as yet no war in Europe, but the fact that Roosevelt authorized them indicated his growing pessimism that war might come after all, and his determination that, should it happen, the United States must play a role in strengthening the democratic nations.

In Asia, in the meantime, the United States was, if anything, becoming even more assertive. In March 1938 a definite decision was made not to invoke the Neutrality Act in connection with the Sino-Japanese War. This enabled China to purchase arms in the United States, and already in that year some $8.9 million worth of arms was shipped to that country. The money for the transactions came from the Chinese sale of silver to the United States (about $115 million that year). Because silver had been "demonetized" in China in the wake of the silver purchase crisis of 1934, it could ship large quantities of the metal to the United States, and the proceeds from their sale could be used to obtain credits with which to purchase arms and other commodities.

Of course, Japan, too, could buy arms from the United States, and it had been doing so throughout the 1930s. (In 1938 the amount came to $9.1 million.) But there was increasing public criticism of this in the United States, where the uneasy awareness grew that the nation was providing Japan with the aircraft, tanks, and ammunition with which to fight the aggressive war in China. Public rallies were held, letters were written to newspapers, and various groups were organized to protest the practice. Of the latter, the most important was the American Committee for Nonparticipation in Japanese Aggression, created mostly through the initiative of former American missionaries in China. The name of the organization was typical; virtually everyone agreed that Japan was engaged in an aggressive war in China, and although there was no consensus as to whether the United States should become involved by more than moral disapprobation, it seemed to make sense at least to refrain from assisting Japan by the sale of American arms.[10]

10 Warren I. Cohen, *The Chinese Connection* (New York, 1978), 214–18.

This growing public protest was reflected in official policy, which also grew more and more critical of Japan. In July the State Department announced a moral embargo of airplanes to Japan. While not legally binding, it sent a clear signal that Japan would no longer be able to count on making use of American arms in the Chinese war. Then, toward the end of the year, as the Japanese government issued a declaration on the new order in East Asia, Secretary of State Hull immediately denounced it, denying Japan's right to create a new order through its own fiat. The United States would adamantly oppose Japanese unilateralism and would not accept any modification in the regional status quo except through consultation and cooperation. This opposition would characterize U.S.-Japanese relations from this time until the outbreak of their war.

Finally, also in December, the U.S. government announced a loan of $25 million to China to be used for whatever objectives the Chungking authorities considered necessary. Although America had provided China with credits in return for silver, such credits had been largely intended for stabilizing Chinese finances. Now, however, the Chinese would be able to use the money for military purposes, and they first turned to the construction of a road from Burma to Chungking, to facilitate the shipment of arms and goods to the wartime Chinese capital. Although a small amount, this, too, was an important symbolic gesture whose significance was not lost on the combatants. Increasingly, the Japanese were becoming aware that the United States was making itself a strong opponent of their aggression, whereas the Chinese felt that for the first time in years they would be able to count on American, in addition to Soviet, support.

To be sure, there was little expectation either in Tokyo or Chungking then that the United States would become militarily involved in the Asian war. Moreover, America's readiness to do something to help China did not yet mean implementing a global strategy of checking Japan, in the spirit of Roosevelt's quarantine address. In retrospect, nevertheless, it is clear that these tentative steps the United States began to take were laying the groundwork for what would develop into a determined policy of opposing Japan.

The Growth of Geopolitical-Mindedness

On January 4, 1939, President Roosevelt gave Congress his annual message. It was notable for its lack of new domestic initiatives. Instead, the president focused his attention on international developments, stressing that forces of aggression were growing stronger and that there must be serious cooperative efforts to resist aggressors. The United States, he said, must use all means "short of war" to deter aggression.

What did "short of war" mean? The answer became evident the very next day when Roosevelt submitted his budget plan for the fiscal year 1940, which included more than $1.3 billion for defense, out of the total figure of $9 billion. To devote 15 percent of government outlays for defense was unprecedented in peacetime, but the actual defense spending exceeded this amount as the president continued to ask for, and Congress granted, additional appropriations. In other words, starting in 1939, the United States began a massive armament program to cope with the international crisis. As of that year, the arsenal of American military aircraft, ships, and vehicles was smaller than that of most other powers. For instance, aircraft production for the United States in 1939 came to little more than 2,000, in contrast to 10,300 in the Soviet Union, 7,900 in Britain, 8,200 in Germany, and 4,400 in Japan.[11] What the nation must now do, and was determined to do, was to catch up and eventually surpass these other countries' performances in arms manufacturing.

Not that there was the expectation that these arms might actually be used by the United States. Rather, they should serve as an indication of American determination to play a role in international affairs. They could also be placed in strategic positions as a deterrent to would-be aggressors against America. Their increasing volume, of course, would make some of them available to those struggling, or likely soon to be struggling, against aggressive powers.

This last objective was very important – but risky, as was revealed when a plane carrying French officials crashed on the West Coast in January. They were testing American airplanes for possible purchase,

11 Paul Kennedy, *The Rise and Fall of the Great Powers* (New York, 1987), 324.

and the accident revealed perhaps more than the president intended about the nation's commitment to the defense of France. Still, the event did not daunt him or anyone else in the administration who was determined that the United States must take an unequivocal stand against aggression. In July, Lord Riverdale of Sheffield arrived to make a survey of what types of military supplies Britain might be able to count upon from the United States. Combined with the aid to China begun in December 1938, all these steps added up to a policy of defending the current and future victims of German, Italian, and Japanese militarism.

In the meantime, the Roosevelt administration sought to have the existing neutrality legislation repealed. From its point of view, neutrality had clearly outlived whatever purposes it had been intended to serve. There could be no neutrality in a world as transparently divided as it was in 1939. Nothing immediately came of it, as substantial segments of Congress were not yet ready for so drastic a step. Roosevelt was willing to settle for a "cash and carry" principle for trade in arms. (This provision, first written into the Neutrality Act of May 1937, specified that belligerents could obtain goods other than arms from the United States so long as they were paid for by cash and carried away in non-U.S. vessels.) Even so, it was only in November, after the outbreak of World War II, that Congress finally revised neutrality laws and authorized the sale of arms to belligerents on the "cash and carry" basis. Though hemmed in by restrictions, the new law was a landmark, indicating the end of American isolation from world conflicts.

While it stepped up arms production and revised neutrality legislation, the administration also took some initiatives to prevent a further deterioration of international affairs. Here it is interesting to note contrasting approaches to Europe and to Asia. Toward Europe, Roosevelt continued his efforts, begun in 1938, to appeal to world leaders to settle international disputes peacefully and in cooperation. For instance, during the spring and summer of 1939, as tensions arose in Europe and there were expectations of war in the near future, the president sent urgent messages to Hitler and Mussolini for a peaceful settlement of the Polish question. On one occasion, Roosevelt invited them as well as leaders of other countries to name thirty-one countries they would pledge not to invade. He must have known that these overtures would not work, given the irreconcilable positions of Germany, on one hand, and Britain and France, on the other, on the Polish question. He therefore coupled such efforts with an attempt (which did not succeed) to persuade the Soviet Union to cooperate with Britain and France to prevent further German aggression. Beyond such steps, however, he did not want to take his country farther in the direction of direct involvement in European affairs. It seemed enough to be in a state of readiness to provide Britain and France with arms, should they be needed.

Toward Asia, in contrast, President Roosevelt was willing to be more forceful. Perhaps no other step taken at this time was more crucial in defining America's Asian policy than the notification presented to Tokyo in July that the United States intended to abrogate the treaty of commerce between the two countries as of January 1940. This was a more drastic measure than anything the president was doing in Europe; to abrogate a treaty of commerce was tantamount to putting bilateral commercial transactions at the mercy of the U.S. authorities, because Japanese shippers, merchants, and bankers engaged in the American trade would no longer be protected by treaty rights.

Officials in Tokyo were shocked. Although they had noticed the steady hardening of American policy in Asia, they had not realized that Washington was taking such a dim view of the situation and was willing to be so decisive in standing up to Japanese aggression. Actually, President Roosevelt seems to have been persuaded to take such action to preempt a congressional resolution to a similar effect; congressmen, too, had become strongly critical of Japan, no doubt influenced by the growing public sentiment against that country. Moreover, Roosevelt may have sought to prevent a German-Japanese alliance – he knew, as did everyone else, that Germans and Japanese were discussing such a possibility – by diminishing Japan's value as Germany's potential ally. Without the treaty of commerce, Japan would be that much more dependent on American goodwill and therefore less attractive to Germany as a partner in a global strategy. (At that time the latter was intent on obtaining a Japanese alliance aimed at Britain, whereas Japan wanted to confine the alliance to joint action against the Soviet Union. In the event, not so much Roosevelt as Hitler and Stalin aborted a German-Japanese alliance; the Japanese were shocked by the Nazi-Soviet nonaggression pact and temporarily lost their appetite for a German alliance.)

It should be noted that all these steps, ranging from military buildups to the abrogation of the treaty of commerce with Japan, were taken before Europe plunged into another war in September. They amounted to a significant transformation of American foreign policy *before* the outbreak of the European war. This transformation was fundamentally geopolitical; it amounted to significant portions of the American people and their leaders embracing military force, power politics, and international collective action as necessary to preserve the peace and to prevent aggression.

Whence came this geopolitical consciousness? Whatever traces of geopolitics there had been in the period of Theodore Roosevelt would seem to have disappeared, or at least become submerged, by the 1930s. The rise of Nazism or the resurgence of Japanese militarism had not automatically produced power-political thinking; on the contrary, such overseas phenomena had reinforced domestic pacifism, isolationism, and antimilitarism. It was only after 1937 that some began talking about America's geopolitical role. One of the first books to advocate the new thinking was Livingston Hartley's *Is America Afraid?,* published in 1937. The author, a journalist, argued that the domination of Europe by one country (Germany, or it could be the Soviet Union) and Asia by another (Japan, or even China) would be a threat to the United States. Either development could bring about the fall of Britain and the British Empire, whose resources could be put at the service of the hegemonic powers. The United States, Hartley noted, was sandwiched between two landmass powers: the European landmass under German or Soviet control, and the Asian landmass under Japanese or Chinese control. The danger to American security would increase especially if Germany and Japan, emerging as the strongest powers in the two spheres, should combine. They would be not only military powers but autocratic states as well, and thus would menace the democratic nations.

In such a situation, the author asserted, the United States must be prepared to ally itself with Britain; the two shared a great deal in basic policies and interests.[12]

Few at first noticed the book, but the sort of argument it contained steadily grew in influence. Of its two themes – that democracy was in danger and that the United States must be willing once again to become involved in world politics – the first may have been easier to accept, for by 1937 some confidence in democracy had returned to America. No longer were commentators or politicians speaking defensively or wistfully about democracy, as they had done during the first few years of the Roosevelt administration. Having survived the worst phase of the Depression without having had to abandon democratic government, the Americans of all political affiliations and persuasions could feel that somehow American democracy had weathered its severest test. But just when they regained confidence in their own domestic institutions, they awoke to the danger posed to them from antidemocratic forces overseas. The definition of this national danger was the important first step in redefining their attitude toward international affairs.

In coping with this newly realized threat to national security and institutions, advocates of U.S.-British (or U.S.-Chinese) cooperation steadily grew in number. Although they did not always speak the language of geopolitics, the direction was clear, because once it was decided that the United States had to do something to prevent total German victory in Europe or Japanese victory in Asia, it followed that it must use its full resources for the defense of the global status quo and otherwise involve itself in the affairs of Europe and Asia.

Such thinking began to be promoted with vigor by a small group of scholars, some of whom were recent arrivals from Europe and saw developments there in a geopolitical framework. For them (men like Nicholas Spykman and Felix Gilbert), and for those who came under their influence (some of whom established research centers on strategy at Princeton, Yale, and elsewhere), it was axiomatic that "the realities of power" were the existential given of world affairs, and

12 Livingston Hartley, *Is America Afraid?* (New York, 1937).

that whether the United States wanted to be or not, it was involved in global power politics by virtue of its very existence with its enormous size, population, resources, and productivity. This being the case, it had no choice but to assert its role in international affairs rather than passively responding to developments elsewhere.

The emergence of geopolitical-mindedness was a major phenomenon of American intellectual and diplomatic history. The consciousness of power and the readiness to consider war as an instrument of national policy – such a "realist" response to world affairs was to have a profound impact on the way the American people viewed external events. The new assertiveness in Roosevelt's foreign policy dovetailed with this intellectual development. It was perhaps fortunate for the United States and for the world that this conjunction of policy and thought had begun to take place by 1939. But, at the same time, the earlier tradition of Wilsonianism would not be totally submerged under the new realism. Henceforth, American foreign policy would have the task of combining geopolitics with Wilsonian internationalism. How the combination would work was not yet clear.

11. The Road to Pearl Harbor

The European War and U.S. Neutrality

The several months between September 1939, when Germany invaded Poland, and the spring of 1940, when the target of the attack shifted to Western Europe, have been referred to as the period of a "phony war." War had been declared by Britain and France immediately after the German invasion of Poland, but there was actually little fighting between the two sides. After Warsaw fell on September 27, there was little further military action, and there were even some attempts at reestablishing a semblance of status quo in Europe without more bloodshed. Although German and French troops confronted one another along their frontier, they did not exchange fire. There was an atmosphere of unreality, and many doubted if this was actually the beginning of another world war.

And yet there was nothing "phony" about the developments in Eastern Europe. The Soviet Union, taking advantage of the just-signed nonaggression pact with Germany, sent its troops to Poland from the east, in effect partitioning Poland into two. Soviet forces then turned north, invading Finland in mid-October. The severe fighting continued until March 1940, when the parties signed a peace accord, which included some territorial cessions to the Soviet Union. In Asia, the Sino-Japanese War went on. Although the intensity of ground fighting had abated, Japanese air attacks on Chinese railroads, military bases, and the wartime capital of Chungking were stepped up. In the meantime, just before the German spring offensive began in the West, a group of Chinese politicians led by Wang Ching-wei set up a pro-Japanese government in Nanking. This action signaled, among other things, Japan's intention to stay in China, for without Japanese military support no such puppet regime would survive.

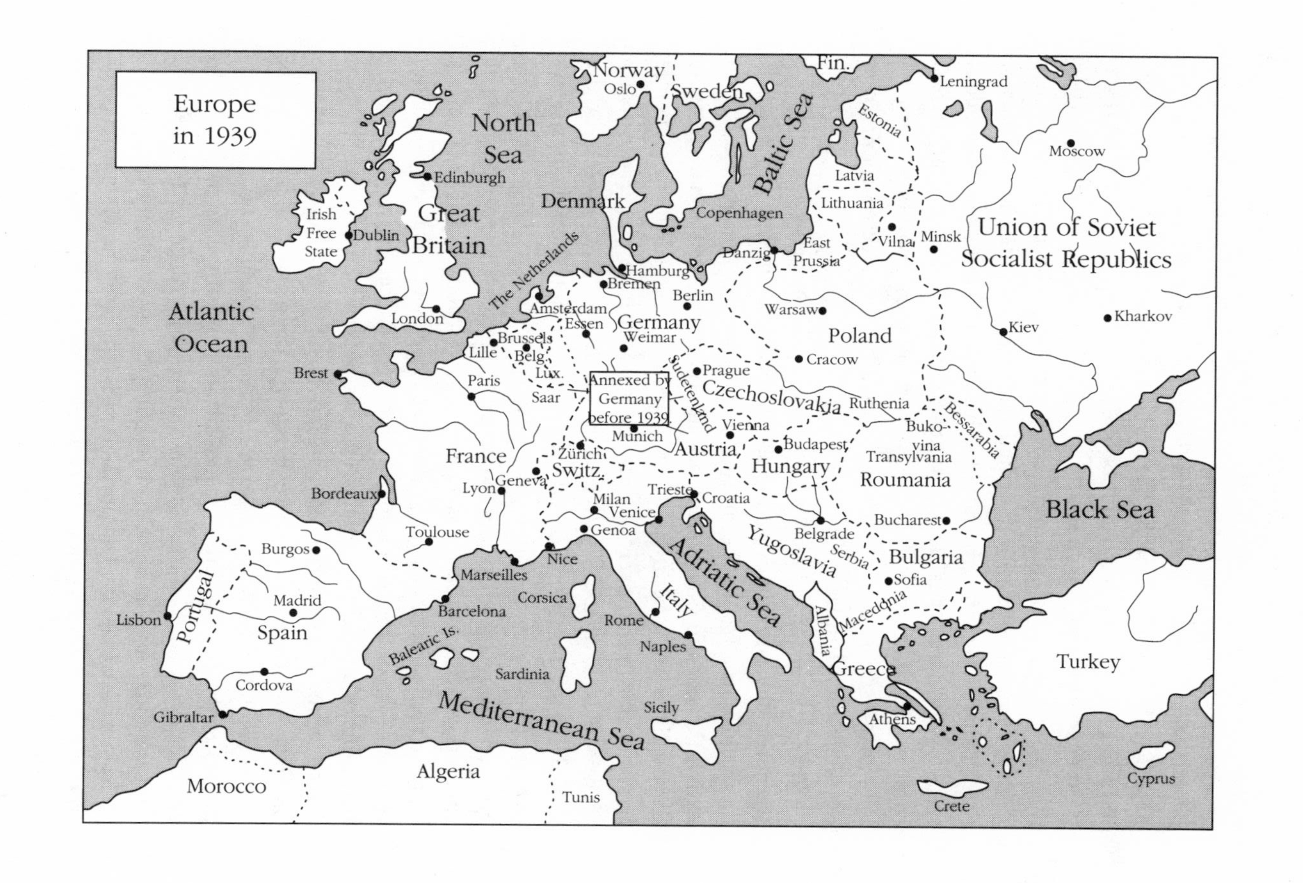

Europe in 1939
North Sea
Atlantic Ocean
Norway
Oslo
Sweden
Fin.
Baltic Sea
Leningrad
Estonia
Latvia
Lithuania
Vilna
Minsk
Moscow
Union of Soviet Socialist Republics
Kharkov
Kiev
Edinburgh
Great Britain
Irish Free State
Dublin
London
Denmark
Copenhagen
Danzig
East Prussia
Hamburg
Bremen
Berlin
Warsaw
Poland
Cracow
The Netherlands
Amsterdam
Essen
Germany
Weimar
Brussels
Belg.
Lille
Lux.
Saar
Annexed by Germany before 1939
Sudetenland
Prague
Czechoslovakia
Ruthenia
Buko-vina
Bessarabia
Transylvania
Roumania
Brest
Paris
Munich
Vienna
Budapest
Austria
Hungary
France
Zürich
Switz.
Geneva
Lyon
Bordeaux
Toulouse
Milan
Venice
Trieste
Croatia
Genoa
Nice
Marseilles
Belgrade
Yugoslavia
Serbia
Bucharest
Bulgaria
Sofia
Black Sea
Burgos
Madrid
Spain
Portugal
Lisbon
Cordova
Gibraltar
Barcelona
Balearic Is.
Corsica
Sardinia
Rome
Naples
Italy
Adriatic Sea
Albania
Macedonia
Greece
Athens
Sicily
Mediterranean Sea
Turkey
Crete
Cyprus
Morocco
Algeria
Tunis

These events revealed that, although the European war may have been "phony," momentous developments were occurring on the global scale, with Germany, Japan, and now the Soviet Union clearly intent on revising territorial boundaries by force. Would the three powers combine as "revisionists" challenging the status quo? If they did, what response would come from the rest of the world, especially from the one major nation that had remained outside the conflicts of the decade, the United States? Although Washington had taken steps to support actual and potential victims of aggression, it had confined its assistance to means "short of war." Would it long be able to persist in such a stand, especially if the three totalitarian regimes should unite?

That was not a far-fetched prospect. The Nazi-Soviet pact had shattered the worldwide coalition of antifascist forces, the popular front, and, as a result, Communists, radicals, and many others who had followed the Soviet lead in international issues had become demoralized and disoriented. In Japan, in the meantime, voices began to be heard, even within the army, which had traditionally viewed Russia as the key hypothetical enemy, that in view of the rapidly changing international events, the nation should completely overhaul its foreign policy and seek an accommodation with the Soviet Union so as to form a tripartite arrangement consisting of the three powerful antidemocratic nations. Although this was still a minority view, it was significant that the Soviet invasion of Poland coincided with the signing of a Nomonhan cease-fire agreement, bringing to an end the series of clashes between Soviet and Japanese forces along the Siberian-Mongolian-Manchurian border. German officials, for their part, were becoming interested in the idea of renewing talks with the Japanese for an alliance – not, however, aimed at the Soviet Union but at Britain and the United States. In the meantime, it would be of paramount importance for Germany to prevent U.S. involvement in the European war, phony or real.

In such a situation, the position of the United States was becoming of critical importance. It had many choices. It could freeze its position as of September 1939 and do nothing. It could openly proclaim its support of the democracies and continue to assist them by all means "short of war." It could try to detach the Soviet Union from Germany by differentiating its responses to the two aggressors. It could seek to prevent a German-Soviet-Japanese coalition from developing by negotiating a compromise settlement of its differences with Japan. Or it could step up its support of China so as to tie Japan down on the Asian continent and make it less valuable as a potential ally of either Germany or the Soviet Union.

These were hard choices. Geopolitical thinking, which, as seen in the preceding chapter, had become evident in America by 1938–9, might have called for a policy of identifying the main threat, for example Germany, and isolating it from its would-be partners by offering some inducements to the latter, in this instance the Soviet Union and Japan. Or, if Japan were to be viewed as the major threat to peace, the United States might find it prudent to concentrate on the Asian war and seek a new Munich-type settlement in Europe.

The trouble was that by then American official and public opinion had become antagonized against all three, so that it was extremely difficult to differentiate among them. The public had supported neutrality revision, assistance to China, and the termination of the Japanese commerce treaty. Now it had become enraged by Soviet behavior in Poland and Finland, and there were pressures on the Roosevelt administration to enact sanctions against the Soviet Union. (That nation was expelled from the League of Nations in December.) Under the circumstances, even if President Roosevelt had wanted to keep his options open so as to prevent collusion among Germany, the Soviet Union, and Japan, he would have found it extremely difficult to obtain public support.

There is evidence that Roosevelt did in fact want to treat the Soviet Union differently, in the belief that sooner or later the Nazi-Soviet marriage of convenience would disintegrate and that Germany in Europe and Japan in Asia were the major threats to peace, rather than the Soviet Union. But others, like the popular isolationist Charles Lindbergh, were asserting that the Soviet Union was a greater menace to civilization than Germany, and so the president had to be circumspect in anything he did toward that country.[1]

1 Warren Kimball, *The Most Unsordid Act* (Baltimore, 1969), 29. See also H. W. Brands, *Inside the Cold War* (New York, 1991), 93–5.

Toward Germany and Japan, the American public seemed satisfied with the "cash and carry" provision in the latest neutrality law that enabled Britain, France, and China to buy American arms legally. Beyond this, however, it would appear that the Americans were much more willing to take stronger measures in Asia than in Europe. Not that they favored conciliating Germany so as to concentrate on frustrating Japanese ambitions in China, but at least for the time being they were opposed to going beyond the "cash and carry" arrangement – for instance, lending money – with Britain or France. That would have further involved the United States in the European situation at a time when Germany was being very cautious not to arouse American hostility. Hitler well recognized that, no matter what he decided to undertake next in Europe, he would have to reckon with the United States as the major supplier of Britain and France as well as the key potential obstacle in the way of his ambitions. "The Germans have nothing against the Americans, and the Americans have nothing against the Germans," he declared shortly after the outbreak of the war, to assure the United States that he did not want trouble with the latter and also to prevent its intervention in European affairs.[2] If the United States could somehow be kept away from the European conflict, then, he thought, Germany might be able to establish its domination over Central and Eastern Europe without much further interference from Britain or France.

In this, Hitler was partially successful. In the absence of overt German attacks on American individuals, goods, or ships, public opinion in the United States remained opposed to going beyond the "cash and carry" formula to help the democracies. And in February 1940 President Roosevelt sent Under Secretary Sumner Welles to Europe to explore possibilities for peace. Had the Germans succeeded in impressing on Welles their peaceful intentions, U.S. foreign policy might have remained unchanged much longer than it did. In reality, however, Welles returned convinced that the best way of preventing the phony war from developing into something more serious was through making clear America's intention to come to the aid of Britain and France should Germany decide to plunge

2 Saul Friedlander, *Prelude to Downfall* (New York, 1967), 41.

Europe to a war of devastation. The episode indicates that there was a limit beyond which the United States would not go. It would not actively seek to mediate between the two sides in the European conflict lest such an attempt should bring about a relative weakening of the democracies' stand against Germany. The two sides were simply not equal in the eyes of the majority of the American people; rather, one side was the obvious aggressor, and so to mediate as if both sides had to make concessions would be untenable.

In Asia the situation was even more clear-cut, and here, too, there was little inclination to conciliate Japan. Tokyo extended several overtures in late 1939 and early 1940 as its officials, like their German counterparts, had become fully aware of America's potential power to frustrate Japanese ambitions. Japanese policy toward the United States during this period aimed primarily at persuading the latter to restore normal trade relations rather than going through with the announced abrogation of the treaty of commerce. Washington, however, rebuffed such overtures and went ahead with the abrogation of the treaty, which took effect on January 26, 1940. The two nations now entered "the period of no treaties," as the Japanese called it. The firmness of U.S. policy toward Japan was derived from the conviction that only such an approach would keep Tokyo's leaders from a more reckless path.

To the degree that the American policy of firmness toward Germany and Japan was intended to moderate their behavior, it did not achieve the objective. As noted earlier, the Japanese went ahead with the establishment of the Nanking puppet regime. More gravely still, Germany launched a devastating offensive against Scandinavia, France, and the Low Countries in April, conquering most of Western Europe by June. One after another, these countries fell to German forces, and the climax came in June when German troops occupied Paris. A German-French armistice was signed on June 22. To compound the gravity of the situation, Soviet forces proceeded against Lithuania, and on July 21 the three Baltic states of Lithuania, Estonia, and Latvia were incorporated into the Soviet Union. (The United States promptly froze the assets of these countries.) Thus the three totalitarian powers were further aggrandizing themselves as though nothing stood in their way. If there had been any intention in Washington of trying to prevent such a development, it had obviously failed.

The sense of failure was devastating, but it also brought about significant changes in U.S. policy, changes that were destined to frustrate the ambitions of Germany and Japan, while at the same time inclining the nation to separate out the Soviet Union from these two.

The Axis Versus the Democracies

Germany's spring offensive (the Blitzkrieg) was undertaken when Hitler calculated that the Western democracies were still weak and chances for U.S. military intervention slim – whereas the longer he hesitated, the readier all these powers would become to resist. It was imperative to strike quickly and decisively, first against France and the nearby countries and then against Britain before the United States had a chance to intervene. If all of Western Europe should fall, then Germany would be able finally to turn against the Soviet Union and bring all of Europe under its control.

It is clear that the position of the United States was of critical importance in such calculations. No matter what America did, or did not do, it was bound to affect the course of the European conflict. Quite predictably, therefore, Hitler sought to prevent U.S. intervention through a number of ways. First, he continued to assure the Americans that "Germany has never had any territorial or political designs on the American continent, and has none at present."[3] He was postulating a divided world – "Europe for the Europeans and America for the Americans," as he said – which he thought the Americans would accept rather than go to war to prevent such a development. At the same time, Hitler made use of propaganda, through subtle hints as well as covert activities, to influence American opinion and promote isolationism. Third, he also tried to tie the United States down in the Pacific by insinuating that he might make a pact with Japan. The idea was to alarm the United States and keep it preoccupied with Japanese aggression

3 Ibid., 95.

in Asia, which would presumably prevent it from intervening in Europe.

None of the tactics worked, for after the spring offensive American public opinion turned decisively against Germany and in favor of assisting Britain – although advocates of outright military intervention were still small in number. The public was now clearly coming to the realization that American security and interests would be menaced should Germany defeat Britain. Germany could then assault the Soviet Union or South America, in either eventuality bringing its threat closer home to the United States. A victorious German Navy would disrupt American trade. Most fundamentally, a totalitarian Europe (and South America) would endanger what was left of democratic governments and ultimately American democracy itself. On top of that, if Japan were formally tied to Germany, the threat would become even more formidable.

In such a situation, American response was quick and clear-cut. Even before the German-Japanese alliance was consummated on September 27, the United States took decisive steps to try to prevent Britain's defeat. As the government in London, headed by Winston Churchill since May, sent Roosevelt urgent pleas for assistance, the United States began shipping large quantities of arms and aircraft to Britain. In an address at the University of Virginia on June 10, the day Italy declared war against France and Britain, Roosevelt asserted, "we will extend to the opponents of force the material resources of this nation." Hitherto, such assistance had taken the form of commercial transactions under the "cash and carry" principle, but the president now made it clear that he was not talking of sale but of aid; it was expected that sooner or later Britain would run out of cash to pay for American arms, so the United States must be prepared to consider other ways of helping out. One arrangement was the "destroyer deal" of September, involving a barter arrangement between fifty U.S. destroyers transferred to Britain in return for the U.S. lease of some British bases in the Western Hemisphere, such as those in Newfoundland, Bermuda, and Trinidad. This agreement was preceded by a U.S. military mission to Britain, which reported that the latter was likely to hold out against the German assault, and therefore that the arms supplied by the United

States would not end up in German hands. All the more reason, then, to ship munitions, ships, and aircraft to Britain.

These measures were supported by the public, some of the most articulate and prominent of whom established, in May, the Committee to Defend America by Aiding the Allies. Its spokesmen reiterated the theme that America's survival was bound up with Britain's, and that these two were now the last hope for the preservation of civilization itself.[4] Such rhetoric was rebutted by the isolationists, who organized their openly anti-British America First Committee, committed to keeping the nation detached from external complications and to erecting a "Fortress America," an impregnable state that would withstand any threat from the outside.[5] Opinion polls indicated, however, that an increasing number of Americans were siding with the Committee to Defend America rather than with the America First Committee. The growing national consensus was symbolized by President Roosevelt's decision to ask two prominent Republicans, Frank Knox and Henry L. Stimson, to join the administration, as secretaries of the navy and of war, respectively. The government was now more bipartisan, and, even more important, the participation of two Republican leaders served to reestablish a close connection between the administration and the business community. No longer would the Roosevelt administration seek to maintain a distance from Wall Street and the world of corporate executives and lawyers; it would forge a new corporatist synthesis in the name of national defense.

In the meantime, the defense of the Western Hemisphere became even more urgent in view of German naval campaigns in the Atlantic and Nazi propaganda activities in Latin America. In late July, Secretary of State Hull traveled to Havana to attend an inter-American conference for the fourth time since taking office. The twenty-one American republics agreed that they should be prepared, collectively and individually, to take over any European possession in the hemisphere that was endangered by aggression and to estab-

4 On the Committee to Defend America, see Mark Chadwin, *Warhawks* (New York, 1968).

5 On the America First Committee, see Wayne S. Cole, *America First* (Madison, 1953).

lish a temporary trusteeship over such territory. The conferees also adopted a declaration stating that any attempt by a non-American power to interfere with the sovereignty of a nation in the hemisphere would be considered an attack against all American states, which would devise means for stopping the threat. Like the "destroyer deal" that followed the Havana conference by a month, these measures were additional steps taken in order to frustrate German ambitions and opened the way for U.S. military reinvolvement in Latin America.[6]

The United States would also help in the defense of the British Empire in Asia. Japan was evidently intent upon taking advantage of Britain's distress to put pressure on the latter's possessions. For instance, on June 24, two days after the German-French armistice was signed, the Japanese government demanded that Britain stop shipments of goods to Chungking through Hong Kong and Burma. Earlier, the Japanese had warned France against sending trucks and gasoline through Indochina to the Chinese Nationalists. Britain had no choice but to give in, as did France.

The situation left the United States as the only power that could still protect the British Empire in Asia – and the French and the Dutch empires as well, for, while their metropolitan governments had succumbed to Germany, the Asian colonies still retained their autonomous existence. The Japanese were counting on Britain's defeat in Europe so that they could control the European colonies in Southeast Asia, a region fabulously rich in natural resources, which in turn should enable them, they believed, to bring the long war in China to satisfactory conclusion. Tokyo's propagandists began mouthing slogans about "Asia for Asians," the idea being to rid the region of Western influence and return it to its "authentic" past when its inhabitants had presumably pursued their traditional ways of life uncontaminated by the West's corrupting cultural influences or economic exploitation.

Such an Asia under Japanese domination could be combined with a German-dominated Europe. This was the horrible prospect the Americans had to contemplate – unless they acted in Asia as well as

6 Irwin F. Gellman, *Good Neighbor Diplomacy* (Baltimore, 1979), 100–1.

in Europe. The Roosevelt administration took a number of decisive steps in this direction. The bulk of the United States fleet was kept at Pearl Harbor after April, instead of being sent back to the Atlantic after its spring exercises in the Pacific. The fleet would serve as a deterrent against hasty Japanese action. Equally important were trade restrictions imposed on the sale of certain goods to Japan. Hitherto, there had been a moral embargo on shipments of aircraft to that country, but in June the United States banned the sale of industrial machinery to Japan. In July the export of aviation fuel to countries outside of the Western Hemisphere was banned, and on September 26 the embargo was extended to all grades of scrap iron.

On the very next day, Japan signed a treaty of alliance with Germany and Italy. It should be noted that America's firm policy toward Japan as well as Germany had been well established before the consummation of the Axis alliance. What the tripartite pact did was to confirm the image of Germany and Japan as two aggressors joining hands to try to rule the world. Such a combination had been imagined by the Americans for some time, but now it became a reality. United States policy would henceforth have to become truly global.

What about the Soviet Union? In the determination to contain German and Japanese ambitions, did the Roosevelt administration consider Russia's potential usefulness, or did it view the latter as part of the world's totalitarian, aggressive forces? The moral embargo on arms to Russia, imposed in December 1939 in retaliation against the Soviet invasion of Finland, was still in effect, and the public's increasing readiness to come to the aid of Britain did not translate into a new view of the Soviet Union, as a possible check on the growth of German power. At the same time, many, in and out of the government in Washington, expected that sooner or later the German-Soviet pact would reveal its strains and might even break down as the two powers collided in areas that both coveted, such as the Balkans and Bessarabia. Hitler, in fact, had concluded by the late summer of 1940 that the Soviet Union must be crushed if Britain were to be defeated. The reasoning was simple; with Russia under its control, Germany would have that much more power to bear upon Britain – and upon the United States, which might hesitate to intervene to save the latter under such circumstances. Moreover, should the Soviet Union be weakened, Japanese power in Asia would be considerably strengthened, thus immobilizing the United States.[7] Thus persuading himself, Hitler decided, in late December, on a war against the Soviet Union, to be undertaken by May 1941.

In the United States there was some inkling of such a development in German-Soviet relations, but in the absence of definite information the nation could not proceed on the assumption that a German-Soviet break was imminent. Thus in the war plans the military strategists in Washington worked out in the fall and winter of 1940–1, the Soviet position remained a big question mark. They had to devise strategies without assuming a definite role for the Soviet Union. At least one thing was clear, however: the United States must make plans for a global war against Germany, Italy, and Japan, and on the side of Britain and others still retaining their independence. These war plans were quite appropriately called "rainbow plans," because the next war would involve not just one enemy such as Japan ("orange") or Germany ("black") but many nations.

Of the five "rainbow plans" devised, Rainbow 5, or Plan D as it came to be called, postulated a major concentration of U.S. military efforts on the Atlantic, leaving the Pacific in a defensive situation. It was judged that, because the existing military resources of the United States were inadequate for a two-ocean war, the nation must focus on one principal enemy at a time. The Atlantic was the obvious choice, given the imminent danger to Britain's survival. It was felt that the United States would probably not have to become involved in actual fighting in Asia and the Pacific if it maintained a firm stand against Japan. Such firmness, it was believed, should restrain and deter the latter.[8] It was not entirely clear, however, how the United States would respond if Japan were to join forces with the Soviet Union – or, on the contrary, decided to attack the latter.

7 Friedlander, *Prelude,* 114.

8 On the Rainbow plans, see Louis Morton, *Strategy and Command: The First Two Years* (Washington, D.C., 1962).

These were the critical questions, not only for Asia but for Europe, that would confront the United States in 1941.

Japan Attacks the United States

The Soviet question hung like a cloud over international affairs during the first half of 1941. Everything else, it appeared, had become clear: the German-Japanese combination and the threat it posed to Britain and the United States; the joining of forces by these latter nations; America's support of China. The early months of the new year confirmed these trends. One of the most important events was the passage of the Lend-Lease Act in March, authorizing the president to sell, transfer, exchange, or lease arms or other materials to any country whose defense was deemed vital to American security. This blanket authorization, which would have been denounced only several months earlier as a presidential usurpation of power, passed the Senate with a two-thirds majority and the House with an even more one-sided vote of 317 to 71, a clear indication that the public was firmly behind such an emergency measure. Britain was the immediate beneficiary of the new law, but in May China too became a recipient of lend-lease goods.

In the meantime, American and British officials began conversations (the so-called American-British conversations, or ABC) to coordinate their military strategy – obviously a nonneutral act on the part of the United States, but few were any longer quibbling over such technicalities. The staff talks produced a plan known as ABC-1, which was based on Rainbow 5 and confirmed the Atlantic priority, focusing on eliminating the German threat before taking on the Japanese menace. As part of the strategy, U.S. naval units began patrolling areas in the western Atlantic (initially the "neutrality zone" established at an inter-American conference held in Panama in October 1939, but now further extended), protecting British ships, and notifying them of the presence of a German submarine should one be sighted.[9] The U.S. Navy then occupied Greenland, a Danish possession but included within the U.S. patrol

9 Gellman, *Good Neighbor,* 90–1.

area, to build bases and other facilities. In Asia, in the meantime, American, British, and Dutch officials worked out a joint strategy against Japan. They were also in close communication with oil companies in the region to make sure the Japanese would not obtain larger quantities of petroleum, especially in Sumatra, than were contracted for. (Japanese trade missions to Batavia, the capital of the Dutch East Indies, invariably were unsuccessful in this regard.) The so-called ABD powers would continue to coordinate their policies toward Japan and would in effect establish an ABCD coalition with the addition of China.

The missing link was still the Soviet Union. By early 1941, American officials had become convinced that they had enough reliable information of Hitler's impending attack on that country and that the United States should begin to modify its policy toward Moscow to signal that it was ready to move away from the ostracism of the Soviet Union in the aftermath of the Hitler-Stalin pact of 1939. Hence President Roosevelt approved the lifting of the moral embargo against Russia. Before the Americans could measure the effectiveness of such an approach, however, they were confronted by another development, the April 13 signing of a Japanese-Soviet neutrality treaty, in which each party pledged neutrality in case the other became involved in a war against a third power or a combination of powers. In a joint declaration accompanying the treaty, Japan promised to respect the territorial integrity of Outer Mongolia, and the Soviet Union that of Manchukuo. This latter provision was a remarkable departure in Soviet foreign policy as it amounted to the recognition of the Manchurian puppet regime, a real blow to the Chinese (Nationalists and Communists alike). Hitherto, the Soviet Union had sent more aid to China than any other country had, but the United States was fast catching up. Now, although Soviet officials kept assuring the Chinese that nothing had changed as a result of the Japanese treaty, the latter would have to expect a drastic shift in Russian policy. The Chinese had been urging the Russians to intervene in the Japanese war even by using force. Now such a development could not be contemplated, and they would have to rely more and more heavily on American help.

The Soviet Union under Joseph Stalin in effect betrayed China because it was concerned over the possibility of a German invasion. Through various intelligence agents – most notably, Richard Sorge in Tokyo – Stalin knew such an attack was imminent, although he did not really believe in it until it happened, on June 22. A Japanese neutrality pact, in any event, would ensure that Japan would not join Germany in the act. He had reason to be grateful for the pact, which kept Japan from intervening in the German-Soviet war.

Not that the Japanese did not contemplate such action. In a way typical of those days when pacts were made and unmade at the whims of a dictator, the Japanese Army as well as civilians (most notably Foreign Minister Matsuoka Yōsuke, the architect of the Axis alliance) now urged that the nation scrap the just-signed neutrality treaty with the Soviet Union and invade its Siberian provinces in coordination with German military action in the West. Tokyo's supreme headquarters tentatively scheduled such an assault for the first week of September.

Had the plan been carried out, the subsequent course of the war – indeed, the subsequent history of the world – would have taken a very different shape. Would the United States have stood by as Japanese forces attacked Russia's Pacific provinces, or would it have intervened? In the absence of a strong American response, would Germany and Japan have defeated Soviet forces? Would that have brought down the Stalin government? Would the combined forces of Germany, Japan, and defeated Russia then have taken on the United States? Would Britain have succumbed in the meantime? What would have happened to China? Would the Chinese have sought to take advantage of the Japanese-Russian conflict to regain some lost ground, or would the prospect of a German-Japanese dominated world have disheartened them and emboldened pro-Japanese factions?

Merely to list such questions is to underline the momentous significance of the German invasion of the Soviet Union *and* of Japan's ultimate decision not to attack the latter. Instead, Japan ended up attacking the United States, Britain, and the Asian colonies of France and The Netherlands – almost every country in the region except the Soviet Union. Herein lies one of the keys to the understanding of the road to Pearl Harbor.

By coincidence, the signing of the Japanese-Soviet neutrality pact was followed by the initiation of diplomatic talks in Washington (the so-called Washington conversations) between American and Japanese officials. Their origins had little to do with the Soviet Union. Rather, they reflected an interest, on America's part, in postponing, if not avoiding, a showdown with Japan while it was preoccupied with the European situation and, on Japan's part, in reducing American support of China.[10]

These were, of course, incompatible objectives, and there was little chance that the negotiations would get anywhere. But at least the conversations served to highlight the areas of conflict between the two countries, without some resolution of which there could be no return to a normal relationship. Most fundamental remained the China question. The United States wanted Japan to end the Chinese war and respect the country's independence and territorial integrity – in short, to return to the status quo of 1937, if not of 1931. Japan, on the other hand, wanted America to exercise its influence over the Chinese Nationalists so as to bring the latter around to accepting some sort of a settlement with Japan. Such a settlement would have to entail the retention of Japan's privileged status in China, but Japanese officials believed the United States would be willing to see the Asian war wind down while its attention remained focused on Europe.

In that connection, the second point of contention, the Axis pact, arose between the United States and Japan. The former wanted the latter to repudiate the pact explicitly as evidence of its good faith in seeking an accommodation with Washington. So long as Tokyo remained tied to Berlin, no protestation of goodwill would persuade the Americans that the Japanese sincerely desired a peaceful relationship with them. The Japanese government, however, was convinced that the German alliance kept America from intervening more forcefully in Asia, so that to give it up before the United States became more accommodating on the China question would make little sense. Thus the first round of Washington conversations got no-

10 The best account of the Washington conversations is in Robert Butow, *The John Doe Associates* (Stanford, 1974).

where. At least for the United States, however, they served to prevent a two-front collision.

The next and most crucial stage in U.S.-Japanese relations came in the wake of the German invasion of the Soviet Union. President Roosevelt did not have precise knowledge of the Japanese Army's plan to attack Siberia, but he realized there was such a possibility, something he was determined to prevent from becoming a reality. He marshaled all his efforts to deter Japanese aggression in the north, ranging from directly warning the Tokyo government against such action to freezing Japanese assets in America.

This last act, which virtually ended commercial transactions between the United States and Japan, was taken on July 25. Three days later Japanese troops occupied the southern part of French Indochina. This was in continuation of the policy of "southern advance," first undertaken in September 1940 when Japanese forces were sent to northern Indochina, designed to bring China under control by sealing off the border areas. Through intercepted and decoded Japanese messages, Washington knew of Tokyo's plans for occupying southern Indochina, so that the freezing of Japanese assets was in part in retaliation against Japan's "southern advance." Obviously, if Japan were allowed to occupy Indochina with impunity, it might go farther south and endanger the British and Dutch colonies as well, with their rich natural resources. At this time, however, it seems that President Roosevelt was even more concerned with Japanese-Soviet relations, and so the freezing order was intended as a clear signal that Japan risked U.S. retaliation if it should turn north against the Soviet Union.[11] As if to make doubly sure that the Japanese got the message, Washington instituted a de facto embargo of oil shipments to Japan. (There was no formal embargo, but export licenses for selling petroleum to Japan were denied by an administrative committee set up to administer the freezing order, so in effect no U.S. oil reached Japan after August 1.)

This proved to be the point of no return. The United States would stand in the way of Japan's turning north. Japan, alarmed, would cancel its plans to attack Siberia in the fall. Relations between the

11 Waldo Heinrichs, *Threshold of War* (New York, 1988).

United States and Japan consequently would now focus on the oil question. Denied American oil, the Japanese Navy, hitherto dependent on it, would insist on obtaining petroleum from the Dutch East Indies, by force if necessary. But both the Japanese Army and Navy recognized such action would bring about U.S. retaliation, resulting in certain war between the two countries. Thus Japan would have to be prepared for war against the United States if it were to undertake further "southern expansion." To prepare for such a war, it would be all the more necessary to have the oil of Sumatra. Such circular reasoning steadily inclined the Japanese military to the contemplation of an impending war with the United States, and with the European powers over their Asian possessions.

It must be noted, then, that to the extent that the prevention of a Japanese attack on the Soviet Union was a cardinal objective of Roosevelt's diplomacy, it was a clear success. But, of course, he was concerned with more than the fate of Russia. Most fundamental remained the preservation of Britain. In addition to ensuring Soviet survival – the lend-lease program was applied to Russia in November – the president took other steps to hold Germany in check. In early July, U.S. forces landed in Iceland to prevent a possible German invasion and use of the country as a base against the Western Hemisphere. In nearby areas, U.S. warships continued to patrol the seas, and when, two months later, one of them, the destroyer *Greer,* was attacked by a German submarine, President Roosevelt issued a "shoot on sight" order to the naval commanders in the Atlantic; they were to prevent German and Italian ships from entering U.S. "defensive waters," covering most of the region west of 26 degrees of longitude. When two other American destroyers were attacked by German submarines in October, Congress approved the arming of U.S. merchant vessels. Undeclared war had come to the Atlantic.

In the meantime, President Roosevelt and Prime Minister Churchill, who had been frequently communicating with each other since the spring of 1940, met in person for several days in early August on American and British warships off the coast of Newfoundland. They further exchanged strategic information and coordinated their military plans for Europe and Asia. In the latter connection, Roosevelt agreed to transmit to Japan a strongly worded warning against further advances southward. The message was considerably toned down when the president met the Japanese ambassador after his return to the capital, as his aides cautioned him against provoking Japan at that point, but the important thing was that the United States and Britain were fully cooperating in Asia as well as in the Atlantic. More than ever, the world was becoming divided between violators and defenders of order, the latter now being joined by the Soviet Union.

Soviet participation in the U.S.-British de facto alliance became evident when the Soviet Union, as well as fourteen other countries (some represented by governments in exile) endorsed the Atlantic Charter, a document of fundamental principles enunciated at the end of the Roosevelt-Churchill meeting. The charter was a ringing statement of the values for which the democratic leaders asserted their countries were fighting, including self-determination, the Open Door, disarmament, and global economic cooperation. The declaration was World War II's equivalent of the Fourteen Points, and for those familiar with the Wilsonian principles, the Atlantic Charter contained little new. At the same time, in mentioning "freedom from fear and want," improved labor standards, and social security, the declaration broadened the scope of its appeal to all people suffering from poverty, exploitation, and insecurity. The document made clear that the principles enumerated would apply to all countries, whether victors or vanquished, after the war, and thus enunciated a vision of postwar world order in which even Germans, Italians, and Japanese could anticipate living well – once their totalitarian, aggressive policies had been crushed.

Thus the months preceding Japan's attack on Pearl Harbor revealed the world divided not only militarily but economically and ideologically as well. On one side were the Axis partners bent on establishing a new world order through conquest and based on revisionist principles. They visualized a globe divided into several regional blocs, each a self-contained economic unit. On the other side stood a coalition of anti-Axis nations, already numbering some seventeen, which struggled to prevent the Axis domination of the world. The former espoused particularism, totalitarianism, and antidemocratic thought, the latter universalism, internationalism, and democratic thought.

The crisis in Asia and the Pacific was part of the global developments, with Japan seeking to establish an Asian regional bloc under its control, aimed at expelling Western power from the region, while the United States and its de facto allies stood in its way in order to keep Asia open to Western interests and to uphold the rights of China and the colonial empires. There could be no compromise between two such opposing forces unless one were willing to retreat, and that could only be Japan.

The United States stepped up its pressures on Japan to prod it to retreat. General Douglas MacArthur was named commander in chief of U.S. forces in Asia, including Filipino soldiers. Fighter aircraft were sent to China and the Philippines to deter Japan. And President Roosevelt refused to meet with the Japanese prime minister when the latter sought such a conference in a last-minute attempt to avoid war, unless Japan agreed beforehand to restore sovereignty to China. Most important, when negotiations were resumed in Washington, Secretary of State Hull presented the Japanese representatives a statement (the "Hull note" of November 26) reiterating the basic principles for which the United States stood and which Japan must accept if it wanted peace:

1. The principle of inviolability of territorial integrity and sovereignty of each and all nations
2. The principle of noninterference in the internal affairs of other countries
3. The principle of equality, including equality of commercial opportunity and treatment
4. The principle of reliance upon international cooperation and conciliation for the prevention and pacific settlement of controversies and for improvement of international conditions by peaceful methods and processes

These principles summed up traditional American objectives. The Japanese could have accepted them and avoided war, but that would have called for a bold political leadership, which did not exist. Instead, they regarded the Hull note as tantamount to an ultimatum, and made the fatal decision to go to war. The Pearl Harbor attack came eleven days later. Simultaneously, Japanese forces bombed, invaded, and otherwise engaged in military action throughout Asia. The European war and the Asian war had become joined, with the United States to become the most deeply involved in both theaters.

12. The Global Conflict

The Diplomacy of War

World War II (1939–45) was far more global than World War I. Few areas of the world, if any, were untouched by the conflagration that had begun in Europe, spread to Russia and the Middle East, merged with the Asian war, and even involved Latin America. The entire world became divided into the allies (officially termed the United Nations) and the Axis, with a few nations (e.g., Spain, Sweden, and Switzerland) maintaining neutrality.

Only the United States, however, could be said to be involved in all theaters of the war, in the Atlantic as well as the Pacific, in North Africa as well as Southeast Asia, and in the Middle East as well as South America. In this sense the war was the culminating point in the story of the steady globalization of the United States; having established its leadership position during World War I, it now exercised its role militarily, economically, and ideologically so forcefully that the world after World War II could truly be said to have been a product of American power and influence.

This is not the place to recount in detail the course of the war. Suffice it to say that in terms of military developments there were three stages in the history of World War II as far as the United States was concerned: from December 1941 to January 1943; from January 1943 to August 1944; and from then on to the end of the Pacific war in August 1945. The first three sections in this chapter briefly describe the course of the war in these three stages and point to some key themes in U.S. strategy and foreign policy as the nation fought the war and at the same time prepared for the peace.

In the immediate aftermath of Japan's attack on Pearl Harbor, which had brought the United States into the war, the most important development was the forging of a wartime alliance, especially the strategy of coalition warfare on the part of the United States and Great Britain. Although the two powers had established a de facto alliance, only the latter had been actually engaged in war. Now, however, not only had Japan attacked both (as well as the Dutch East Indies), but Germany also declared war against the United States. (This action came on December 11, four days after Pearl Harbor. During the interval there was much uncertainty in Washington whether the nation should go to war against Germany as well as Japan. Had Adolf Hitler decided not to join Japan in the war, President Franklin D. Roosevelt would have been placed in a predicament, given the American people's outrage at Japan's surprise attack and determination to punish the latter. Hitler evidently reasoned that with Japan winning spectacular initial victories in the Pacific, little would be lost in honoring the Axis pact and going to war against America; the latter would be preoccupied with the Pacific war and in the meantime the German Navy would legitimately harass U.S. ships in the Atlantic. Such a decision, of course, proved as great a blunder for Hitler as his invasion of the Soviet Union six months earlier.)

Germany's entry into the U.S.-Japanese conflict was immediately followed by a visit of Prime Minister Winston Churchill to Washington, which resulted in the establishment of the Combined Chiefs of Staff. The CSS, situated in the American capital, was the symbol of the wartime alliance between the two English-speaking peoples. Key strategic decisions were coordinated there, although the ultimate authority lay with Roosevelt and Churchill, who met on numerous other occasions during the war and regularly exchanged cables. An obvious consequence of this was that the United States deferred to Great Britain on matters of strategy much more than to other allies such as China or the Soviet Union.

These nations, too, had now become America's allies, although the Soviet Union was not technically involved in the Pacific war (due to the neutrality treaty with Japan which had been signed in April 1941). The United States continued to send lend-lease shipments to them and exchanged strategic information with their leaders. But there was nothing like the close coordination with Britain.

One case in point at the earlier stages of the war was the decision to put off the establishment of a second front in Europe, an assault on German forces in Western Europe to relieve pressures on the eastern (Soviet) front. Most American military leaders, including General George C. Marshall, chairman of the Joint Chiefs of Staff, favored an early execution of the second-front strategy, involving a massive buildup of expeditionary forces in England and then an invasion of the northwestern French coast. The British, on the other hand, believed the allies would not be ready to undertake such a strategy for some time to come, and in the meantime suggested a North African campaign, to invade the French colonies of Morocco, Algeria, and Tunisia which remained under the authority of the "Vichy French" – those in France and overseas who collaborated with the Germans. To attack these areas would be to violate their nominally neutral status (because France had left the war), but Churchill persuaded Roosevelt that this strategy would serve to bring the North African coast to allied control, which in turn would enable the allies to prepare for an assault on Sicily and Italy. Although Marshall and others protested that such a strategy was a waste of resources and that, if the cross-Channel invasion were not to take place, U.S. forces should focus on the Pacific theater of the war, in the end they went along with the president's decision. The African campaign was successfully carried out in the last months of 1942.

This did not mean that the Pacific was neglected. Actually, next to driving out the Germans from Africa, launching a counterattack against Japanese forces became a principal U.S. objective in the early part of the war. Indeed, here the United States had virtual autonomy since neither Britain nor the Soviet Union interfered with American strategy or operations in the Pacific. Although the bulk of the U.S. fleet had been destroyed at Pearl Harbor, that did not prevent Americans from engaging in major battles in the southwestern Pacific. One objective was to prevent Japanese forces from advancing toward Australia, and another to weaken as much Japanese naval power as possible so as to deny the enemy the luxury of establishing an enlarged Asian-Pacific empire. In the meantime, in the central Pacific, effective use was made of the American aircraft carriers that had escaped the Pearl Harbor disaster (they had fortuitously been out of the naval base). In a crucial battle near the island of Midway in

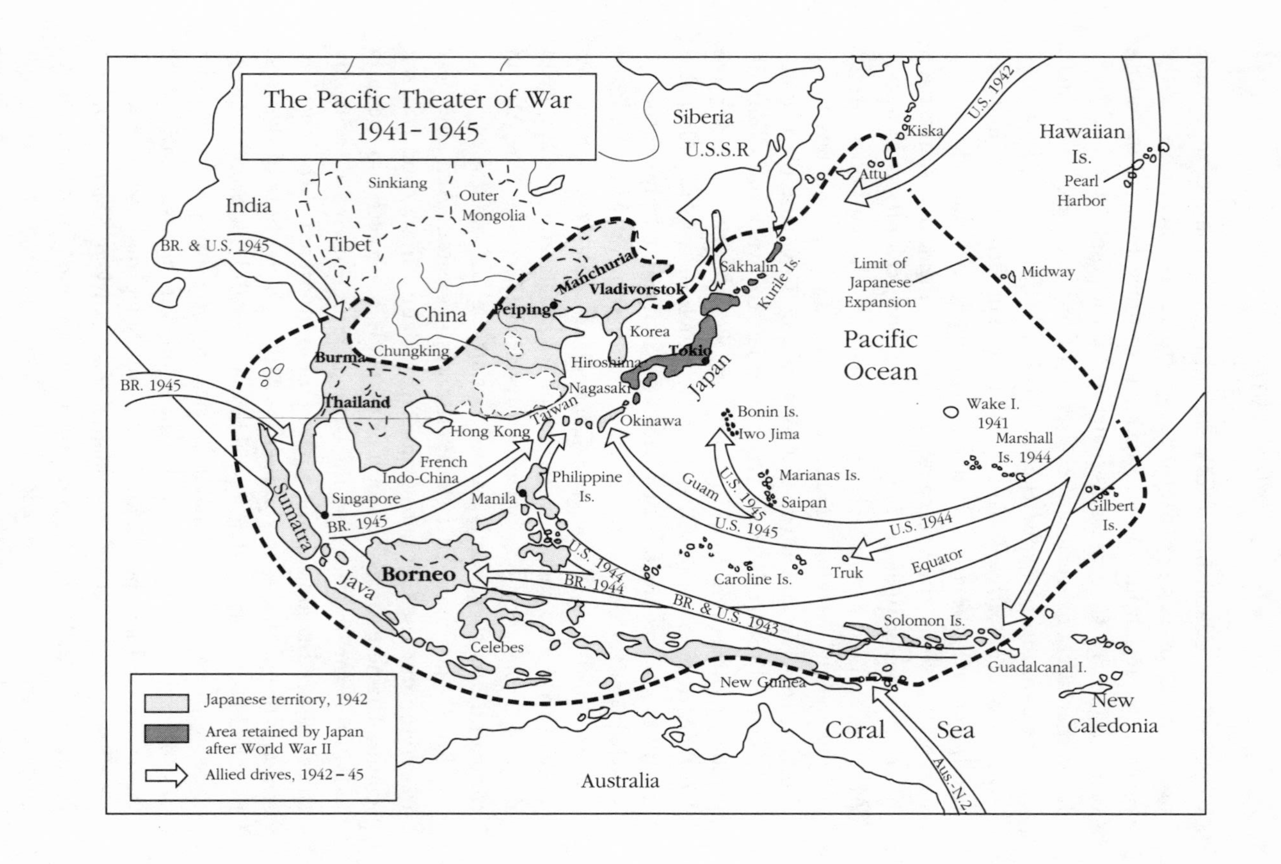

The Pacific Theater of War
1941–1945
Siberia
U.S.S.R
India
Sinkiang
Outer
Mongolia
Tibet
China
Chungking
Burma
Thailand
Manchuria
Vladivostok
Peiping
Korea
Hiroshima
Nagasaki
Tokio
Japan
Sakhalin
Kurile Is.
Kiska
Attu
U.S. 1942
Hawaiian
Is.
Pearl
Harbor
Midway
Limit of
Japanese
Expansion
Pacific
Ocean
Wake I.
1941
Marshall
Is. 1944
Gilbert
Is.
Bonin Is.
Iwo Jima
Marianas Is.
Saipan
Guam
U.S. 1945
U.S. 1945
U.S. 1944
Truk
Equator
Caroline Is.
Okinawa
Taiwan
Hong Kong
French
Indo-China
Philippine
Is.
Manila
Singapore
BR. 1945
BR. 1945
BR. & U.S. 1945
Sumatra
Java
Borneo
U.S. 1944
BR. 1944
BR. & U.S. 1943
Celebes
Solomon Is.
Guadalcanal I.
New Guinea
New
Caledonia
Coral
Sea
Aus.-N.Z.
Australia
Japanese territory, 1942
Area retained by Japan
after World War II
Allied drives, 1942–45

June 1942, U.S. aircraft and ships inflicted heavy losses on an advancing Japanese naval force intent on capturing the island on the way to an invasion of the Hawaiian Islands. This proved to be a turning point in the Pacific war, barely six months after Pearl Harbor.

There was less U.S. involvement elsewhere, but it was no less significant. On the continent of Asia, a China-Burma-India (CBI) theater was proclaimed, an arena of three-nation cooperation among Americans, British, and Chinese. This joint venture made the war there a more complicated proposition than the Pacific campaign, but President Roosevelt sought to ensure its smooth operation by sending General Joseph Stilwell to Chungking to command America's CBI forces and to administer lend-lease disbursement in China, as well as serving as chief of staff to Chiang Kai-shek. This task proved difficult, as Stilwell had to contend with the different objectives and priorities of the allies; the Chinese leadership, already convinced that America's entry into the war ensured China's eventual victory over Japan, became as interested in domestic political affairs (where Nationalists and Communists had never been able to establish a unified government) as in fighting the war. The British, for their part, focused on the defense of India but had trouble obtaining the wholehearted cooperation of nationalist leaders such as Mohandas Gandhi who insisted on a promise of independence in return for support of the war. There was little that the combined CBI forces could do at this time except passively resisting Japanese offensives in Malaya and Burma.[1]

In the Western Hemisphere, Pearl Harbor was followed by another inter-American conference, this time held in Rio de Janeiro in January 1942, where the American republics (with the exception of Argentina) agreed to break diplomatic ties with the Axis powers. Mexico and Brazil soon declared war against them and were eventually to send some of their men to battle scenes (a Mexican air squadron to the Philippines, Brazilian troops to Italy). In March, an inter-American defense board was set up in Washington to devise

1 On the Stilwell mission, see Barbara Tuchman, *Stilwell and the American Experience in China* (New York, 1971).

joint strategy. Although no actual fighting took place in the hemisphere, initially there was anxiety over the activities of German submarines in the western Atlantic. Of greater relevance at this time, however, was the "bulge" of Brazil, which lay fewer than two thousand miles from the western edge of North Africa, where an allied invasion was to take place. In order to defend the bulge and also to prepare for the African campaign, the U.S. Army undertook the construction of air bases in the area. During the war, forty such airfields were to be constructed in various parts of Latin America, although after 1943 serious danger to the continent was judged to have diminished so that the need for hemispheric defense would lose its urgency. (Lend-lease shipments to Latin America continued, but they would comprise only 1.1 percent of total military aid offered by the United States.)[2]

United States forces were not directly involved in the fiercest fighting of the war at that time, that in the eastern front, where the summer (1942) offensive by German forces brought them to Stalingrad. Leningrad had been besieged for several months, and Moscow lay only a hundred miles from the German front line. America's role here was to step up the shipment of lend-lease goods. Special offices were established in Washington and Moscow to expedite the transaction, and the United States also supported the British and Soviet military occupation of Iran in view of the latter's crucial importance as a supply route to the Soviet Union. The Middle Eastern Supply Centre was as important a symbol of American commitment to defeat the Axis as more overt military acts.

Even during this first phase of the war, however, military strategy was only part of the picture. From the beginning, the United States saw its role as much more than strategic and, increasingly, it found itself involved in complicated political questions as a result of its wartime alliance. This could not have been otherwise, given the already extensive involvement of American power and resources throughout the world, and given the even greater power the nation was expected to command as the war progressed.

For one thing, the wartime military occupation of any territory

2 Irwin F. Gellman, *Good Neighbor Diplomacy* (Baltimore, 1979), 136–7.

would create problems of governance: how to deal with the leaders and populace of the occupied areas, how to coordinate policies with other occupying powers in case the United States was not the sole occupier, and how to balance day-to-day administrative affairs with the question of the future status of the land. Thus the first major territory that U.S. forces occupied in 1942–3, North Africa, gave a foretaste of what had to be expected throughout the duration of, and even beyond, the war. The politics of occupied North Africa was particularly vexing in view of the presence of Vichy and Free French factions, British forces, and many neutral nationals, not to mention the indigenous population, some of whom aspired to a measure of autonomy. President Roosevelt tried to be pragmatic, postponing larger political issues, but even that entailed working with the Vichy French authorities, such as Admiral J.-F. Darlan, after the allied forces landed in Morocco and Algeria. But the British had recognized a Free French government in exile in London under General Charles de Gaulle, who insisted on being established as the power in liberated North Africa. In the end, an arrangement was worked out with the two French factions sharing power, but it was never a satisfactory solution.[3]

In the meantime, the wishes of the Moroccans, Algerians, and Tunisians could not be ignored, for their cooperation would be crucial for the war effort, especially as German propaganda was trying to turn them against the allies. This was part of the larger question: In view of the lofty proclamation (the Atlantic Charter) of August 1941, should the United States and its allies not clarify their position on the future status of the colonial and dependent areas of the world? Should the United States push colonial self-determination as one of its war aims? Under Secretary of State Sumner Welles, for instance, was echoing a main theme in American public opinion when he declared in May 1942 that "our victory must bring in its train the liberation of all peoples."[4]

President Roosevelt sought to resist such pressures as long as possible so as to avoid making hasty commitments or giving rise to

3 See Arthur L. Funk, *The Politics of TORCH* (Lawrence, Kans., 1974).

4 W. Roger Louis, *Imperialism at Bay* (New York, 1978), 155.

extravagant hopes when he had to concentrate on the war effort. But he could not ignore public discussions of war aims, nor forget that the Atlantic Charter had clearly spelled out visions of the peace that would follow the defeat of the enemy. And in fact there is sufficient evidence to indicate that he was already giving serious thought to the shape of the world after victory. In May 1942, for instance, when Soviet Foreign Minister Vyacheslav Molotov visited him in Washington, Roosevelt suggested that after the war four powers – the United States, the Soviet Union, Britain, and China – might function as "policemen" in ensuring global security. If the "four big policemen" could cooperate in policing the world, other, lesser nations would not have to maintain large armed forces to prepare against the resurgence of German or Japanese power. The president seems also to have hoped that if such big-power cooperation could be upheld, neither the Soviet Union nor Britain would have to maintain colonies or spheres of influence. In fact, he reasoned that the four big powers could serve as "trustees" for the colonial and dependent peoples while they prepared themselves for eventual freedom.[5]

These were rather vague ideas without precise definition, but at least they indicated that Roosevelt's principal concern was with preserving the wartime alliance so as to make it the linchpin of the postwar world order. Such a conception was less Wilsonian than it was couched in the framework of Theodore Roosevelt's power politics, and it revealed Franklin D. Roosevelt's conviction that power was the basic reality in international relations. Still, power had to be exercised in a responsible manner, and for him it made sense to call on the world's four greatest military powers in the aftermath of the Axis defeat to continue their cooperation on behalf of the whole world. While he did not want to make any specific commitment, it is clear that, like Wilson, he took it for granted that the United States would remain a principal participant in the postwar world order.

If the president was too preoccupied with military and strategic problems to give much thought to the specific shape of the world after victory, others had more time to devote to postwar planning.

5 Akira Iriye, *Power and Culture* (Cambridge, Mass., 1981), 53–4.

Particularly notable were the efforts of the State Department, which began organizing study groups and advisory committees on future world issues almost as soon as war came. They brought together not only department officials but also congressmen, journalists, scholars, military officers, and others for broad-ranging discussions of postwar issues, including the occupation of enemy countries, territorial readjustments, international security, and the reestablishment of commercial links. Although in this period these committees' deliberations did not go much beyond exchanging information and viewpoints, certain ideas were already emerging, ideas that would constitute part of official U.S. policy once Washington began formulating specific guidelines toward the end of the war.[6]

These ideas were clearly Wilsonian. Most members participating in the study groups agreed that the restoration of the principle of international cooperation, rather than old-fashioned balance of power, should be the principal framework for maintenance of order and security after the Axis had been defeated. The enemy countries' totalitarianism and militarism must be eradicated to ensure a stable peace, but their citizens should be treated leniently. The assumption here was that, despite totalitarian control in Germany and Japan, there were democratic forces in those countries that had been temporarily suppressed but could be encouraged to reemerge once the national leaders had been crushed. These countries should be reintegrated into a new international order, which would be quite different from the 1930s but not altogether a radical departure from what had existed before the Depression. For instance, the committees agreed that all postwar territorial changes should be in accordance with the wishes of the peoples involved and that there should be no sphere of influence politically or economically.

One sees here a Wilsonian agenda not only because these principles had been articulated by the United States during World War I but also because it was generally believed that the evils of the 1930s were an aberration and that the world of the 1920s, which had reflected some of the Wilsonian principles, had been fundamentally

6 See ibid., chaps. 2 and 3, for a discussion of wartime planning for the treatment of Japan.

sound. State Department meetings, in other words, were visualizing a return to the pattern of international affairs that had existed before the rise of totalitarianism and aggressive militarism. Of course, it was well recognized that something had to be done to prevent a repetition of the same history, the progression from the hopeful beginnings of the first post–World War I decade to the horrors of the second. The answer, many Americans believed, lay in two elements: America's active participation in international politics, and the institution of some built-in mechanisms to guard against excessive economic nationalism. Both these had been lacking in the 1920s. If the new peace were to be more successful, therefore, it would be necessary to promote these additional policies. Both, of course, assumed continued U.S. involvement in world affairs. Though more an expression of aspirations than a specific program, such ideas were to become more and more important as the war entered its second phase.

The New Internationalism

If there ever was a point during World War II when "the tide turned," as the cliché goes, it was January 1943, when Soviet forces relieved the siege of Leningrad and forced the Germans to give up Stalingrad. The Soviet counteroffensive was followed elsewhere by the allied invasion of Sicily and Italy (July 1943) and attacks on Japanese-occupied central-Pacific islands, notably the Gilbert Islands (November). The climax in Europe came in June 1944, when U.S. and British forces entered Rome and also landed on France's Normandy coast. That landing opened the long-promised second front and culminated in the liberation of Paris in August. At about the same time, U.S. troops invaded the Marianas, turning some of them (in particular, Saipan and Tinian) into air bases from which to bomb the Japanese homeland.

With the turning of the tide, this second period saw as much interallied goodwill and cooperation as there was ever going to be during the war. Not surprisingly, the attention of the allied powers began shifting to postwar issues. By coincidence, January 1943 saw a meeting of Roosevelt and Churchill at Casablanca. The Casablanca Conference became famous because at its conclusion the two leaders announced the "unconditional surrender" formula, that is, the policy of not discussing peace terms or postwar questions until after the enemy surrendered. The policy was in reaction against the armistice making of 1918, when, as mentioned earlier, the Germans approached President Wilson to obtain a peace on the basis of the Fourteen Points. This time, Roosevelt was determined never to let the enemy dictate such conditions.

The matter, however, was never that simple. Actually, although the allies might insist on continuing the war until the enemy surrendered, that did not mean they would not start thinking seriously about the shape of the peace. This second period of the war was significant precisely because the United States, Britain, the Soviet Union, and China conferred with one another on postwar problems.

The very fact that Roosevelt and Churchill traveled all the way to Casablanca to meet belied their professed lack of interest in considering postwar issues, for they went there in part to settle the question of which French faction should be supported in North Africa. The answer: both the Vichy and the Free French groups, the former represented by Henri Giraud and the latter by Charles de Gaulle. The marriage of convenience did not work, and by the time of the liberation of Paris, de Gaulle would emerge as the undisputed voice of Free France. Although Roosevelt did not appreciate what he took to be de Gaulle's sense of self-importance, the fact that the two met in Casablanca had political significance and indicated how difficult it was to avoid making decisions that had implications for the shape of the postwar world.

Italy was specifically excepted from the "unconditional surrender" formula, and in the fall of 1943 the allies were willing to deal with a successor government to Benito Mussolini's rule after the dictator fled Rome and half of the country had been liberated. But who should lead the successor government was a troublesome question, and there was no easy solution at this time. The allies, however, were willing to provide economic aid to occupied Italy and also to set up a control commission for setting occupation policies.[7]

Regarding the treatment of the two principal enemies, too, this

7 On the treatment of Italy after 1943, see Norman Kogan, *Italy and the Allies* (Cambridge, Mass., 1956).

period saw substantial developments. Starting in the spring of 1943, Washington and London began exchanging ideas about the occupation of Germany, and soon there emerged agreement on two points. First, eastern Germany (Prussia) should be separated from the rest of the country and possibly incorporated into Poland; two, Germany should be divided into three zones of occupation, to be administered by the United States, Britain, and the Soviet Union.

These two policies were endorsed by Roosevelt, Churchill, and Joseph Stalin when they met together for the first time in Teheran at the end of 1943 and the beginning of 1944. That the "big three" met to discuss these and other matters – for instance, the removal of foreign troops from Iran after the war – showed that they were quite willing to consider postwar issues. As far as they were concerned, even before the opening of the second front in Europe, the time had come to start thinking about the shape of the postwar world.

Postwar Europe was in fact already taking shape. The Soviet Union would retain the Baltic states and the eastern half of Poland, which it had absorbed during 1939–40. Although nothing specific was said about these matters at Teheran, the discussions on Germany implied the setting up of new boundaries between defeated Germany and Poland, and therefore between Poland and the Soviet Union. As for the Baltic states, neither Roosevelt nor Churchill was willing to challenge Stalin on the issue when they had been postponing the opening of the second front time and again. These appeared to be a small price to pay for obtaining continued cooperation of the Soviet Union in the war and in postwar arrangements. Big-three cooperation in Europe was to be the basic principle.

President Roosevelt, as noted earlier, had already visualized adding China to the three, in effect creating the framework of big-four cooperation after the war. In Asia, as in Europe, such cooperation would be founded upon acceptable territorial adjustments. The Soviet Union, for one, would regain the Kurile Islands and Southern Sakhalin, ceded to Japan in 1875 and 1905, respectively. Britain would regain its empire in Asia, although both Roosevelt and the State Department pushed for some assurances about future self-determination. Little was forthcoming at this time, however.

Neither was the United States above contemplating its own territorial adjustments. The U.S. Navy, for one thing, was keen on retaining some of the Pacific islands after the war to safeguard against resurgent Japanese military power. Roosevelt supported the idea and sent a naval mission to the Pacific in 1943 to investigate possibilities. At the same time, he preferred some kind of trusteeship to outright possession of the islands in question. The form of the trusteeship would depend on the postwar world organization through which it would be carried out, but there was no doubt that the United States would be the sole trustee over the islands.[8]

But the key to postwar Asia, as distinct from the Pacific Ocean, was to be the inclusion of China in any scheme. The emergence of China as a great power was unmistakably signaled when its leader, Chiang Kai-shek, was invited to meet Roosevelt and Churchill in Cairo at the end of the year to confer on the Asian war and postwar settlements. The Cairo gathering took place while Roosevelt, Churchill, and Stalin were meeting in Teheran, but the two affairs were kept separate as Stalin did not want to attend a conference to discuss the Japanese war toward which the Soviet Union was maintaining neutrality. (This did not prevent him from promising that the nation would enter the war against Japan after Germany had been defeated.) In any event, at Cairo it was agreed that China should regain all territory Japan had "stolen" from it since the 1890s, in particular Taiwan and Manchuria. Korea, another Japanese colony, would be given independence "in due course." The idea was that until the Koreans were ready for independence, the country might be placed under a trusteeship arrangement, the trustees likely being the United States, the Soviet Union, and China. This was another boost to China's standing in international affairs.

Earlier in 1943, the United States had acted to remove two sources of inequities about which the Chinese had complained for decades, first by terminating extraterritorial privileges in China and second by ending the exclusion of Chinese immigrants from America. All these were gratifying developments from the Chinese point of view. For the United States they were an expression of the policy to look to China as the main Asian partner after Japan's defeat. With

8 The best study of the trusteeship arrangement is Louis, *Imperialism at Bay.*

American naval power predominant in the Pacific, and with China the new power on the continent, the future of the region could be expected to be much stabler than heretofore. (At a foreign ministers' conference, meeting in Moscow in October, the representatives of the United States, Britain, and the Soviet Union confirmed that China would play a role as one of the four principal powers after the war.)

Japan, as could be seen in such decisions, was to be reduced to the ranks of a minor power, back where it had been before the 1890s. Neither at this time nor later, however, was there much thought given to dividing Japan into zones of occupation. State Department officials persisted in the idea that the United States would control the occupation of defeated Japan and, therefore, that it would be unnecessary to establish separate zones of occupation by other powers, as was being contemplated for Germany. This was to have far-reaching consequences, as was the conviction on the part of American officials that it should be possible to obtain the cooperation of "friendly" Japanese – prewar liberals, businessmen, and others who had been active in the 1920s and developed close contacts with Americans – in carrying out occupation policies. While there was clearly an asymmetry between the emerging notion of U.S.-Chinese partnership and the more or less benevolent U.S. occupation of Japan after the latter's defeat, all these attested to the existence of serious planning for postwar international affairs.

Most of these were power-political arrangements. The allies were contemplating a postwar world in which the Axis powers would be kept weak and the big four would replace them as definers of international order. The United States would emerge as the major power in the Pacific and in the Western Hemisphere (where there was much interest in maintaining hemispheric strategic coordination into the postwar period). It should also be noted in this connection that the United States was already, by 1943–4, visualizing itself as a nuclear power, equipped with atomic weapons, which were being developed in great secrecy in Los Alamos, New Mexico. The idea of using atomic energy (created either by fission or fusion of uranium atoms) to make an unprecedentedly explosive and destructive bomb had existed for several years, and both sides in the war were avidly trying to manufacture such bombs. Once they were developed, there was little doubt that they would be used. But there was the equally important question of their future use, when the enemy had been defeated, with or without the new weapon. At a meeting they held in Quebec in August 1943, Roosevelt and Churchill discussed the question and signed a secret protocol to the effect that the two nations would continue to share atomic secrets and consult with one another regarding their use in the future. Neither the Soviet Union nor any other power would be brought into their confidence. Because the United States would clearly be the senior of the two atomic partners, this memorandum – and the ideas there expressed were reiterated by the two leaders at the second Quebec conference of August 1944 – suggests that in addition to the various territorial arrangements being discussed with the allies, there was a presupposition of the United States emerging as the sole superpower out of the victory, at least insofar as military force was concerned.[9]

What about the other aspects of international relations, economic and cultural? The Wilsonian impulse evinced by the State Department's postwar planning committees never abated, and during 1943–4 they were joined by an increasing number of American individuals and groups calling for a new internationalism – an internationalism that would be Wilsonian in inspiration but would be "new" in the recognition of the need to work closely with other military powers, such as China and the Soviet Union, as well as Great Britain. Their hope was that these nations would share the principles and values embodied in the Atlantic Charter and cooperate together in implementing them after the war. More specifically, by 1943 there was a clear public consensus in the United States in support of the nation's participation in a new world organization. Even erstwhile isolationists, notably Senator Arthur Vandenberg of Michigan, came out in favor of such a step, and the Republican party issued a policy statement endorsing U.S. membership in a postwar international organization. Such membership, however, would mean little unless it were supported by economic underpinnings. This was the task the Bretton Woods Conference undertook. In the mean-

9 See Martin Sherwin, *A World Destroyed* (New York, 1975).

time, the United Nations established the Relief and Rehabilitation Administration (UNRRA) to distribute food and supplies to war-devastated areas as they were liberated by the allies.

In the cultural realm, it was well recognized that for the duration of the war all belligerents – United Nations and Axis powers alike – would have to concentrate on propaganda work, aimed both at the home front and at enemy countries. Cultural internationalism was a luxury, if it was not irrelevant to the war effort. Nevertheless, it is worth noting that earlier activities sponsored by the League of Nations in promoting cross-cultural cooperation were never forgotten; those who had taken part in them, as well as many others who shared their views, sought to keep alive the legacy, and they were determined to resurrect it once the war came to an end. This can be seen, for instance, in the series of meetings of allied ministers of education that began to take place in London as early as 1942. Although the initial aim of the meetings was to help schoolchildren suffering from wartime destruction and deprivation, in time the delegates became equally interested in preparing for a postwar agenda. Americans began participating in these meetings in 1943, and in April 1944 a high-level delegation, including Congressman J. William Fulbright and Librarian of Congress Archibald MacLeish, was sent to London to join colleagues from elsewhere in discussing the establishment of a successor to the League's intellectual cooperation committee. There was a basic continuity from these beginnings to the postwar founding of UNESCO.[10]

Toward a Postwar World

Whether the hopeful beginnings of the new internationalism could develop into a solid structure of postwar world affairs depended on what the allies would do, individually and collectively, with the areas they were fast recovering and occupying from the summer of 1944 onward. With the liberation of France and the Low Countries in the west, and the Soviet counteroffensive and occupation of Po-

10 My account of the founding of UNESCO is based on documents in the FO 394 series, Foreign Office Archives, Public Record Office, London.

land, Bulgaria, Rumania, Yugoslavia, and then eventually eastern Germany, the wartime alliance was clearly reaching its climactic successes. In the Pacific, too, the same months witnessed the beginning of the bombing of Japan proper as well as the invasion of the Philippines, leading to their reconquest by U.S. forces. The big question now was the impact of such successes, which would surely bring the war to an end in the near future, upon the alliance. Would victory perpetuate the alliance, or would the allies go their separate ways once the war ended? How could they perpetuate their wartime cooperation and form a solid framework for postwar international order?

These questions had been raised before, but now they gained great urgency as it appeared that Germany would soon capitulate, to be followed by Japan's defeat a year or so later. The Soviet Union appeared eager to establish its control over much of the occupied territory in the Balkans and Eastern Europe, and Prime Minister Churchill became so alarmed over these developments that he offered to recognize Soviet spheres of influence in some of these countries in return for Stalin's agreement to let the British keep their spheres. Roosevelt would not accept such explicit arrangements, but he was not averse to agreeing to de facto spheres of influence so long as this could be made a basis for continued big-power cooperation.

The idea of big-power cooperation, however, underwent subtle changes after mid-1944 because two of the big four, Britain and China, became weaker relative to the other two. Officials in and out of Britain readily admitted that the nation was bankrupt, and that its economic difficulties and financial stringencies would make problematic whether it could continue to play the role of a world power–unless the United States helped out. The latter did not want Britain weakened, and Roosevelt, as noted, made sure that the American-British monopoly of atomic weapons technology would be retained. The idea was that Britain could still be important as a balancer of Soviet power. Nevertheless, at this time there was no commitment to offer postwar economic assistance to Britain.

China, too, began to shed some of its power and prestige in the fall of 1944. This was in part a reflection of the Pacific strategy of the United States, whose successful "island-hopping" campaign was making the CBI theater of the war less crucial for the defeat of Japan. President Roosevelt did want to use Chinese and U.S. forces on the Asian continent to tie Japanese troops down, to prevent their return to Japan to defend the home islands. But he got into trouble with Chiang Kai-shek for suggesting that General Stilwell be placed in command of all forces in China, including Communist troops. The request infuriated Chiang, who was determined to prevent a Communist takeover of power after the war. With Japan's defeat a matter of time, factions in China were positioning themselves for the postwar struggle, and Chiang believed that accepting Roosevelt's suggestion was tantamount to committing suicide. So Chiang remained adamant, Stilwell was recalled, and U.S.-Chinese relations visibly cooled.

Such a situation left the United States and the Soviet Union as possibly the only great military powers after the war, although the former would undoubtedly be the stronger of the two, not least because it was expected to possess (and monopolize for the foreseeable future) atomic weapons. The shape of the postwar world, in any event, would hinge on whether the two would be able to continue to work together after the Axis defeat. The question was more than military in nature, for by then American officials were getting ready to endorse specific plans for the postwar international community that would be defined as much economically and culturally as geopolitically – and as much through international cooperation as through America's unilateral initiatives.

This became clear at two important international conferences of 1944, at Bretton Woods (July) and Dumbarton Oaks (October). The former was an occasion for reestablishing international economic order after it had been destroyed by the Depression and by the autarkic policies of the powers. The conferees, including John Maynard Keynes, the famous British economist, agreed that the kind of chaotic economic nationalism that had been the rule since the 1930s must be replaced by some arrangement for international cooperation. But they also knew that merely to return to the situation existing before 1929 would not be enough; international economic transactions of the 1920s, as seen earlier, had been based on a gold exchange system, which worked well so long as trade and investments across national boundaries flowed without interruption, and so long as governments were willing to control spending in order to bolster the values of their currencies. The Depression had indicated how fragile the whole structure was. What was now needed, it was thought, was an institutional mechanism with which stable rates of exchange among different currencies could be preserved, without, however, each country's having to adopt a fiscally conservative policy to maintain the value of its own currency. (It was widely accepted that such a policy had kept consumption down and unemployment high.) This task, the forty-four countries represented at Bretton Woods agreed, could be accomplished by establishing an international monetary fund (IMF) that would provide temporary relief to countries experiencing trade and exchange difficulties so that they would not have to resort to protectionism or devaluation – or to domestic retrenchment policies that would give rise to unemployment. The IMF, with its initial capital of $8,800 million, would be a new experiment; nothing like that had ever existed in world economic affairs, and it marked a new era of international cooperation that would go much beyond such traditional areas as security and arms control.

The Bretton Woods Conference also proposed the establishment of an international bank for reconstruction and development, or the World Bank as it would come to be known. This, too, was something novel; the idea was to pool the richer countries' resources – $10 billion was initially envisaged – so as to help less developed and dependent countries undertake economic transformation. Although neither the IMF nor the World Bank was yet a reality, it was clear that once they were established, the United States would be called upon to provide the bulk of the initial capital for both. Here clearly was a lesson of the Depression well learned. The nation would not again revert to economic nationalism but would on the contrary take the lead in the spirit of economic internationalism.

In the meantime, at Dumbarton Oaks, delegates from the United States, the Soviet Union, Britain, and China established a basis for a postwar international organization. The idea itself was not new, but now they were ready to start drafting the specifics of such an organization, which was to be called the United Nations, an indication that they were determined to continue their wartime cooperation into the postwar period. The delegates also knew that the United Nations would have to be more effective than the League of Nations. Reflecting Roosevelt's long-standing conception of big-power cooperation, with which the other three governments were in agreement, the conference proposed the setting up of a security council, with the big four as the permanent members. They would cooperate with one another and in effect seek to police the world. The Soviet Union, however, insisted on complete unanimity among the four before the security council took any action. The United States was opposed to giving blanket veto power to any permanent member, and the conferees were unable to resolve the difference at this time. Still, Dumbarton Oaks marked the point when a postwar world organization took definite shape.

The fact that the Soviet Union participated in both these important conferences showed its interest in remaining part of a cooperative international arrangement after the war, even as it was fast claiming its unilateral control over the areas its troops occupied. Whether these two aspects of Soviet policy – adherence to some framework of cooperative action and the establishment of its own spheres of influence – were compatible was not clear; many felt that they were not and that, so long as the Soviet Union insisted on unilateral action, it would have to be viewed as a serious obstacle in the way of establishing postwar order. Some believed power-level arrangements were the only framework in which the big powers could still work together. Others, including President Roosevelt, however, continued to hope that in security, economic, and other areas it would be possible to maintain big-power cooperation. (After all, Soviet delegates were still regularly attending the London meetings of education ministers to establish an international cultural organization.)

Such optimism appeared at least partially vindicated at the Yalta Conference of February 1945, the second and the last meeting of Roosevelt, Churchill, and Stalin together. With Germany's surrender expected momentarily, the leaders' attention focused on defeating Japan as expeditiously as possible. Stalin renewed his pledge that the Soviet Union would enter the war against Japan about three months after the German surrender. He also agreed to continue to deal with the Nationalists in China as the legitimate government, even though their authority was now openly being challenged by the Communists. In return Roosevelt and Churchill supported Russia's special interests in Manchuria, in particular its railways and southern (ice-free) ports.

The three leaders also agreed on other matters. For instance, Stalin gave up his insistence on blanket veto power at the United Nations security council and agreed that the veto power would not be used over "procedural" issues. He also agreed to have France join in the occupation of Germany. Roosevelt and Churchill, on their turn, formally endorsed the new Soviet-Polish boundary. There was, however, disagreement over the nature of new governments being set up in liberated areas, most notably Poland. Stalin insisted on their control by Communist politicians, most of whom had spent the war in the Soviet Union, whereas Roosevelt and Churchill wanted to broaden the bases of government. In the end a compromise was struck, and the big three agreed to support the principle of democratic government for these countries, although initially Soviet-oriented Communists were to constitute its core.

The Yalta compromise seemed to augur well for continued interallied cooperation. It was, to be sure, a largely power-level arrangement in which the big three accepted, tacitly or explicitly, the new realities of power as the basis for postwar spheres of influence, and these spheres as the key to world order. But so long as the United States and the Soviet Union could continue to cooperate in some fashion, there was hope that eventually their cooperation might come to cover other areas and bring Soviet policy into closer conformity to the principles of the Atlantic Charter, the ideological foundations of the coalition during the war.

In this sense, the end of the German war, on May 8, 1945, may be said to have come too soon. Roosevelt had died on April 12, and the new president, Harry S. Truman, had not had time to develop his own approach to postwar problems before the European war was completed. Having crushed Germany, the allies were now tempted to go their separate ways. The Japanese war still necessitated their cooperation, but to a much lesser extent, and some in the United

States even began to argue that Soviet participation in the Pacific war might not be necessary – it might not even be desirable, as it would further extend Soviet power in Asia. Some officials wanted a political end to the Japanese war; believing, perhaps correctly, that the Japanese could be induced to stop fighting once they were assured that the allies did not intend to destroy their emperor institution, they advocated approaching Japan for a possible cease-fire on this basis. President Truman, however, did not agree, convinced that public opinion would not accept any promise to save the emperor and that Soviet participation was strategically imperative to minimize the costs of the American invasion of the Japanese homeland, which was visualized for 1946.[11]

In the meantime, State Department officials, now joined by War and Navy Department personnel, finalized their plans for the occupation of Japan. Now, more than ever before, they were determined not to divide the country into zones of occupation. Rather, the United States would control Japan's destiny. China was still viewed as America's principal postwar partner in postwar Asia, but with the Nationalist-Communist conflict flaring up again, it was becoming more and more difficult to envisage that country as a unified and strong power in the immediate future.

The result was that, during the months following Germany's defeat, the wartime coalition, already strained after the autumn of 1944, was put to a severe test. With the disappearance of the common enemy, the task was not easy. The alliance would now have to be redefined for peace, but the shape of the peace itself depended on their cooperation, or lack thereof. In such a fluid situation, only a determined effort at preserving the coalition would have worked. It is to the credit of Truman, Stalin, and Churchill (as well as Clement Attlee who replaced him after the Conservative party's defeat at the elections in July) that they did continue their efforts in this direction. For instance, much was accomplished at a conference of fifty nations, meeting in San Francisco from the end of April through the end of July, to complete the drafting of the charter of the United

11 On the emperor question toward the end of the Pacific war, see Iriye, *Power and Culture,* 251–7.

Nations. The charter was a ringing declaration of the nations' determination to work together to preserve the peace, and to cooperate in punishing future aggressors through collective action. The preamble also enumerated the fundamental principles (self-determination, human rights, "equal rights of men and women," "social progress," "better standards of life") for which the postwar world was to strive.

These were as satisfactory an achievement as could have been obtained at that time. Together with the more frankly power-level arrangements worked out at Yalta, the San Francisco conference could be said to have defined the framework of the postwar world order.

In such a context, Japan's surrender, which came on August 15, could have been seen as a footnote, one final act before the new drama, the history of the postwar world, was to begin. The way the surrender was brought about, however, served in many ways to make it the beginning not merely of the postwar peace but of the Cold War. First, the Soviet entry into the Japanese war (on August 8) confirmed the emergence of the Soviet Union as a formidable Asian, as well as European, power, one whose influence in China could be expected to be considerable. Second, the decision of the United States to drop atom bombs on Japan ushered in the age of nuclear weapons. Neither of these developments had been unanticipated, but their actual occurrence immediately created novel realities and made postwar international relations that much more difficult to conceptualize.

The atomic decision had been preceded by a big-three conference at Potsdam, outside of Berlin, where Truman, Stalin, and Churchill (as well as Attlee) conferred on the treatment of Germany and on the war against Japan. Regarding the former, it was decided to set up a conference of foreign ministers of these three powers plus France to prepare peace treaties with Germany and its former allies. Toward Japan, the conferees issued a declaration, warning of its catastrophic destruction (atom bombs were implied, though not mentioned) unless the nation surrendered immediately. By then Tokyo's civilian leaders, including the emperor, had come to the conclusion that the war had been lost and that an honorable way must be sought to bring it to conclusion. But they did not respond forthrightly to the

Potsdam declaration because they first had to persuade the military, particularly the army, to accept ending the war, and also because they hoped to obtain Soviet intercession in the war. As the Soviet Union still remained technically neutral, it was hoped that it might serve as an intermediary between Japan and the United States and its allies.

Such hesitation not only cost Japan more destruction, but it also brought the world into the atomic age. President Truman, who was told about the successful detonation of an atom bomb while attending the Potsdam Conference, decided that the new weapon must be used to bring a speedy end to the conflict. Two atom bombs were dropped, on Hiroshima (August 6) and Nagasaki (August 9), causing instant or indirect (through radiation) death to hundreds of thousands of civilians. The bombings, coupled with the Soviet entry into the war, finally forced the Japanese emperor and his top advisers to accept the Potsdam declaration. The formal announcement came on August 14 (August 15 in Asia), when the emperor conveyed the decision to his people in an unprecedented radio broadcast. The long war, which had killed and maimed more than 40 million people, more than 2 percent of the world's population, and otherwise affected an even larger number through forced migration, property destruction, disease, and hunger, was at last at an end.

But the way the war came to an end – through Soviet entry into the Pacific war and the U.S. use of atom bombs – suggested that the postwar world would be enormously complicated. It would not be easy to develop effective big-power cooperation, one key foundation on which all believed the future of world peace rested, when any such cooperation would have to reckon with the vastly expanded territorial control exercised by the Soviet Union and with the awesome new weapon the United States had developed but other countries could also be expected to acquire soon.

At the same time, however, there were two other pillars of the postwar international order that had been developed through the American initiative but with the cooperation of other nations. One was economic, and it remained to be seen to what extent the IMF, the World Bank, and other mechanisms would serve to integrate all countries, including the Soviet Union and ultimately the former

Axis powers, into an interdependent and open world economic order. The second was cultural and ideological, as expressed in the United Nations charter. It envisioned a world free of tyranny, oppression, and insecurity. All nations and peoples would be united in their search for, and commitment to, freedom, justice, and compassion. This, too, was a product of the American tradition and imagination.

In other words, the world at the end of World War II was one in which America's military power, economic resources, and cultural influence were more pronounced than ever before. Presumably, they would shape the peace; if they failed to do so, that would be because American power and influence would be challenged by others, not just by the Soviet Union and other would-be military superpowers but also by countries and peoples that would want to take better advantage of the new economic opportunities and to embrace more fully the visions of freedom that were appearing on the horizon. For the world was becoming Americanized just as America had become globalized.

Conclusion

The history of the world transformation of 1913–45 is also a story of the transformation of America's role in the world. Europe, the center of international relations into which other parts of the globe, including the United States, had been fitted, lost its primacy after World War I. The years after 1917 marked the emergence of the United States as the world's leader. Even when it did not actually lead through military force (such as the 1920s), it provided economic and cultural resources to define and sustain global order. The mid-1930s were an exception in that the nation eschewed international leadership or cooperation at all levels and retreated to nationalism and unilateralism, but even then it was clear that sooner or later it was "bound to lead," to use Joseph Nye's phrase.[12] It could not have done otherwise, unless its leaders and people – *and* millions of others elsewhere – had been content to live in a world divided

12 Joseph Nye, *Bound to Lead* (Boston, 1990).

into separate spheres, many of them under totalitarian control. And the moment for leadership came sooner than expected, with the German invasion of Poland in 1939 and the Japanese attack on Pearl Harbor two years later. Now the United States became involved, militarily, economically, and politically, in all parts of the world: the Western Hemisphere, the Atlantic, Europe, Africa, the Middle East, Asia, the Pacific. The globalization of America was virtually complete.

The emergence of the United States as world leader also brought about the transformation of other countries politically, economically, and culturally. That was why so many observers during World War II spoke of the world in revolution – revolution in the sense of unprecedented changes. The changes were particularly notable in colonial and dependent areas of the globe, where the big-power conflict had brought about the dislocation of entrenched authority, massive destruction as well as mass mobilization, and emerging political movements for autonomy. The story of the awakening of the non-West was to become a major theme in postwar history, but in fact it had begun in parallel to the emergence of the United States as the world's leader. And the two phenomena were interrelated, as the non-Western peoples looked to America for support and inspiration.

Americanization of the globe would be destabilizing, even as the globalization of the United States was an attempt to redefine world order in the wake of Europe's relative decline. It remained to be seen how these twin phenomena would develop, and whether there would emerge a new international order in which the United States and the world would become even more interdependent without having to pay the cost of millions of lives as they had during 1913–45.

Bibliographic Essay

1913–1921

On the origins of World War I, the best summary of various factors and interpretations is offered by James Joll, *The Origins of the First World War* (London, 1984). On United States neutrality during 1914–17, the standard work is Ernest R. May, *The World War and American Isolation* (Cambridge, Mass., 1959). There is a voluminous amount of writings on President Woodrow Wilson's diplomacy both during the period of neutrality and after the decision for war. The most detailed and reliable study is the multivolume biography by Arthur S. Link, of which two volumes are particularly relevant: *Wilson: The Struggle for Neutrality* (Princeton, 1960), and *Wilson: Campaigns for Progressivism and Peace* (Princeton, 1965). For a more compact survey, see Robert H. Ferrell, *Woodrow Wilson and World War I* (New York, 1985). An extremely interesting contrast between Wilson and former president Theodore Roosevelt is drawn in John Milton Cooper, *The Warrior and the Priest* (New York, 1983). See also the same author's *The Vanity of Power* (Westport, Conn., 1969) for a discussion of antiinterventionism during the war.

Perhaps the most influential interpretation of Wilsonian foreign policy in peace and war has been offered by N. Gordon Levin, *Woodrow Wilson and World Politics* (New York, 1968), which places Wilsonianism squarely in the middle between traditional power politics and Bolshevik radicalism. The best analysis of Wilson's struggle to go beyond traditional patterns of diplomacy is Frederick Calhoun, *Power and Principle* (Kent, Ohio, 1986). The relationship between Wilsonianism and Leninism is given further elaboration in such works as Klaus Schwabe, *The World War, Revolutionary Germany, and Peacemaking* (Chapel Hill, 1985); Arno Mayer, *Politics and Diplomacy of Peacemaking* (New York, 1967); and John M. Thompson,

Russia, Bolshevism, and the Versailles Peace (Princeton, 1967). On America's expedition to Siberia, the most authoritative historian has been George F. Kennan. See his *Russia Leaves the War* (Princeton, 1956) and *The Decision to Intervene* (Princeton, 1958). The Siberian intervention is put in the framework of American relations with the Czechs and wartime developments in Central Europe in Betty Miller Unterberger's massive *The United States, Revolutionary Russia, and the Making of Czechoslovakia* (Chapel Hill, 1989).

There are many accounts of American relations with specific countries and regions of the world in the era of World War I. Anglo-American relations are treated extensively in such works as Lloyd C. Gardner, *Safe for Democracy* (New York, 1984); Seth P. Tillman, *Anglo-American Relations at the Paris Peace Conference* (Princeton, 1961); and W. B. Fowler, *British-American Relations* (Princeton, 1969). The literature on U.S. involvement in Latin America and East Asia is particularly rich. On Mexico, see Friedrich Katz, *The Secret War in Mexico* (Chicago, 1981), a study of U.S.-German rivalry in that country. The American expeditions to Santo Domingo and Haiti are chronicled in David Healy, *Gunboat Diplomacy in the Wilson Era* (Madison, 1976); and Hans Schmidt, *The U.S. Occupation of Haiti* (New Brunswick, N.J., 1971).

Regarding the wartime friction with Japan and Wilson's pro-Chinese orientation, see Tien-i Li, *Woodrow Wilson's China Policy* (New York, 1969); James Reed, *The Missionary Mind and American East Asian Policy* (Cambridge, Mass., 1983); and Roy Watson Curry, *Woodrow Wilson and Far Eastern Policy* (New York, 1959). There is less work on the Middle East, but some useful data may be obtained in John A. DeNovo, *American Interests and Policies in the Middle East* (Minneapolis, 1963); Laurence Evans, *United States Policy and the Partition of Turkey* (Baltimore, 1965); Daniel Yergin, *The Prize* (New York, 1991); and Burton Kaufman, *Efficiency and Expansion* (Westport, Conn., 1974). This last, in addition to discussing the American pursuit of Middle Eastern oil fields, presents a fresh interpretation of Wilsonian foreign policy in terms of the movement in the United States for government-business cooperation in the interest of efficiency and maximization of overall national interests. This theme, that the development of a framework for state-society cooperation steadily came to characterize American national and international affairs, is known as a "corporatist" interpretation and has informed such other important works as Michael J. Hogan, *Informal Entente* (Columbia, Mo., 1977), and Emily Rosenberg, *Spreading the American Dream* (New York, 1982). Both stress the initiatives taken by the nation's political and business leaders to reform domestic institutions and decision-making mechanisms so as to realize the efficient use of resources at home and the expansion of interests and opportunities abroad. See also Jerry Israel, *Progressivism and the Open Door* (Pittsburgh, 1971), and Carl P. Parrini, *Heir to Empire* (Pittsburgh, 1969).

1921–1933

United States foreign relations after World War I used to be dismissed as little more than a story of isolation, a less than honorable period in the nation's history when it abdicated its responsibility in the world arena. This view has been steadily undermined by scholarly publications since the 1960s, and today it is much more common among historians to stress continuities rather than discontinuities between wartime diplomacy and the foreign affairs of the 1920s. For a good survey of this topic, the best place to start is Warren I. Cohen, *Empire Without Tears* (New York, 1987), a scholarly synthesis and a comprehensive survey. Further factual details on American-European relations, particularly on the thorny debt question, are provided by Melvin Leffler, *The Elusive Quest* (Chapel Hill, 1979), and Frank Costigliola, *Awkward Dominion* (Ithaca, 1984). As the titles of these books suggest, there was something tentative about American involvement in postwar European affairs, but one could argue that the United States was much more self-confident and less hesitant in its relations with other parts of the globe.

A great deal has been written on postwar America's role in stabilizing Asian-Pacific affairs. The Washington Conference, the point of departure, is well analyzed by Roger Dingman, *Power in the Pacific* (Chicago, 1976). More critical assessments of the disarmament initiatives of the interwar period are offered by Robert E. Osgood, *Ideals and Self-Interest in American Foreign Relations* (Chicago, 1953), and Betty Glad, *Charles Evans Hughes and the Illusions of Innocence* (Urbana, Ill., 1966). For the London Conference of 1930, see Raymond O'Connor, *Perilous Equilibrium* (Lawrence, Kans., 1962). On the response to the growth of Chinese nationalism and the emergence of the Nationalists as the new leaders in China, see Akira Iriye, *After Imperialism* (Cambridge, Mass., 1965); Dorothy Borg, *American Policy and the Chinese Revolution* (New York, 1947); Paul A. Varg, *Missionaries, Chinese, and Diplomats* (Princeton, 1958); L. Ethan Ellis, *Frank B. Kellogg and American Foreign Relations* (New Brunswick, N.J., 1961); and Russell D. Buhite, *Nelson T. Johnson and American Policy Toward China* (East Lansing, Mich., 1968). Warren I. Cohen, *The Chinese Connection* (New York, 1978), is a study of three Americans representing different backgrounds and interests in China.

On Latin American relations, Bryce Wood, *The Making of a Good Neighbor Policy* (New York, 1961), is still useful as a history of the redefinition of the Monroe Doctrine in the 1920s, as is Alexander DeConde, *Herbert Hoover's Latin American Policy* (Stanford, 1951). Responses to Mexico's radical nationalism are given a masterful treatment in Robert Freeman Smith, *The United States and Revolutionary Nationalism in Mexico* (Chicago, 1972). The continued intervention in Nicaragua is discussed in William Kamman, *A Search for Stability* (Notre Dame, Ind., 1968). On the overall commercial links between North and South America, see Joseph Tulchin, *Aftermath of War* (New York, 1971).

American relations with Bolshevik Russia are a story in themselves – or, one could say a nonstory in that there was no formal diplomatic relationship between the two governments. But there were commercial interactions and, besides, Americans of all political persuasions were fascinated by the Soviet experiment. These developments are described in such books as William Appleman Williams, *American-Russian Relations* (New York, 1952); Joan Hoff Wilson, *Ideology and Economics* (Columbia, Mo., 1974); and Peter G. Filene, *Americans and the Soviet Experiment* (Cambridge, Mass., 1967).

There is much interesting work on public attitudes toward foreign affairs during the 1920s. Warren I. Cohen, *The American Revi-*

sionists (Chicago, 1967), studies the controversy on the origins of World War II; Peter Novick, *That Noble Dream* (New York, 1988), offers an intriguing account of the impact of that controversy on historians; and Selig Adler, *The Isolationist Impulse* (New York, 1957), while more traditional in interpretation, contains much valuable information on American opinion in the interwar years. Robert D. Schulzinger, *The Wise Men of Foreign Affairs* (New York, 1984), looks at the Council of Foreign Relations, established in 1921 as an elite organization to influence American foreign policy. The same author's *The Making of the Diplomatic Mind* (Middletown, Conn., 1975) describes what may be termed the official ideology of the period concerning international relations. The increasingly active peace movement in postwar America is treated extensively in Charles Chatfield, *For Peace and Justice* (Knoxville, 1971). See also Charles DeBenedetti, *Origins of the Modern American Peace Movement* (Millwood, N.Y., 1978), and Robert H. Ferrell, *Peace in Their Time* (New Haven, 1952). This latter focuses on the making of the Kellogg-Briand Pact of 1928. Slightly different in character but essential reading for understanding American attitudes in the interwar years is John P. Diggins, *Mussolini and Fascism: The View from America* (Princeton, 1972). It not only shows how Americans responded to the rise of fascism in Italy but how they defined their mental universes at a time of steady economic, political, and cultural interpenetration among nations.

Economics was a crucial medium of American foreign relations in the 1920s, and its importance is reflected in such standard works as Herbert Feis, *The Diplomacy of the Dollar* (Baltimore, 1950); Joan Hoff Wilson, *American Business and Foreign Policy* (Boston, 1971); and Joseph Brandes, *Herbert Hoover and Economic Diplomacy* (Pittsburgh, 1962). The collapse of economic diplomacy that came with the Depression is the subject of Ferrell, *American Diplomacy in the Great Depression* (New Haven, 1957). For a penetrating discussion of the structural problems in the global economic system during the 1920s with its heavy dependence on the United States, consult Charles P. Kindleberger, *The World in Depression* (Berkeley, 1973).

Japan's invasion of Manchuria, the first overt challenge to world order during the Depression, has been a subject of numerous studies. In the context of U.S.-Japanese relations, an excellent account, besides Ferrell's *American Diplomacy,* is Christopher Thorne, *The Limits of Power* (New York, 1973). See also Armin Rappaport, *Henry L. Stimson and Japan* (Chicago, 1973); Gary Ostrower, *Collective Insecurity* (Lewisburg, Pa., 1979); and Justus Doenecke, *When the Wicked Rise* (Lewisburg, Pa., 1984). Rappaport's book takes a harshly critical view of Stimson's foreign policy, the others much less so. The best study of Japan's decision for continental expansionism and its implications for the United States is Michael Barnhart, *Japan Prepares for Total War* (Ithaca, 1987).

1933–1939

The period between 1933, when Franklin D. Roosevelt entered the White House, and 1939, when World War II began in Europe, has not been as extensively studied by historians in the recent decades, in part because they have tended to focus on the New Deal and other domestic developments, and also because the nation's foreign affairs were much more circumscribed during those years than earlier. Still, many interesting works exist and help us explore how the United States, going through an unprecedented economic crisis, coped with serious world problems ranging from Japan's aggressive war in China to Nazi Germany's repudiation of the Versailles peace settlement.

Lloyd C. Gardner, *Economic Aspects of the New Deal Diplomacy* (Madison, 1964), examines the efforts of Secretary of State Cordell Hull and others to solve the acute economic crisis at home through reestablishing an orderly system of multilateral trade. See also Frederick C. Adams, *Economic Diplomacy* (Columbia, Mo., 1976). On the impact of the Depression on American opinion, especially the rise of extremism with obvious implications for foreign relations, see Alan Brinkley, *Voices of Protest* (New York, 1982), and Geoffrey S. Smith, *To Save a Nation* (New York, 1973).

The isolationist bent of American public and congressional opinion during much of the 1930s is an extremely important phenomenon. We must realize, however, that it was filled with contradictions. One person's isolationism could mean another's interventionism. The various shades of isolationist thought are lucidly analyzed by Manfred Jonas, *Isolationism in America* (Ithaca, 1966). On congressional isolationists, the best study is Wayne S. Cole, *Roosevelt and the Isolationists* (Lincoln, Neb., 1983). Cole has devoted his career to the study of isolationism and published many other important works, including *Gerald P. Nye and American Foreign Relations* (Minneapolis, 1962) and *Charles A. Lindbergh and the Battle Against American Intervention in World War II* (New York, 1974). The congressional enactment of neutrality laws is given authoritative treatment in Robert A. Divine, *The Illusion of Neutrality* (Chicago, 1962). On the persistence of pacifist opinion, see Lawrence S. Wittner, *Rebels Against War* (New York, 1969).

Despite America's self-imposed isolation, external events mercilessly intruded upon national consciousness and forced the policymakers to respond. President Roosevelt's thinking, in which he had to weigh domestic opinion as well as the threat to world peace, is carefully traced in Robert Dallek, *Franklin D. Roosevelt and American Foreign Policy* (New York, 1979). Readers interested in Roosevelt's foreign policy should first turn to this book and then supplement it with other studies of specific challenges and responses in various parts of the world. For instance, on U.S. responses to various initiatives undertaken by Nazi Germany, the best account is found in Arnold A. Offner, *American Appeasement* (Cambridge, Mass., 1967). See also J. A. Compton, *The Swastika and the Eagle* (Boston, 1967). On German propaganda activities in the Western Hemisphere, see Alton Frye, *Nazi Germany and the American Hemisphere* (New Haven, 1967).

The uneasy state of U.S.-British relations in the 1930s is well described in Offner's book. The fascinating question of how, despite such uncertainty, even profound mistrust at times between Washington and London, there eventually emerged a cooperative framework for dealing with German and Japanese aggression, is discussed in two excellent books: James R. Leutze, *Bargaining for Supremacy* (Chapel Hill, 1977), and David Reynolds, *The Creation of the Anglo-American Alliance* (Chapel Hill, 1981). See also Ritchie Ovendale, *"Appeasement" and the English Speaking World* (Cardiff, 1975). Concerning Fascist Italy, there is, in addition to the previously noted book by Diggins, Bryce Harris, *The United States and the Italo-*

Ethiopian Crisis (Stanford, 1964). On the turmoil of 1931–9 and American responses, among the most useful works are Douglas Little, *Malevolent Neutrality* (Ithaca, 1985), and Richard Traina, *American Diplomacy and the Spanish Civil War* (Bloomington, Ind., 1968).

On Latin American policy, in addition to the book by Frye, one may consult E. D. Cronon, *Josephus Daniels in Mexico* (Madison, 1960); Irwin Gellman, *Roosevelt and Batista* (Albuquerque, 1973); the same author's *Good Neighbor Diplomacy* (Baltimore, 1979); and Joseph Tulchin, *Argentina and the United States* (Boston, 1990). On the Asian crisis, the best study remains Dorothy Borg, *The United States and the Far Eastern Crisis of 1933–1938* (Cambridge, Mass., 1964). The book chronicles America's failure to come to the aid of China until very late in the 1930s. The same theme is treated from various angles in two collections of scholarly essays: Dorothy Borg and Shumpei Okamoto, *Pearl Harbor as History* (New York, 1973), and Akira Iriye and Warren I. Cohen, *American, Chinese, and Japanese Perspectives on Wartime Asia* (Wilmington, Del., 1990). These volumes are useful as they contain contributions by Chinese and Japanese, as well as American, scholars. James C. Thomson, *While China Faced West* (Cambridge, Mass., 1969), discusses America's difficulties in assisting China because of the Depression. The decision to reverse the trend and to come to the support of China during 1938–9 is ably described in Michael Schaller, *The U.S. Crusade in China* (New York, 1979). For a survey of Asian international relations that led to the Pacific war, see Akira Iriye, *The Origins of the Second World War in Asia and the Pacific* (London, 1987). One American diplomat's heroic endeavor to preserve the peace with Japan is detailed in Waldo Heinrichs, *American Ambassador* (Boston, 1966), a biography of Joseph C. Grew. Sandra Taylor, *Advocate of Understanding* (Kent, Ohio, 1984), offers a portrait of a former missionary, Sidney Gulick, who struggled for the same end.

Although the Soviet Union would emerge as a key factor in U.S. dealings with Japan as well as with Germany, there has been little systematic study of U.S. relations with Moscow, probably because historians have not had time to digest the mass of archival documents that have been opened up in the former Soviet Union. But Robert C. Tucker, *Stalin in Power* (New York, 1990), does make use of these documents and gives a sinister portrait of the Soviet dictator's opportunistic diplomacy. To understand the impact of the Comintern's call in 1935 for the establishment of a global antifascist front, an event that held real significance for a large number of American intellectuals, one may profitably turn to personal reminiscences such as Malcolm Cowley, *The Dream of the Golden Mountains* (New York, 1980).

1939–1945

The best account of the coming of World War II in Europe is D. C. Watt, *How War Came* (London, 1989). The way in which the United States became steadily drawn into the European conflict during 1939–41 is chronicled in detail in William L. Langer and S. Everett Gleason, *The Undeclared War* (New York, 1953). On Roosevelt's growing readiness to support Britain by all means short of war, see, besides the works by Dallek and Reynolds cited in the previous section, James M. Burns, *Roosevelt: The Soldier of Freedom* (New York, 1970); Theodore A. Wilson, *The First Summit* (Boston, 1969); and Warren F. Kimball, *The Most Unsordid Act* (Baltimore, 1969). This last is an important study of the making of the Lend-Lease Act. Its application to the Soviet Union after June 1941 is described in Raymond H. Dawson, *The Decision to Aid Russia* (Chapel Hill, 1959), and George C. Herring, *Aid to Russia* (New York, 1973). The American public's increasing willingness to help the democracies against Nazi Germany is documented in such works as Mark L. Chadwin, *Warhawks* (New York, 1968); Walter Johnson, *The Battle Against Isolation* (Chicago, 1944); and James C. Schneider, *Should America Go to War?* (Chapel Hill, 1989). On the less well known aid to France, which also began around 1939, consult Julian Hurstfield, *America and the French Nation* (Chapel Hill, 1986).

There is an enormous amount of scholarly literature on "the road to Pearl Harbor." The standard "orthodox" presentation is Herbert Feis, *The Road to Pearl Harbor* (Princeton, 1950), and the most extreme "revisionist" interpretation – that the Roosevelt administration was engaged in a conspiracy to maneuver the Japanese into firing the first shot so that the United States might enter the war in

Europe through the Asian "back door" – is in Charles C. Tansill, *Back Door to War* (Chicago, 1952), and Charles A. Beard, *President Roosevelt and the Coming of the War* (New York, 1948). Most studies reject the conspiracy theory but add many nuances to the story climaxing in the Pearl Harbor attack. The role of the Axis pact in the deteriorating U.S.-Japanese relations is analyzed critically in Paul W. Schroeder, *The Axis Alliance and Japanese-American Relations* (Ithaca, 1958), and Saul Friedlander, *Prelude to Downfall* (New York, 1967). The crucial petroleum question as a determining factor is discussed in Irvine H. Anderson, *The Standard Vacuum Oil Company and United States East Asian Policy* (Princeton, 1975). The story is brought up to date in an excellent chapter in Yergin's *The Prize* (New York, 1991). See also Jonathan G. Utley, *Going to War with Japan* (Knoxville, 1985). The Washington "conversations" of 1941, in which the United States and Japan sought to avoid a final showdown, are ably presented in Robert Butow, *The John Doe Associates* (Stanford, 1974). See also the same author's *Tojo and the Coming of the War* (Princeton, 1961). By far the best account of the U.S.-Japanese crisis in the summer and fall of the year is Waldo Heinrichs, *Threshold of War* (New York, 1988). The book stresses Roosevelt's concern with preventing Soviet collapse as the main factor behind his get-tough policy toward Japan.

Among the voluminous literature on the Pearl Harbor attack, the most detailed and reliable is Gordon W. Prange, *At Dawn We Slept* (New York, 1981). See also the same author's *Pearl Harbor: The Verdict of History* (New York, 1986). The influential book by Roberta Wohlstetter, *Pearl Harbor: Warning and Decision* (Stanford, 1962), argues that it was the volume of the cable traffic that created confusion in official Washington and made it impossible to communicate relevant messages to the commanders in Hawaii in time to avert the disaster.

Thousands of books have been written on American strategy and diplomacy during World War II. The best brief summary is Gaddis Smith, *American Diplomacy During the Second World War* (New York, 1985). On overall strategy, see Maurice Matloff and Edwin M. Snell, *Strategic Planning for Coalition Warfare* (Washington, D.C., 1953). There are two excellent studies of military preparedness and mobilization undertaken by the United States and other countries: Alan S. Milward, *War, Economy, and Society* (Berkeley, 1977), and Paul Kennedy, *The Rise and Fall of the Great Powers* (New York, 1987).

The Anglo-American alliance is best understood by reading the letters exchanged between the two wartime leaders, ably edited by Warren F. Kimball: *Churchill and Roosevelt* (Princeton, 1984). On the relationship among the big three, Herbert Feis, *Churchill, Roosevelt, Stalin* (Princeton, 1957), is still useful, but it should be supplemented by Martin Sherwin, *A World Destroyed* (New York, 1975), a study of the development of nuclear weapons and of their implications for postwar world affairs. Diana Clemens, *Yalta* (New York, 1970), shows that there was as much U.S.-Soviet agreement as disagreement at the 1945 conference.

Because the latter part of the war was also the period of preparation for the defining of the postwar world, and because the postwar world was to be characterized by the breakup of the wartime alliance into two camps, many accounts of World War II are also, in effect, descriptions of the origins of the Cold War. Among the most important in tracing this transition in Europe are William H. McNeill, *America, Britain, and Russia* (London, 1953); John W. Gaddis, *The United States and the Origins of the Cold War* (New York, 1972); Daniel Yergin, *The Shattered Peace* (Boston, 1977); Vojtech Mastny, *Russia's Road to the Cold War* (New York, 1979); and Lynn E. Davis, *The Cold War Begins* (Princeton, 1974). Hugh DeSantis, *The Diplomacy of Silence* (Chicago, 1980), is unique in its focus on State Department officials' changing perceptions of the Soviet Union. Also see, in this connection, Ralph Levering, *American Opinion and the Russian Alliance* (Chapel Hill, 1976).

On the Pacific theater of the war, Christopher Thorne, *Allies of a Kind* (New York, 1978), offers a fascinating account of Anglo-American cooperation as well as differences over such matters as the future of China and of the British Empire. Akira Iriye, *Power and Culture* (Cambridge, Mass., 1981), suggests areas of convergence in official American and Japanese wartime thinking. On China's role in the war, see Barbara Tuchman, *Stilwell and the American Experience in China* (New York, 1971). The subtle ways in which the Asian war developed into an Asian Cold War is treated in such works as Herbert Feis, *Dilemma in China* (Hamden, Con., 1980); Russell Buhite, *Patrick J. Hurley and American Relations with China* (Ithaca, 1973); Kenneth Shewmaker, *Americans and Chinese Communists* (Ithaca, 1971); Marc Gallicchio, *The Cold War Begins in Asia* (New York, 1988); Tang Tsou, *America's Failure in China* (Chicago, 1963); Akira Iriye, *The Cold War in Asia* (New York, 1974); and the essays contained in Yōnosuke Nagai and Akira Iriye, *The Origins of the Cold War in Asia* (Tokyo, 1977). Frank Ninkovich, *The Diplomacy of Ideas* (New York, 1981), offers interesting observations on wartime American cultural diplomacy in China and elsewhere.

Because of the global character of the war, no part of the world escaped American attention and influence. Some flavor of the way in which the nation's military presence became intertwined with the destiny of people everywhere may be gathered by reading such books as Gary Hess, *America Encounters India* (Baltimore, 1971); Martin W. Wilmington, *The Middle East Supply Centre* (Albany, 1971); Arthur L. Funk, *The Politics of TORCH* (Lawrence, Kans., 1974), a study of the occupation of North Africa; and Donald M. Dozer, *Are We Good Neighbors?* (Gainesville, Fla., 1959), which recounts the activities of American airmen in Brazil and other countries.

What did World War II mean to the American people? The question has been examined from various angles. Paul Fussell, *Wartime* (New York, 1989), looks at the war from the common soldier's perspective. John Dower, *War Without Mercy* (New York, 1986), examines wartime stereotypes of the Japanese enemy. Robert A. Divine, *Second Chance* (New York, 1971), is an excellent study of the "new internationalism." American politics and society during the war are described in John Morton Blum, *V Was for Victory* (New York, 1976); Richard Polenberg, *War and Society* (Philadelphia, 1972); Richard Darilek, *A Loyal Opposition in Time of War* (Westport, Conn., 1976); and Martin Melosi, *The Shadow of Pearl Harbor* (College Station, Tex., 1977).

On planning for the enemy's surrender and occupation by the allies, Harley Notter, *Postwar Foreign Policy Preparation* (Washington, D.C., 1949), provides essential raw material from the minutes of numerous State Department meetings. Regarding the treatment of defeated Germany, see Tony Sharp, *The Wartime Alliance and the*

Zonal Division of Germany (Oxford, 1975). On Japan, Frederick Dunn, *Peacemaking and the Settlement with Japan* (Princeton, 1963), is useful. The best study of the important Bretton Woods Conference is Richard N. Gardner, *Sterling-Dollar Diplomacy* (New York, 1980). See also Alfred Eckes, *A Search for Solvency* (Austin, Tex., 1975). On the dropping of the atom bomb and its implications for American policy and opinion, see, besides Sherwin's *World Destroyed,* mentioned earlier, Herbert Feis, *The Atomic Bomb and the End of World War II* (Princeton, 1961), Leon Sigal, *Fighting to a Finish* (Ithaca, 1988), and Paul Boyer, *By the Bomb's Early Light* (New York, 1985).

Index

WITHDRAWN

MORRIS AUTOMATED INFORMATION NETWORK
0 1004 0105737 5